Preface

Dear Student,

General Knowledge is an integral part of various entrance examinations in India. The General Knowledge part in the examination not only tests the Current Affairs but also tests the fundamental understanding of History, Geography, Science , Sports, Constitution of India ,Culture, Basic Economics and Indian Economy since independence and other important areas like, Books and Authors, Days, Awards, Organization etc., that forms the core of what we call as Static General Knowledge.

This book is compiled precisely to take care of this need of guiding you in Static General Knowledge. The book is divided in three parts.

Part – I takes care of History, Geography, Science, Sports, Constitution of India, Culture and Miscellaneous General Knowledge.

Part – II addresses the area of Basic Economics and Indian Economy since independence.

Part – III has five tests of static general knowledge to give you an idea and practice of the type of the questions that are asked in the examination.

Please understand very clearly that this book is basically a compilation of important General Knowledge facts from quality sources and in no way can be interpreted as the complete book that can take care of a subject of the stature of General Knowledge. This compilation is up-to-date as on **20th August, 2019.** The whole purpose of this book is to make you aware about the important General Knowledge topics and guide you to prepare them in detail. Hence you should use this book as only a precursor to your thorough preparation in the area of Static General Knowledge with the help of other recommended sources.

Remember that General Knowledge is a very vast subject and therefore, demands time to prepare. Therefore, it is advisable that you should start early and be patient and perseverant in you approach towards General Knowledge.

Happy reading!

All the best

Team CL

CL MEDIA (P) LTD.

Edition : 2019

© *PUBLISHER*

No part of this book may be reproduced in a retrieval system or transmitted, in any form or by any means, electronics, mechanical, photocopying, recording, scanning and or without the written permission of the publisher.

Typeset by : *CL Media DTP Unit*

Administrative and Production Offices

Published by : **CL Media (P) Ltd.**

A-45, Mohan Cooperative Industrial Area,
Near Mohan Estate Metro Station,
New Delhi - 110044

Marketed by : **G.K. Publications (P) Ltd.**

A-45, Mohan Cooperative Industrial Area,
Near Mohan Estate Metro Station,
New Delhi - 110044

For product information :
Visit *www.gkpublications.com* or email to *gkp@gkpublications.com*

Contents

Part – I : General Knowledge

1. Indian History

Introduction 03

Ancient India 03

Medieval India 07

India Under British Rule 09

List of important historical events in India 17

Important Battles in the Indian History 18

List of important Presidents of Indian National Congress 19

Important Newspaper brought out by National leaders 19

Important visitors to India and the Kings whose courts they visited 20

Important National Days 21

Record Makers (India) 22

2. Geography

Basic geographical facts 24

Important Countries, Capitals and Currencies 29

Important Countries and their Parliaments 33

Geographical facts of India 34

Industries In India 38

Oil Refineries 39

Nuclear Power Stations 39

Major Thermal Power Plants 39

Ultra Mega Power Plants 39

3. Constitution of India 40

4. Science 61

5. Sports 68

6. Culture of India 71

7. Miscellaneous General Knowledge

Important International Organizations 75

Heads of Important International Organizations 80

Important Awards 80

Important Days 91

Important Sobriquets 93

Important Books and Authors 95

Important Abbreviations 102

Important Facts about World and India 113

Important Demographic Facts of India (Census - 2011) 119

Different UN Agencies 120

Anti-Poverty And Employment Generation Programs 122

Part – II : Basics of Economics and Indian Economy since Independence

Important Basic Concepts of Economics 129

Important Economics Terms 133

Stock Market Glossary 138

Important Economics Abbreviations 139

Important Financial Institutions 141

Performance of Indian Economy under various Plans 145

Part – III : General Knowledge Tests

Test – 1 153

Test – 2 155

Test – 3 157

Test – 4 159

Test – 5 161

Answer Keys 163

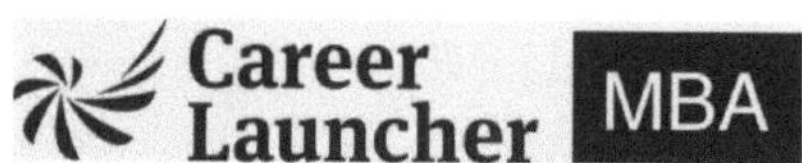

Part – I
General Knowledge

Indian History

The history of India has been broadly divided into three distinct periods, viz.:
1. Ancient India
2. Medieval India
3. India Under British Rule

The history of modern India is further sub-divided into two major periods, viz.:
(a) The British Period
(b) The Indian Freedom Struggle and Partition of India

Ancient India

Indus Valley Civilization: The most important period of ancient Indian history is the development of Indus Valley Civilization. This civilization was developed on the banks of river Indus. It extended from Jammu in the north to Ahmednagar in the south, and in various regions of Gujarat. The main sites which have been found in the excavation are: Kalibangan in Rajasthan, Lothal in Gujarat, Banwali in Haryana and Ropar in Punjab. Indus Valley Civilization period lies between 3000 BC and 1500 BC. The main cities associated with it are Harappa, Mohenjo-Daro and Lothal. The main feature of this civilization was the town planning. They had great buildings, well-planned roads, cities and drainage system. Hunting and agriculture were their main sources of livelihood. They were the first to produce cotton.

Indus Valley Civilization: This was the earliest civilization that flourished in India on the banks of the river Indus, from frontiers extending from Manda on the Chenab near Jammu in the north to Daimabad, on the Godavari in Ahmednagar in the South, embracing 200 sites in the Kutch-Saurashtra region of Gujarat out of more than 1000 and above sites all over.

Period: Between 2500 BC and 1800 BC. Early Harappan (C. 3200 - 2600 BC);

Cities: More than 800 sites related to Harappan civilization have been discovered. Some important ones are:

Harappa: Located on the banks of the Ravi in Punjab was the first settlement where the Indus civilization was discovered. In terms of its size and variety of objects discovered, it ranks as the premier city of the Indus Civilization.

Mohenjodaro: Mohenjodaro in Sind on the bank of Indus is the largest known Indus city. Most of the information about the Indus Civilization is derived from the study of town planning, houses, seals and sealings from this place.

Kalibangan: Similar to Mohenjodaro, the site of Kalibangan in Rajasthan excavated in 1960s seems to have been a provincial capital.

Lothal: The site of Lothal in Gujarat was an outpost for sea-trade with the contemporary West Asian Civilizations.

Alamgirpur: Located towards the east in the Ganga-Yamuna Doab

Analysis of Location of Harappan Towns: Most of the Harappan sites were located in the flood-plains of the Indus and Ghaggar-Hakra rivers.

Features

Political : Its seems that there was a central government, as per the evidence from the existence of assembly hall and citadels.

Socio-economic: The Indus Valley Civilization people sowed seeds in the flood plains in November, when the flood water receded and reaped their harvest of wheat and barley in April, before the advent of the next flood. Wheat, rice, barley, milk, dates, fish, eg and animal flesh formed their staple food. Cotton was first produced by the Indus valley people. Spun and woven cotton and wool dresses were used by them. Agriculture, hunting, fishing and rearing of animals/birds was their main source of livelihood.

Society: The people had a highly developed artistic sense which is reflected in their pottery, and painting on vases.

Town Planning: Great buildings, double-storeyed dwellings, and drainage system were in existence. There were planned cities and roads.

The Vedic Period: The Aryans

Early Vedic age (1500 BC- 1000 BC)

(A)   Early Vedic Period:

This is marked by the entry of Aryans, who were originally inhabitants of Central Asia around the Caspian Sea and probably came through Hindukush mountains.

Their period lies between 2500–2000 BC.

The main features of Aryans were:

They were the admirers of nature and worshipped sun, fire and water. *Yagna* was an important part of their religion. They had organized system of living, and were quite matured socially and politically.

They had following religious books:

(i)   **Vedas:**

These books were their most sacred books. (These are also the oldest known books of Indus Valley Civilization). They were four in number, viz.

(a) *Rig Veda:* The oldest, and contained prayers of God, Vayu, Varun, Indra and Agni.

(b) *Sam Veda:* It dealt with music.

(c) *Yajur Veda:* It dealt with formulae and rituals.

(d) *Atharva Veda:* It dealt with medicines.

(ii)   **The Puranas:** The Puranas were 18 in number and contained details of Aryan civilization, like their rituals, traditions and formulae, etc.

(iii)   **The Upanishads:** They are the main source of Indian philosophy and are 300 in number.

The **Brahmanas** and **Aranyakas** are the other important religious books of Aryans.

Who were the Aryans: The Aryans were semi-nomadic pastoral people who originally inhabited the area around the Caspian Sea in Central Asia. The Aryans entered India, probably, through the Khyber Pass (Hindukush Mountains) around 1500 BC in more than two waves in search of new pastures. The holy book of Iran, Zend Avesta, whose language has close resemblance with the Indo-European Languages indicates the possibility of entry of some Aryans to India via Iran. The word 'Aryan' comes from 'ari', which in the Vedic times meant 'foreigners' or 'strangers'. The first reference to the Aryans is found in the Bagharkai Peace Treaty (in Western Asia 1350 BC), concluded between the kingdoms of Mitanni and Hittites in which the Aryan gods, Varuna , Indra, Mitra and Nasatya were invoked as witnesses.

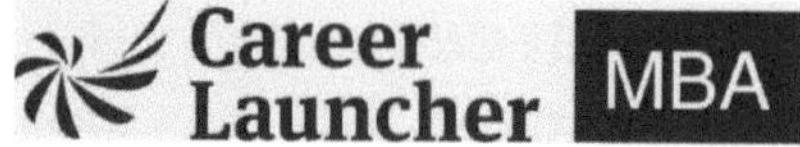

(B) **The later Vedic Period:**

This period ranges from 2000–700 BC. The important features of this period are:

(i) It is also known as the period of **Brahmanical Age** which resmbles modern-day, Hindu religion.

(ii) Society was divided into four castes: (a) **Brahmins,** (b) **Kshatriyas,** (c) **Vaisyas** and (d) **Sudras,** depending upon the work they did in the mentioned order of preference. Brahmins were the priestly class, Kshatriyas were the fighters, Vaisyas were the business class and Sudras represented the labour class.

(iii) Two great epics were written in this period, namely Mahabharata by Ved Vyas, and Ramayana by Maharishi Valmiki. The shastras basically dealt with Indian philosophy and concepts of birth, death and God.

(C) **Rise of religions (other than Hinduism):**

(i) **Buddhism:** Initiated by a Kshatriya prince of **Shakya clan,** Siddhartha, (later came to be known as **Buddha**) around 6th century BC, who was born at **Lumbini** (in present day Nepal) near Kapilavastu. He was the son of king Shuddhodhana. He went in search of truth and attained enlightenment under a *pipal* tree at **Bodh Gaya,** and delivered his first sermons at Sarnath in UP. He spread his message for many years and died at **Kusinagar in** present day **UP. There are many sects of Buddhism, out of which three are important viz.**

- **Mahayan** (the higher vehicle): It believes Buddha to be a God.
- **Hinyan** (the lesser vehicle): It does not believes that Buddha was a God. It is a more pristine form of budhism.
- **Vajrayan** It is the tantric form of buddhism. Now prevelent in Laddakh and Bhutan.

Buddhism got divided into Hinyan and Mahayan at the fourth buddhist council held during the reign of Harshavardhan.

The main Buddhist teachings are: The eight-fold path of right faith, thought, action, livelihood, efforts, speech, remembrance and concentration, **belief in nirvana (freedom from the cycle of birth and death), ahimsa, law of karma.**

(ii) **Jainism:** Founded by Rishabha (a Kshatriya), Jainism attained peak under Vardhamana Mahavira (the 24th Tirthankara). Mahavira was born at **Kundagrama** in 540 BC in present day Bihar, and attained perfect knowledge, **'Kaivalya',** after he became ascetic at the age of 30. He became a 'Jina' (one who has conquered happiness and misery) and died at **Pawapuri** near Rajagir in present day Bihar. Jainism is also divided into two sects, viz., **digambars** and **shwetambara.** Former is a more pristine form, and remain naked, while latter, wear white clothes.

The main features of Jainism are:
The *tri-ratna* concept, consisting of: (a) right knowledge, (b) right faith, and (c) right conduct. Belief in karma and belief in ahimsa, are the other two great teachings of this religion.

(D) **Various important empires and dynasties:**

Name of empire/dynasty	Period	Important characteristics
Magadha empire	Around 542 BC	Prominent kings were Bimbisara, Ajatashatru, Shishunaga and Nanda
Mauryan dynasty Ashoka: 273–232 BC Both of Kaling: 261 BC	321–232 BC	Founded by Chandragupta Maurya, Ashoka was the other prominent king of this dynasty
Gupta dynasty (Golden Age)	AD 320–550	Prominent rulers were Chandragupta I, Samudragupta and Chandragupta II
Harshavardhana	AD 606–647	He was the last Hindu king of North India
Rajputs	AD 650–1200	Prominent rulers were Prithvi Raj Chauhan and Jaichand Rathore

Other important dynasties:

(i)	Chalukyas (AD 550–642)	Prominent rulers were Pulkeshin I and II
(ii)	Cholas – Founded by Rajaraja-I	Prominent rulers were Rajendra Chola and Rajendra III
(iii)	Rashtrakutas (AD 753–973)	Prominent rulers were Krishna I, Amogha Varsha
(iv)	Yadavas (AD 1191–1318)	Prominent rulers were Ramachandra and Singhana
(v)	Vijayanagar's empire (AD 1336–1646)	Krishnadevaraya was the only prominent ruler of the empire and ruled in the Deccan part of India

Religious Books

1. **The Vedas:** These are the most sacred books of early Aryans. There were four Vedas and the Brahmanas concerned with these Vedas are:

   i. Rig Veda (Aitaraya Brahamana and Kaushitika Brahamana) Book of Hymns

   ii. Sama Veda (Jaminya Brahamana and Tandyamaha Brahamana) Book of Malodies and Charts

   iii. Yajur Veda (Satpatha Brahamana) book of Sacifices

   iv. Atharva Veda (Gopatha Brahamana) Book of magical and Technical formulae

2. **The Brahamanas :** Throw light on the socio-political life of the Aryans and form a sort of explanation of their religion, especially, sacrifice. It also contain ritualistic formulae for the respective Veda and Priests.

3. *The Aranyakas:* These forest books are treaties on mysticism and philosophy and are the concluding portion of the **Brahmanas**. It explains the metaphysics and symbolism of sacrifice.

4. **The Upanishads:** The Upanishads are the main source of Indian philosophy. There are about 300 Upanishads of which 10 have attracted worldwide attention as they deal with philosophy and theology of the Aryans . These are commentaries which are appended to the Aranyakas and deal mainly with philosophy and religion.

5. **The Puranas:** Are 18 in number, of which the Bhagawat Purana and Vishnu Purana are the most important. They give religious and historical details of the Aryan civilization, and contain legends, rituals, tradition and moral codes.

6. **Manu Smriti:** Manu was the great law-giver in the Aryan period and his book, Manu Smriti, deals with the laws of inheritance, duties of kings and his subjects. As Manu established a detailed legal system for the Aryans, he is considered the first law-giver of India.

Doctrines	Priest/Teacher	Important Information
1. Nayasutra (Logical Doctrine)	Gautama Maharshi	Hindu doctrines based on logic
2. Vaisheshika (Monic Doctrine)	Karnad and Ramanuja	This is basis of Vishistadwaita
3. Yogasutra (Yoga Doctrine)	Maharishi Pathanjali	A hormonic doctrine that deals with harmony between mind and body through yoga.
4. Sankya sutra (Numerical Doctrine)	Kapil Maharishi and Madhvacharya	Duite Siddhanata which deals with numerals
5. Uttara Meemamsa	Badatayans	Major upanishadic work taken up by the rishis of that time
6. Poorva Meemamsa	Jaimini Maharshi	About worship via Yajna (rituals) and also become the basis of Karmamarga.

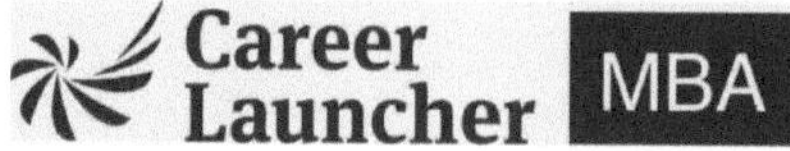

Later Vedic Period (1000 - 600 BC): Rishis who were the authors of the Vedas are Madhuchandra Vaisvamitra, Gurutsamida, Afri, Bhardvaj, Kanva, Kashypa Rashikas, Vamadevas, Yami Vaivasratai, Sasvathi and other.

Growth of Buddhism and Jainism: In sixth BC, also called the period of religious unrest.
As a result of revolt against the supremacy of Brahmanical priests, several schools of philosophy opposing Brahmanism developed, led by the Kshatriyas of the royal families of Magadha who later helped in the propagation of Jainism and Budhism.

Buddhism: The fourth greatest religion in the world originated in India. Buddhism received state patronage of king like Ashoka the Great, and it spread to neighbouring countires like Myanmar, Sri Lanka, Japan Vietnam, Thailand.

The Schism (or split) in Buddhism: During the 4th Buddhist council held in Kashmir, the Budhists split into two groups: the Himanyas (believed in simple teachings of Buddha) and the Mahayamas (the preachers with doctrine of bhakti as their integral part) Pali was the main language for Himanyas and Sanskrit for Mahayanas.

Founder: Founded by Gautama Siddhartha who was a Kshatriya prince of the Saka clan. He was born in 567 BC (or 576 BC as is believed by some historians) at Lumbini in Nepal and was the son of Suddhodana, *Raja of Kapilavastu.*

Influence of Buddhism: *Political* Buddhism destroyed the rising militant spirit and fostered a sense of national unity and universal brotherhood.
Educational centres were founded at Buddhist Viharas and Indain culture spread to regions outside India during the reigns of emperor Ashoka and Kanishka.

Decline of Buddhism: Buddhism declined as Hinduism reformed with the rise of the Rajputs as a military force. Muslim invasions in the 11th and 12th centuries led to its further disintegration.

Founder: Founded by Rishabha, who was father of King Bharata, the first Chakravarti of India. Jainism became a major religion under Vardhamana Mahavira who was the 24th Tirthankara or Prophet of Jainism.

Doctrine
1. Attainment of Nirvana (release from rebirth) through Tri-Ratna (three jewels) consisting of (a) Right faith, (b) Right knowledge, (c) Right conduct,
2. Belief in Ahmisa or non-violence in world, thought or deed towards all living beings.
3. Belief in Karma through denying the existence of God and dismissal of ritual.

///////Medieval India///////

Marked by the beginning of the Sultanate of Delhi, which was established after the conquest of Muhammad Ghouri. The period of Sultanate of Delhi, ranges from AD 1206–1526. This is considered as the beginning of Muslim rule in India.

Important dynasties:
(i) The **Slave dynasty's** period ranges from AD 1206–1290. It was founded by Qutub-ud-din Aibak and the prominent rulers of this dynasty were Iltutmish and **the only Muslim woman ruler of India, Razia Sultana.**
(ii) The **Khilji dynasty** was founded by Jalal-ud-din Khilji and its period ranges from AD 1290–1320. Alaud-din Khilji was one of the most prominent rulers of this dynasty.
(iii) The **Tughlak dynasty** was founded by Ghiasuddin Tughlak and the period ranges from AD 1320–1414. **Ibn Batuta was an important African traveller who visited India in 1333**.
(iv) The **Lodhi dynasty** was founded by Bahlol Lodhi and the period of this dynasty ranges from AD 1451–1526. Sikander and Ibrahim Lodhi were the other two prominent rulers belonging to this dynasty.

Decline of Delhi Sultanate

The main causes were:
(a)   Despotic and military type of governments which did not have the confidence of the people
(b)   Degeneration of the Delhi sultans
(c)   The Sultanate became too vast and could not be controlled effectively
(d)   Financial instability
(e)   Number of slaves increased to 1,80,000 in Firoz Shah's time which was a burden on the treasury

First Battle of Panipat: The first Battle of Panipat was fought in 1526 between Ibrahim Lodhi, the Sultan of Delhi and Babur, the ruler of Kabul, Babur invaded India and established the Mughal dynasty.

The Mughal Dynasty (1526 - 1540 and 1555 - 1857)

Extent: Stretched from Punjab to Bengal, including Jaunpur and Bihar, in the 16th century. Included Kabul in the north-west, Kashmir in the north; Sindhi, Multan , Ajmer and Gujarat in the west; Malwa and Benar in the south; and Odisha and Bengal in the east at the time of Akbar's death. Stretched from Kabul, kandhar and Peshawar in the north of Kaveri in the south by the end of the 17th century.

Important rulers of Mughal dynasty:

One of the most important dynasties of India is **Mughal dynasty,** which reigned almost continuously from AD 1526–1857 **(the longest period).**

Important Rulers

Babur (1526 - 1530): Is said to have founded the Mughal empire. He defeated Ibrahim Lodhi in the First Battle of Panipat on 20 April 1526 and became emperor of Delhi. In 1527, he defeated rana Sanga at Khanwa a near Fatehpur Sikri and occupied Agra. In 1527, in the Battle of Gorge, he defeated the Afghans and thus, became the master of the entire India.

He Wrote his autobiography, Tuzuk-i-Babri in which he gives an excellent account of India and his empire. He died in 1530.

Humayun (1530 - 1540): He was the son of Babur and ascended the throne in 1530. His succession was challenged by his brothers Kamran, Hindal and Askari along with the Afghans. He fought two battles against Sher Shah at Chausa (1539) and at Kannauj (1560) and was completely defeated by his enemies. He escaped to Persia where he passed 12 years of his life in exile.

After Sher Shah's death, he invaded India in 1555 and defeated his brothers and the Afghans. He once again became the ruler of India. He died in and accident in 1556, just two years after he regained his kingdom.

Sher Shah Suri (1540 - 1545): An Afghan who ruled the country for a brief period from 1540 - 1545 after defeating Humayun. His empire extended from the Brahmaputra in the east to the Indus in the west, from the Himalayas in the north to the Narmada in the south. During his reign of five years, he introduced a brilliant administration, land revenue policy and several other measures to improve economic conditions of his subjects. He issued the coin called 'Rupia' and fixed standard weights and measures all over the empire. He also improved communications by building several highways. He built the Grand Trunk Road (G.T.Road), that runs from Peshawar to Calcutta. He also introduced military reforms; he recruited and paid the soldiers directly and every soldier had hic *Chehra* (face) recorded and his horse branded with the imperial sign. He set up cantonments in various part of his empire and a strong garrison was posted in each cantonment.

Akbar **(1556-1605):** The eldest son of Humayun, he ascended the throne at the young age of 13 on 14 February 1556 and his tutor Bairam Khan was appointed as the regent. The most successful Mughal emperor. An excellent leader, who separated religion and politics, started a new religion called **Din-e-Ilahi.**

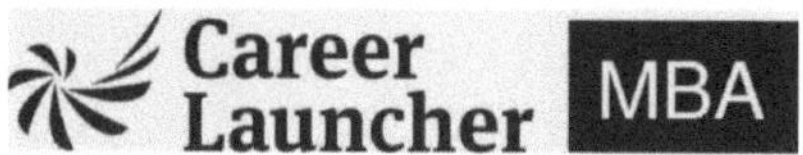

Jahangir (1605-1627): Salim, son of Akbar, came to the throne after Akbar's death in AD 1605. He is known for his strict administration of justice. In May 1611 Jehangir married Mihru-un-nisa, widow of Sher Afghan, a Persian nobleman of Bengal. Later on, she was given the title 'Nur Jahan'. Nur Jahan took an active interest in the matters of the state and also ruled the empire when Jahangir was ill for a long time.
Jahangir issued coins jointly in Nur Jahan's named and his own.

Relation with Foreigners: In 1608, Captain William Hawkins, a representative of the East India Company came to Jahangir's court. In 1615, Sir Thomas Roe, an ambassador of King James of England also came to his court. Though initially Jahangir resisted, he later on granted permission to the English to establish a trading post at Surat.

Revolts: Guru Arjan Dev was martyred during his period, thus alienating the Sikh Community.

Aurangzeb (1659 - 1707): After imprisoning Shahjahan, his son Aurangzeb was crowned at Delhi under the title *Alamgir*. He ruled for 50 years till his death in February, 1707 in Ahmednagar.

Extent of the Empire: Aurangzeb's empire extended from Kashmir in the north to Jinji in the south, and the Hindu-kush in the west to Chittagong in the east.

During this period, the Marathas, under Shivaji, rose to power and were a force to reckno with.

The Execution of Sambhaji in 1689 saw the collapse of the Maratha empire. Aurangzeb's empire now extended But in certain parts of south India (Mysore, Maharashtra, etc), he was not entirely successful in thwarting his enemies. Aurangzeb never returned to the north and died in Ahmednagar in February, 1707.

Intolerance of other religions: He was Muslim fanatic and thus was an intolerant autocrat. Many Hindu temples were demolished and religious festivals, idol worship and pilgrimages were banned during his reign.

Sikh Revolt: Aurangzeb captured Guru Teg Bahadur, the 9th Guru of Sikhs in 1675 and executed him when he refused to embrace Islam. Guru Gobind Sing, son of Guru Teg Bahadur, organized his followers into a militant force called 'Khalsa' to avenge the murder of his father. Guru Gobind Singh continued the war against Mughals but he too was put to death.

Decline of the Mughal Empire

After Aurangzeb, the Mughal empire rapidly declined. Important causes for the decline were:
(a) Aurangzeb's Rajput, Deccan and religious policies;
(b) Stagnation in agricultural production, trade and manufacture;
(c) Rapidly rising demands of the ruling classes, leading to attempts to realize more from Jagirs, causing peasant and Zamindari discontent;
(d) Jagirdari crisis: Nobel tried to corner the most profitable Jagirs, leading to corruption;
(e) Factionalism among nobility after Aurangzeb; development of powerful Irani, Turani, Deccani, Hindustani blocs in the court who vied for power in order to destabilize the central administrative machinery;
(f) Rise of independent kingdoms;
(g) Rise of European power in India;
(h) Nadir Shah's invasion in 1739.

Third Battle of Panipat: The third battle of Panipat fought between Ahmed Shah abdali and the Marathas, ended Maratha power.

In 1498, a Portuguese sailor Vasco da Gama discovered the sea route to India. East India Company of Britain came here with the excuse of trading and soon started developing its political dominion in India and, finally, succeeded in establishing their rule over India.

(A) **Important events related to modern Indian history:**
  (i) **First War of Independence (Mutiny of Sepoys):** It took place in 1857, when soldiers refused to touch the new rifle cartridges which were said to have been greased with cover made of animal fat. **Mangal Pande** was a prominent figure, who surfaced during this mutiny. He killed two Britishers at Barrackpore, and this was also one of the causes of the mutiny.
  (ii) **Government of India Act, 1858:** This proclaimed the direct governance of British crown over India.
  (iii) **Formation of Indian National Congress:** A.O. Hume is credited with the formation of Indian National Congress in **December 1885,** which held its **first session at Bombay,** under the **presidentship of W.C. Bonnerjee.**
  (iv) **Partition of Bengal:** It took place in 1905.

(B) **Other significant events related to Indian Freedom Movement:**

Year	Important events happenings in that year
1885	Formation of Congress by A. O. Hume
1905	Partiton of Bengal, launching of swadeshi movement
1906	Formation of Muslim League by Nawab Salimullah of Dacca
1907	Surat session of Congress, where congress got split into moderates and extremists
1909	Morley-Minto Reforms, in which separate electorates for Hindus and Muslims was introduced for the first time.
1911	Capital shifted from Calcutta to New Delhi (architectured by Lutyen)
1916	Lucknow session of Congress, where the famous Lucknow pact was signed between congress and muslim league. Formation of home rule league by Annie Besant.
1917	Champaran satyagraha (champaran is a place in Bihar) by Mahatma Gandhi. His first satyagraha in India.
1919	The draconian Rowlatt Act, Jalliyawallah massacre at Amritsar on the orders of General O'Dyer; Montague-Chemlsford reforms.
1920	Khilafat Movement against British by Shaukat and Muhammad Ali. Launching of non cooperation movement by Mahatama Gandhi.
1922	Chauri chaura, incident in UP and widhrawl of NCM by Gandhi, **formation of Swaraj party** by Motilal Nehru, C.R. Das and N. C. Kelkar.
1927	Simon Commission to India, which was protested by Lala Lajpat Rai. He died during a lathi charge during the protest.
1929	Passing of Purna Swaraj resolution at Lahore session of Congress under the presidentship of Jawaharlal Nehru.
1930	Dandi March (Salt Satyagrah) by Mahatma Gandhi from Sabarmati ashram (a palce in Gujrat). First round table conference in London
1935	Government of India Act
1937	Formation of Congress Ministries in provinces
1939	Out break of World War II, resignation of Congress ministries
1942	Quit India Movement, Wavell plan and Shimla conference. Maulana Abul Kalam Azad attended the conference representing Congress
1945	Cabinet Mission Plan which envisaged forming of the interim government and to determine means of transferring power.
1946	Formation of Constituent Assembly under Rajendra Prasad (Muslim league did not participate)
1947	Mountbatten Plan (June 3 plan) and partition of India

General Knowledge

(C) Important Governor General and Viceroys associated with British rule and related events:

Name	Events associated with
Lord Dalhousie (1848-1856)	Mainly known for **Doctrine of Lapse**, responsible for annexing number of states on the basis of this philosophy. First train from Bombay to Thane started during his reign in 1853.
Lord Cornwallis (1786-1793)	Credited with a **new revenue system** under the **permanent settlement of Bengal. Introduction of Civil services.**
Lord Canning	The revolt of 1857. The first Viceroy of India
Lord Wellesley (1798-1805)	The subsidiary alliance system.
Lord Curzon (1899-1905)	Partition of Bengal
William Bentinck (1828-35)	**Abolition of Sati** and reducing the female infanticide.
Thomas B. Macaulay	His advice was instrumental in **introducing English, under the leadership of William Bentinck.**
Lord Hastings(1813-1823)	Associated with **Ryotwari settlement.**
Robert Clive	He was the **first British Governor of Bengal.**
Warren Hastings (1773-1785)	The **first Governor-General of India; Regulating Act 1773 and Pitt's India Act of 1784 were passed during his tenure.**
Lord Mountbatten	The **first Governor-General of Free India.**
C. Rajagopalachari	**First Indian and last Governor-General of Independent India.**

Reforms under British period and important people carrying them

Warren Hastings (1772 - 1758): Warren Hastings succeeded Clive in 1772 and became the first Governor-General of India. He passed The Regulating Act 1773, giving a legalized working constitution to the Company's dominion in India. It envisaged a Council of Ministers headed by the Governor - General.

The Pitt's India Act of 1784 was passed by the British Parliament to put the Company's affairs in permanent centralized control of the British Parliament.

Lord Cornwallis (1786 - 93): Hasting in 1787. He introduced a new revenue system under the permanent Settlement of Bengal in 1793 with a view to stabilize land revenue and create a loyal contented class of Zamindars.

Lord Wellesley (1798 - 1805): During the governor-generalship of Lord Wellesley, the Fourth Mysore War (1799) was fought. Tipu Sultan, after regaining lost strength, set out again on his plan to oust the British from India with the help of Napolean and the Persian king.

Lord Hastings (1813 - 23): Under the governorship of Lord Hastings, Nepal was defeated in 1814, resulting in Nepal ceding Garhwal and kumaon to the British. In 1818, the Marathas made a last attempt to regain their independence. This led to the third Anglo-Maratha war in which the Marathas were completely crushed.
During Hasting' tenure various reforms were initiated such as the Ryotwari settlement according to which direct settlement was made between the government and the Ryots (cultivators).

Lord William Bentinck (1828 - 35): He was famous for the social reforms he introduced , such as abolition of Sati (1829), suppression of Thuggee, suppression of female infanticide and human sacrifices, English was introduced as a medium of higher education on the advice of his council member, Lord Bentinck also made a pact with Maharaja Ranjit Singh, the ruler of Punjab . By the charter Act 1833 , the company ceased to be a trading company and bacame an administrative power.

Raja Rammohan Roy: Lived during his period . He was a religious and social reformer who helped bentinck in the abolition of Sati. In 1829, a new society called Brahmo Samaj was started by Rammohun Roy which discarded idol worship, caste system and several complicated rites and rituals.

Sir Charles Metacalfe (1836 - 44): He was notable for removing restriction on the press and media.

Lord Hardinge (1844 - 48): During his period the First Sikh War (1845) was fought between the Sikhs and the British. The Sikhs were defeated and were brought under British control.

Lord Dalhousie (1848 - 56): Lord Dalhousie succeeded Lord Harding in 1848 . During his period the Second Sikh War (1849) was fought in which the Sikhs were defeated again and Dalhousie was successful in annexing the whole of Punjab to the British administration.

The Doctrine of Lapse was introduce by Lord Dalhousie, whereby in the absence of a natural heir, the sovereignty of Indian states was to lapse to the British and such rulers were not permitted to adopt a son to inherit their kingdoms.

Reforms: The first railway line between Bombay and Thane was opened in 1853 and in the same year Calcutta and Agra were connected by telegraph. Other reforms include setting up of P.W.D and passing of the Widow Remarriage Act (1856).

Lord Ripon: He was appointed Viceroy of India in 1880. During his time in India, Ripon introduced legislation (the "Ilbert Bill", named for his secretary, Courtenay Ilbert), that would have granted native Indians more legal rights, including the right of Indian judges to judge Europeans in court. He was known for introducing the Local Self Government in 1882. He is often referred as father of Local Self Government in India.

Ramakrishna and Vivekananda: Ramakrishna Paramahansa (1836 - 1886), a priest at a temple in Dakshineshwar near Calcutta emphasized that there are many roads to God. His great disciple, Swami Vivekananda (1863 - 1902) popularized his religious message and founded Ramakrishna Mission in 1896.

Arya Samaj: The Arya samaj was founded in 1875 by Swami Dayanand Saraswati in order to reform Hindu religion in north India. Swami Dayanand believed that there was only one God who was to be worshipped in spirit and not in the form of idols and images. He also wrote Satyarth Prakash.

Lord Wavell (1944 - 47): The Cabinet Mission Plan (1946) provided for an interim government and laid down the procedure for the framing of the Indian Constitution. The observation of direct Action Day in Calcutta by the Muslim League led to riots and bloodshed. On 20 February 1947 the Prime Minister of England, Clement Atlee, announced that transfer of power would take place before June 1948 . Riots and disturbances continued vigorously in demand for Partition of India.

Lord Mountbatten (1947 - 1948): Lord Mountbatten was the last Viceroy and the first Governor-General of Free India. The partition of India was decided by the June 3rd Plan and the Indian Independence Act 1947 and Pakistan a free nation on 14 August 1947. Lord Mountbatten retired in June 1948 and was succeded by C. Rajagopalachari, who became the first Indian Governor-General of Independent India.

Important events and incidents during British rule

Partition of Bengal: On 30 December 1898, Lord Curzon took over as the new Viceroy of India. The partition of Bengal came into effect on 16 October 1905 , through a Royal Proclamation, reducing the old province of Bengal in size by creating a new province of East Bengal, which later on became East Pakistan and present day Bangladesh. The government explained that it was done to stimulate growth of underdeveloped eastern region of the Bengal. But, actually, the main objective was to 'Divide and Rule' the most advanced region of the country at that time.

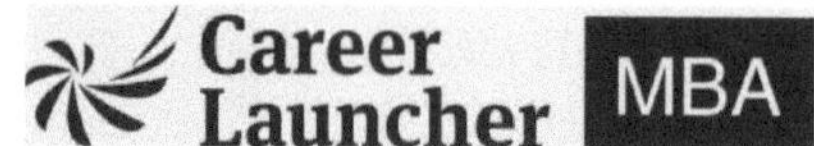

Reasons for Partition of Bengal: To destroy the political influence of the educated middle class among whom the Bengali intelligentsia were the most prominent. It also set up a communal gulf between Hindus and Muslims. The Indian national Congress unanimously condemned the partition of Bengal.

Surat Congress: The Indian National Congress split into two groups - the extremists and the moderates - at the Surat session in 1907 held on the banks of the river 'Tapti'. The extremists were led by Tilak, Lajpat rai and Bipin Chandra Pal and the moderates were led by Gopal Krishna Gokhale. At the Surat session, the moderate and extremist delegates of congress met in an atmosphere surcharged with excitement and anger.

The suddenness of the Surat fiasco took the extremist leaders by surprise and they offered their cooperation to the working committee of the Congress by accepting presidentship of Ras Behari Ghose. But the Moderates would not relent as they found themselves on firm ground. The government observing the opportunity lunched a massive attack on the Extremists by suppressing their newspaper and arresting their main leader, Tilak, and sending him to Mandalay Jail for six years. The Extremists were not able to organize an effective alternative party or to sustain the movement. Aurobindo Ghosh gave up politics and left for Pondicherry. Bipin Chandra Pal, also left politics temporarily and Lajpat Rai left for Britain. After 1908, the national movement as a wholed declined.

The Gandhian Era (1918 - 1947): Mahatma Gandhi dominated the Indian political scene from 1918 - 1947. This period of the Indian National Congress is also referred to as the Gandhian Era. It was the most intense and eventful phase of India's freedom struggle. Mahatma Gandhi provided the leadership of the highest order and his philosophy of non-violent Satyagraha bacame the most potent weapon to drive out the British from the Indian soil.

Rawlatt Act (1919): During the viceroyalty of Lord Chelmsford, a sedition committee was appointed by the government in 1918 with Justice Rowlatt which made certain recommendations to curb seditious activities in India. The Rowlatt Act 1919, gave unbridled powers to the government to arrest and imprison suspects without trial.
Gandhiji decided to fight against this Act and he gave a call for Satyagraha on 6 April 1919.
He was arrested on 8 April 1919. This led to further intensification of the agitation in Delhi, Ahmedabad and Punjab.

Jallianwala Bagh Massacre (13 April, 1919): The arrest of Dr Kitchlu and Dr Satyapal on 10 April 1919, under the Rowlatt Act in connection with Satyagraha caused serious unrest in Punjab. A public metting was held the next day, 13 April 1919 in a park called Jallianwala Bagh in Amritsar where thousands of people including women and children assembled. Before the meeting could start General O' Dyer ordered indiscriminate heavy firing on the crowd and the people had no way out to escape. As a result hundreds of men, women, and children were killed and more than 1200 people wounded.

Khilafat Movement (1920): The Caliph, Sultan of Turkey , was looked upon by the Muslims as their religious head. During the First World War, when the safety and the welfare to Turkey were threatened by the British thereby weakening the Caliph's position, Indian Muslims adopted an aggressive anti-British attitude. The two brother, Mohammed Ali and Shaukat Ali launched an anti-British movement in 1920 - the Khilafat Movement for the restoration of the Khilafat. Maulana Abul Kalam Azad also led the movement. It was supported by Gandhiji and the Indian National Congress which paved the way for Hindu-Muslim unity.

Non- Cooperation Movement (1920): Gandhiji to launch his non-violent, non-cooperation movement At the Calcutta Session in September 1920, the Congress resolved in favour of the non-violent, non-cooperation movement and defined Swaraj as its ultimate aim. The movement envisaged: (a) Surrender of titles and honorary officers; (b) resignation from nominated offices and posts in the local bodies; (c) Refusal to attend government. *darbars* and official functions and boycott of British courts by the lawyer; (d) Refusal of general public to offer themselves for military and other government jobs, and boycott of foreign goods. etc.

Apart from educational boycott, there was boycott of law courts which saw major lawyers like Motilal Nehru, C.R.Das, Rajagopalachari, Saifuddin Kitchlu, Vallabhbhai Patel, Aruna Asaf Ali, etc. giving up their lucrative practices in their fields and inspiring thousands of followers.

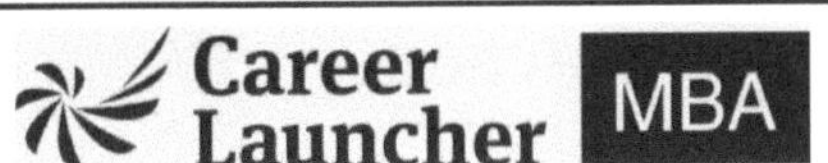

Chauri Chaura Incident (1922): The Congress session held at Ahmedabad in December 1921 decided to launch a Civil Disobedience movement while reiterating its stand on the non-violent, non-cooperation movement of which Gandhiji was appointed the leader. Before Gandhiji could launch the Civil Disobedience Movement a mob of countrymen at Chauri Chaura, a place near Gorakhpur in UP, Clash with the police which opened fire. In retaliation the mob burnt the police - station and killed 22 police man. This completed Gandhiji to call of the Civil Disobedience Movement on 12 February 1922.

Swaraj Party (1922): The foundation of the 'Swaraj Party' were laid on 1 January 1923, as the 'Congress-Khilafat Swarajya Party'. It proposed then an alternative programme of diverting the movement from widespread civil disobedience programme to restrictive one which would encourage its member to enter into legislative councils (established under Montford Reforms of 1919) by contesting elections in order to wreck the legislature from within and to use moral pressure to compel the authority to concede to the popular demand for self-government.

In the election held in 1923, the Swaraj Party captured 45 of the 145 seats. In provincial elections they secured few seats but in the central provinces they secured a clear majority. In Bengal, the Swaraj Party was the largest party. They followed the policy of undiluted opposition. The Swarajists demanded the release of all the political prisoners, provincial autonomy, repealing of the repressive laws imposed by the British government. However, after the death of C.R.Das in 1925 they drifted towards a policy of cooperation with the government. This led to dissension and the party broke up in 1926.

Lahore Session (1929): In December 1929, under the presidentship of Pt Jawaharlal Nehru, the Indian National Congress at its Lahore Session resolved declaring 'Poorna Swaraj' (complete independence) to be the goal of the national movement.

It was Gandhiji again who was the decisive voice in investing Jawaharalal Nehru with the office of President in what was to be a critical year of mass struggle.

Jawaharlal Nehru's Presidential address was a stirring call to action: *"We have now an open conspiracy to free this country from foreign rule, and you, comrades, and all the countrymen and countrywomen are invited to join it".* Nehru also made it known that in his view liberation did not mean only throwing off the foreign yoke: *" I must frankly confess that I am a socialist and a republican, and am no believer in kings and princes, or in an order which produces the modern kings of industry, who have greater power over the lives and fortunes on men than even the kings of old, and whose methods are as predatory as those of old feudal aristocracy."* He also spelt out the method of struggle: *"Any great movement for liberation today must necessarily be a massa movement, and mass movements must essentially be peaceful, except in times of organized revolt... And if the principal movement is a peaceful one, contemporaneous attempts at a sporadic violence can only distract attention and weaken it."*

On 31 December 1929, the newly adopted tricolour flag was unfurled and 26 January fixed as the Independence Day which was to be celebrated every year, pleading to the people not to submit to British rule any longer.

Dandi March (1930): Also called the 'Salt Satyagraha'. To achieve the goal of complete independence, Gandhiji launched another civil disobedience movement. Along with 79 followers, Gandhiji started his famous march from Sabaramati Ashram on 20 March 1930, for the small village Dandi to break the Salt Law. While Gandhiji was marching to Dandi, Congress leaders and workers had been busy at various levels with the hard organizational tasks of enrolling volunteers and members, forming grassroot Congress Committee, collecting funds, and touring villages and towns to spread nationalist messages.

On reaching the seashore on 6 April 1930, he broke the Salt Law by picking up salt from the seashore. By picking a handful of salt, Gandhiji inaugurated the Civil Disobedience Movement , a movement that was to remain unsurpassed in the history of the Indian National Movement for the countrywide mass participation it unleashed. The movement became so powerful that it sparked off partriotism even among the Indian soldiers in the Army. The Garhwal soldiers refused to fire on the people at Peshawar.

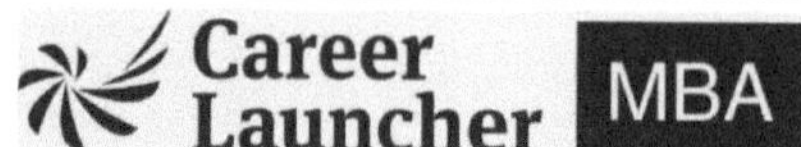

General Knowledge

Gandhiji was arrested on 5 May 1930. This was followed by another round of boycott of foreign goods and it took the shaped of a nationwide civil disobedience movement in which ladies also participated. Soon thereafter followed repressive measures such as mass arrests, lathi-charge, police firing, etc. About 1,00,000people went to jail. There was a massive protest on Gandhiji's arrest. But it was in Sholapur, where the textile workers, who dominated the strike along with the residents of the town, went on to attack alll symbols of the government authority and established a virtual paralled government in the city, which could only be dislodged with the imposition of the martial law after 16 May 1930.

Gandhi-Irwin Pact (1931): Early in 1931 two moderate statesmen, Sapru and Jayakar, initiated efforts to bring about approachment between Gandhiji and the government. Six meetings with Viceroy Lord Irwin, finally, led to the signing of a pact between the two on 5 March 1931, whereby the Congress called off the movement and agree to join the Second Round Table Conference. The terms of the agreement included the immediate release of all political prisoners not convicted for violence, the remission of all fines not yet collected, the return of confiscated land not yet sold to third parties, and lenient treatment of all the government officials who had resigned.

Gandhiji and other leaders were released from Jail as Irwin agreed to release most political prisoners and to return the properties that had been seized by the governments. The government also conceded the right to make the salt for consumption of villages along the coast, and also the right to peaceful and non-aggressive picketing. The Congress on its part, agreed to discontinue the Civil Disobedience Movement and to participate in the next round Table Conference.

The Second round Table Conference (1931): Was held London during the viceroyalty of Lord Willingdon during September-December 1931 and Gandhiji attended it on behalf of Indian National Congress. Nothing much was expected from the Conference for the imperialist political forces, which ultimately controlled the British Government in London, were opposed to any political or economic concession being given to India which could lead to its independence. The Round Table Conference, however, failed as Gandhiji could not agree with British Prime Minister Ramsay Macdonald on his policy of communal representation and refusal of the British government on the basic India demand for freedom. The conference closed on 11 December 1931, without any concrete result.

The Communal Award (1932): While Gandhiji was arrested on his return from London after the Second Round Table Conference, Ramsay Macdonald announced his award on communal representation in August 1931. This was another expression of the age-old British policy of 'Divide and Rule'. Besides containing provisions for representation of Muslims, Sikhs and Europeans, it envisaged communal representation of depressed classes also. Gandhiji was deeply grieved by this and underwent a fast in protest against this award since it aimed to divide India on a communal basis.

While many political Indians saw the fast as a diversion from the ongoing political movement, all were deeply concerned and emotionally shaken: almost everywhere in India mass meetings took place. Political leaders of different persuasions, like Madan Mohan Malviya, B.R.Ambedkar and M.C.Rajah became active. In the end they succeeded in hammering out an agreement, known as the Poona Pact.

Poona Pact (1932): As discussed, the communal award created immense dissatisfaction among Hindus. Gandhiji who was on fast in protest staked his life to get the award repudiated. According to the Pact, the idea of separate electorate for the Depressed Classes was abandoned but seats reserved for them in the provincial legislatures were increased from 71 in the award to 147, and in the Central legislature to 81 per cent of the total. Ultimately, the fast ended with the Poona Pact which annulled the award. The leaders of the various groups and parties among Hindus, and Dr B.R Ambedkar on behalf of the harijans, signed the pact. The Poona Pact between caste Hindus and the depressed classes agreed upon a joint electorate.

The third round Table Conference (1932): It was held in 1932 but again proved fruitless since the national leaders were in prison.

The Government of India Act, 1935: The Simon Commission report submitted in 1930 formed the basis for the Government of India Act received the royal assent on 4 August 1935.

The Act continued and extended all the existing features of the Indian constitution. Popular representation, which went back to 1892, dyarchy and ministerial responsibility, which dated from 1921, provincial autonomy, whose chequered history went back to eighteenth century presidencies, communal representation, which first received overt recognition in 1909, and the safeguards devised in 1919, were all continued and in most cases extended. But in addition there were certain new principles introduced .It provided for a federal type of government. Thus, the act:

i.   Introduced provincial autonomy
ii.   Abolished dyarchy in provinces
iii.   Made ministers responsible to the legislative and federation at the centre

The act of 1935 was condemned by nearly all section of Indian public opinion and was unanimously rejected by the Congress. The Congress demanded instead, the convening of a Constituent Assembly elected on the basis of adult franchise to frame a constitution for an independent India.

Although the Congress opposed the Act, yet it contested the elections when the Constitution was introduced on 1 April 1937; and formed ministries, first in six provinces and then in another two . The Congress high command exercised a great hold upon ministries of each province. The Muslim League was, however, not happy with the Congress rule, especially Mr Jinnah, who described it in these words: "Congress was drunk with power and was oppressive against Muslims."

Quit India Movement (1942 - 1945): On 8 August 1942, the Congress in its meeting at Bombay passed a resolution known as 'Quit India' resolution, whereby Gandhiji asked the British to quit India and gave a call for 'Do or die' to his countrymen. On 9 August 1942, Gandhiji was arrested but the other leaders continued the revolutionary struggle. Violence spread throughout the country, several government offices were destroyed and damaged, telegraph wires, were cut and communication paralyzed. The movement was, however, crushed by the government.

Cabinet Mission Plan: The struggle for freedom entered a decisive phase in the year 1945 - 46. The British Prime Minister, Lord Attlee, made a declaration on 15 March 1946, the British Cabinet Mission would visit India to make recommendations regarding constitutional reforms to be introduced in India. The Cabinet Mission which constituted of Lord Lawrence, Sir Stafford Cripps and A..V.Alexander visited India and met the representatives of different political parties, but a satisfactory solution to the constitutional difficulties could not be found. The Mission envisaged the establishment of a Constituent Assembly to frame the Constitution, as well as, an interim government. The Muslim League accepted the plan on 6 June 1946, while maintaining its rights of striving for a separate Muslim state. The Congress also partially accepted the plan.

Direct Action Campaign: Provoked by the success of the Congress, the Muslim League launched a direct action campaign on 16 August 1946, which resulted in heavy communal riots in the country.

Interim Government: On 2 September 1946, and interim government was formed. Congress members led by Pandit Jawaharlal Nehru joined it, but the Muslim League did not as it withdrew its earlier acceptance of the Cabinet Mission Plan.

Mountbatten Plan: In March 1947, Lord Mountbatten replaced Lord Wavell. He announced his plan on 3 June 1947. It offered a key to the political and constitutional deadlock created by the refusal of the Muslim Leagues to join the Constituent Assembly formed to frame the Constitution of India. Mountbatten's formula was to divide India but retain maximum unity. The country would be partitioned but so would be Punjab and Bengal, so that the Limited Pakistan that emerged would meet both the Congress and the League's position to some extent. the League's position on Pakistan was conceded in that it would be created, but the Congress position on unity would be taken into account to make Pakistan as small as possible. He laid down detailed principles for the partition of the country and speedy transfer of political powers in the form of dominion status to the newly formed dominion of India and Pakistan. Its acceptance by the Congress and the Muslim League resulted in the birth of Pakistan.

Partition of India: In accordance with the Independence Act 1947, India was partitioned on 15 August 1947 into India and Pakistan The Act made India and Pakistan independent dominions. Bloodshed and violence marked the exodus of refugees. The state of Kashmir acceded to the Indian Union, after the raiders were helped by Pakistan in October 1947. Lord Mountbatten was appointed the Governor-General of free India and M.A. Jinnah, the first Governor-General of Pakistan.

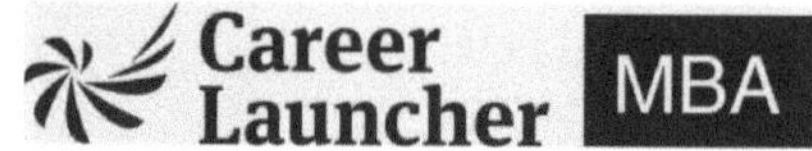

Year	Events
326 BC	Invasion of Alexander the Great on India
58 BC	**Beginning of Vikrami Era**
AD 78	**Beginning of Saka Era**
AD 1001	First invasion of India by Mahmud Ghazni
AD 1236	Accession of only women ruler of India, Razia Sultana, to the throne of Delhi
1498	Discovery of sea route of India by Portuguese traveller Vasco da Gama, via the Cape of Good Hope
1526	**First Battle of Panipat, between Babur and Ibrahim Lodi, Babur won and established Mughal empire.**
1540	Battle of Kanauj
1556	**Second Battle of Panipat (between Akbar and Himu)**
1576	Battle of Haldighati, Akbar defeated Rana Pratap
1600	**East India Company was established**
1675	Execution of the Ninth Sikh Guru, Guru Tegh Bahadur
1757	Battle of Plassey, East India Rule established through Lord Clive
1761	Shah Alam II became Indian emperor and **Third Battle of Panipat** between (Ahmad Shah Abdali and Maratha) took place
1764	Battle of Buxar between Mir Caseem & East India Company
1784	Pitt's India Act
1793	Permanent Settlement in Bengal
1829	Prohibition of Sati Practice
1853	First railway line became operational between Bombay and Thane
1857	First War of Independence or Mutiny of Sepoys
1885	Foundation of Indian National Congress
1905	First partition of Bengal under Lord Curzon
1914	Beginning of First World War
1920	Non Cooperation Movement
1930	Salt Satyagraha
1931	Gandhi-Irwin Pact
1931	Civil Disobediance
1939	Beginning of Second World War
1942-45	Quit India Movement
1943-44	Subhash Chandra Bose took over Azad Hind Fauj (Indian National Army); Bengal famine also occurred during this period.
1947	Independence of India
1948	Mahatma Gandhi assassinated
26 November 1949	Indian Constitution was adopted (Obeserved as National Law Day)
26 January 1950	India Became Republic

B.C.

326	Alexander defeated Porus in the Battle of Hydaspas.
261	Ashoka defeated Kalinga in the Kalinga War.

A.D.

712	Invasion of Sind by Mohd.-bin-Qasim.
1191	First Battle of Tarain in which Prithviraj Chauhan defeated Mohd. Ghori.
1192	Second Battle of Tarain in which Mohd. Ghori defeated Prithviraj Chauhan.
1194	Battle of Chhandwar in which Mohd. Ghori defeated Jaichandra of Kannauj.
1526	First Baffle of Panipat in which Babar defeated Ibrahim Lodhi.
1527	Battle of Khanua in which Babar defeated Rana Sanga.
1529	Battle of Ghaghara in which Babar defeated the Afghans.
1539	Battle of Chausa in which Sher Shah Suri defeated Humayun.
1540	Battle of Kannauj (or Bilgram) in which Sher Shah Suri defeated Humayun and forced him to flee.
1556	Second Battle of Panipat in which Bairam Khan (representing Akbar) defeated Hemu.
1565	Battle of Talikota (or Banihatti) in which an alliance of Ahmednagar, Bijapur, Golkonda and Bidar defeated the Vijaynagar empire (represented by Sadasiva).
1576	Battle of Haldighati in which Akbar defeated Maharana Pratap.
1615	Mewar submitted to the Mughals. A treaty of peace was signed between Jahangir and Rana Amar Singh of Mewar.
1649	Kandahar was lost to Persia forever by the Mughals.
1658	Battle of Dharmatt and Samugarh in which Aurangzeb defeated Dora Shikoh.
1665	Raja Jai Singh defeated Shivaji and the Treaty of Purandar signed.
1708	Battle of Khed in which Shahu defeated Tara Bai.
1737	Battle of Bhopal in which Baji Rao defeated Mohd. Shah.
1739	Battle of Karnal in which Nadir Shah defeated Mohd. Shah.
1757	Battle of Plassey in which the English forces (under Robert Clive) defeated Siraj-ud-daula, the Nawab of Bengal.
1760	Battle of Wandiwash in which the English forces defeated the French forces.
1761	Third Battle of Panipat in which Ahmed Shah Abdali defeated the Marathas.
1764	Battle of Buxar in which the English under Munro defeated the alliance of Nawab Mir Qasim of Bengal, Nawab Shuja-ud-daula of Awadh and Mughal emperor Shah Alam.
1767-69	First Anglo Mysore War in which Hyder Ali defeated the English forces.
1770	Battle of Udgir in which the Marathas defeated the Nizam.
1766-69	First Anglo Maratha War in which the British were defeated.
1780-84	Second Anglo Mysore War. Hyder Ali died during the battle (1 782) and the field was taken by his son Tipu Sultan. The war concluded with the Treaty of Mangalore (1784).

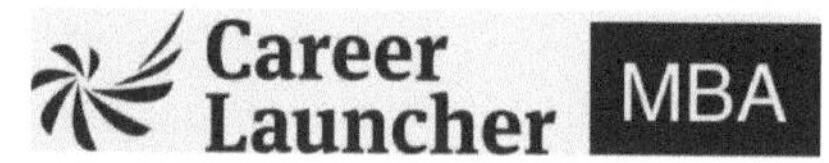

1789-92	Third Anglo Mysore War in which Tipu Sultan was defeated. The Treaty of Serirangapatnam followed.
1799	Fourth Anglo Mysore War in which Tipu was defeated and killed.
1803-06	Second Anglo Maratha War in which the British defeated the Marathas.
1817-19	Third Anglo Maratha War in which the British defeated the Marathas badly.

List of important Presidents of Indian National Congress

Session No.	Year	Place	President
1	1885	Bombay	W.C. Bonnerjee
2	1886	Calcutta	Dadabhai Naoroji
3	1887	Madras	Badruddin Tyabji
4	1888	Allahabad	George Yule (First European, Congress president)
5	1889	Bombay	Sir William Wedderburn
6	1890	Calcutta	Sir Phirozshah Mehta
9	1893	Lahore	Dadabhai Naoroji
21	1905	Banaras	G K Gokhale
22	1906	Calcutta	Dadabhai Naoroji
23	1907	Surat	Dr. Rash Behari Ghosh
33	1917	Calcutta	Mrs. Annie Beseant (First Women President of Congress)
35	1918	Delhi (Annual Session)	M. M. Malaviya
36	1919	Amritsar	Motilal Nehru
40	1923	Special Session	Lala Lajpat Rai
42	1924	Belgaum	M K Gandhi
43	1925	Kanpur	Mrs. Sarojini Naidu
47	1929	Lahore	Jawaharlal Nehru
56	1938	Haripura	S.C. Bose
57	1939	Tripuri	S.C. Bose

Important Newspaper brought out by National leaders

1	Bengal Gazzette	1780, In Calcutta, started by James Augustus Hickey. It was the first newspaper of India
2	Aharatta and Kesari	Bal Gangadhar Tilak
3	New India and Common Wheel	Annie Besant
4	Harijan, Young India	Mahatma Gandhi
5	Al Hilal	Maulana Azad

	Visitor	King
1	Megasthenes (greek)	Chandragupta Maurya
2	Fahien (Chinese)	Chandragupta II
3	Huen Tsang (Chinese)	Harshavardhan
4	Al-Beruni	He accompanied Mehmood of Gazni, when the latter invaded India. Al-Beruni has written an important book on India viz. **Tariq-i-Hind**, also known as **Kitab-i-Hind.**
5	Ibn Batuta	Muhammed bin Tuglak
6	Amir Khusro	Balban, Allaudin Khilzi, Muhammed bin Tuglak
7	Sir Thomas Roe	Jahangir
8	Abul Fazal ibn Mubarak	Akbar (His famous books are The Akbar Nama Ain-i-Akbari

India after Independence

Lord Mountbatten bacame the first Governor - General of free India. Sir C. Rajagopalachari became the first and the only Indian Governor-General of India in 1948. Pt Jawahar Lal Nehru took over as the first Prime Minister in 1950. Sardar Vallabhbhai Patel sing-handedly dealt with the accession of all princely states. All states were merged into neighbouring provinces. The state of Kashmir , Hyderabad and Mysore merged later on . Mahatma Gandhi undertook a fast for the sake of Muslim rights. On 30 January 1948, he was assassinated by Nathuram Vinayak Godse at the Birla House prayer meeting in Delhi.

On 13 September 1948, the Indian Army marched into Hyderabad after the violent actions of the Razakars, and the state was acceded to the Indian union. On 26 November 1949, the Constituent Assembly passed the new Constitution of India On the morning of 26 January 1950, India was proclaimed a republic and Dr Rajendra Prasad took over as the first President, Dr S. Radhakrishnan as the Vice-President and Pt Jawaharlal Nehru as the first Prime Minister of India.

During this period India has fought a number of wars with its neighbours
1948 - Pakistan attacked India and occupied large part of Kashmir.
1962 - China attacked India in retaliation to Indias suport to Tibet. China forcefully occupied large part of India straitching from parts of Ladakh and parts of Arunachal Pradesh.
1965 - Pakistan again attacked India heightened dispute over Kashmir. India defeated Pakistan comprehensively.
1971 - Bangladesh war. The two countries fought against one another and East Pakistan brook away and emerged as independence Bangladesh.

In addition to the wars mentioned above, there were couples of incident brought India close to having war with its neighbours. Operation in Kargil was one of them.

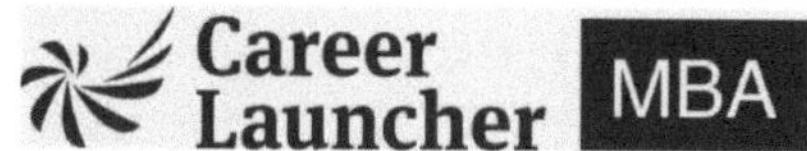

National Day

National Day	Date and Month	Remarks
Independence Day	15 August	India achieved Independence on this day in 1947
Republic Day	26 January	India became a Republic on this day in 1950
Martyr's Day	30 January	Mahatma Gandhi was assassinated on this day in 1948
Teachers' Day	5 September	Birthday of Dr S. Radhakrishnan, first Vice – President of India
Children's Day	14 November	Birthday of Pt Jawaharlal Nehru
Gandhi Jayanti	2 October	Birthday of Mahatma Gandhi

Other Important Days

Day	Date & Month
National Maritime Day	5th April
Quit India Day	9th august
National Rededication Day	31th October
National Integration Day	9th November
National Law Day	26th of November
Flag Day	7th December

Women

1.	First woman Prime Minister	Mrs Indira Gandhi
2.	First woman Chief Minister of a State	Mrs Sucheta Kripalani
3.	First woman Minister	Mrs Vijayalakshmi Pandit
4.	First woman Central Minister	Rajkumari Amrit Kaur
5.	First woman Speaker of Lok Sabha	Mrs Meira Kumar
6.	First woman Governor of a State	Mrs Sarojini Naidu
7.	First Indian woman President of Indian National Congress	Annie Besant
8.	First Indian woman President of UN General Assembly	Mrs Vijayalakshmi Pandit
9.	First Muslim woman to sit on the throne od Delhi	Razia Sultana
10.	First woman to swim across the English Cahnnel	Miss Arti Saha (now Mrs Arti Gupta)
11.	First woman to climb Mount Everest	Bachhendri Pal
12.	First woman to circumnavigate (sail round the world)	Ujwala Rai
13.	First woman IAS Officer	Anna George Malhotra
14.	First woman IPS Officer	Kiran Bedi
15.	First woman Advocate	Corknelia Sorabji
16.	First woman Judge	Annna Chandi
17.	First woman Judge of a High Court	Annna Chandi
18.	First woman Judge of Supreme Court	M. Fathima Bibi
19.	First woman Chief Justice of a High Court	Leila Seth
20.	First woman Doctor	Kadambini Ganguli
21.	First woman to pass MA	Chandra Mukhi Bose
22.	First woman editor of English newspaper	Dina Vakil
23.	First woman Chief Engineer	P.K.Thresia
24.	First woman to receive a Sena Madel	Constable Bimla Devi (88 BN of CRPF)-1990
25.	Youngest woman to climb Mount Everest	Dicky Dolma (19) from Manali - 1993
26.	First woman to climb mount Everest two times	Santosh Yadav (ITBP Officer) - 1993
27.	First Lady Magistrate	Omana Kunjamma
28	First woman to win Nobel Prize	Mother Teresa
29.	First to be crowned Miss India	Pramita (Ester victoria Abraham) - 1947
30.	First to be crowned Miss Universe	Sushmita Sen
31.	First to be crowned Miss World	Reita Faria (1966)
32.	First woman President	Pratibha Devi Singh Patil
33.	The first woman Speaker of a State Assembly	Shano Devi (Punjab)

Career Launcher **MBA**

General Knowledge

Man

1.	First Indian to swim across the English Channel	Mihir Sen
2.	First to Climb Mount Everest	Tenzing Norgay
3.	First to Climb Mount Everest without Oxygen	Phu Dorjee
4.	First Indian to join I.C.S.(ICS now is IAS)	Satyendra Nath Tagore
5.	First Indian to get Nobel Prize	Rabindranath Tagore
6.	First Indian in Space (first Indian cosmonaut)	Sqn Ldr Rakesh Sharma
7.	First British Governor general	Warren Hastings
8.	First Governor General of Free India	Lord Mountbatten
9.	First Viceroy of India	Lord Canning
10.	Last Governor General of Free India	C. Rajagopalachari
11.	First President of India	Dr Rajendra Prasad
12.	First Vice-President of India	Dr S . Radhakrishnan
13.	First Muslim President of India	Dr Zakir Hussain
14.	First Sikh President of India	Giani Zail Singh
15.	Firest Prime Minster	Pt Jawahar Lal Nehru
16.	First Speaker of Lok Sabha	G.V.Mavlankar
17.	First Chief Justice of India	Justice H.L.Kania
18.	First President of Indian National Congress	W.C.Bonnerjee
19.	First Indian to become member of Viceroy's Executive Council	Lord S.P.Sinha
20.	First Indian to become President of International Court of Justice	Dr Nagendra Singh
21.	First Emperor of Mvghal Dyansty	Babur
22.	First Field Marshal	S.H.F.J.Manekshaw
23.	First Indian Commander-in-Chief of India (now Field Marshal)	Gen. K.M.Cariappa
24.	First Chief of the Army Staff (Indian)	Gen . Maharaja Rajendra Sinhji
25.	First Chief of the Naval Staff (Indian)	Vice-Admiral R.D.Katari
26.	First Chief ot the Air Force Staff (Indian)	Subroto Mukherjee
27.	First Indian in British Parliament	Dadabhai Naoroii
28.	First Indian recipient of Victoria Cross (highest gallavtry award before independence)	Khudada Khan
29.	First Indian to circumnavigate the globe	Lt Col K.S.Rao
30.	First Indian to reach the South Pole	Col J.K.Bajaj (1989)
31.	First Indian High Court Judge	Justice Syed Mehamood (1878)
32.	First Indian to make a solo air flight	J.R.D. Tata
33.	First Indian to visit England	Raja Rammohun Roy (1878)
34.	First Indian Member of House of Lords (British)	Lord S.P.Sinha
35.	First Bar-at-Law	J.M.Tagore
36.	First Chairman of Raiya Sabha	Dr S. Radhakrishnan (1952 - 62)
37.	First Air Marshal	Arjan Singh
38.	First Judge to face impeachment in the Lok Sabha	Justice V.Ramaswami (1993)

Geography

Physical geography:

(A) Planets:

As per the International Astronomical Union (IAU), the planet is a celestial body which-
1. is in orbit around the sun.
2. has sufficient mass to assume hydrostatic equilibrium (a nearly round shape) and
3. has 'cleared the neighbourhood' around its orbits.

According to the definition, there are currently eight planets and five dwarf planet in the solar system.

(1)	Mercury	(Closest to the Sun and is the fastest planet to revolve around the Sun)
(2)	Venus	(The Brightest and hottest planet in all)
(3)	Earth	(Only known planet to possess life)
(4)	Mars	(Known as the Red planet. Explored for life by astronomers now, as it is having similarities with Earth)
(5)	Jupiter	(The largest planet of the solar system)
(6)	Saturn	(System of rings are the characteristic feature of this planet)
(7)	Uranus	
(8)	Neptune	

*   Please note that Pluto used to be a planet but recently has been discarded as a planet and is no longer counted as a planet.

(B) Comets:

Comets are cosmic snowballs of frozen gases, rock and dust roughly the size of a small town. When a comet's orbit brings close to sun, it heats up and spews dust and gases into a joint glowing head larger than most planet. The dust and gases form the tail that stretches away from the sun for millions of kilometers. Two famous comets known, are as follows:

(i) **Halley's comet:** Discovered by British astronomer Edmond Halley, takes 76.1 years to encircle the Sun. It was last seen in February 9, 1986.
(ii) **Smith-Tuttle comet:** It's a huge comet heading on a collision course with Earth on August 17, 2116.

(C) Satellites:

A satellite is a moon, planet or machine that orbits a planet or star. For example, Earth is a satellite because it orbits the sun. Likewise, the moon is a satellite because it orbits the Earth. Usually, the word 'satellite' refers to a machine that is launched into space and moves around Earth or another body in space.
Earth and moon are examples of natural satellites. Satellites are mainly used for communication such as beaming TV signals, Phone calls etc. A group of 20 satellites makeup the Global Positioning System (GPS).

These are the bodies which revolve around the planets. Mercury and Venus have no satellites. Earth has only one satellite (natural), i.e. Moon. Jupiter has the maximum number of satellites.
Moon: The first planet of our solar system visited by man. On July 20, 1969, Neil Armstrong and Edwin Aldrin were the first to set foot on the Moon, and between them, Neil Armstrong is the first person to have set foot on the Moon.

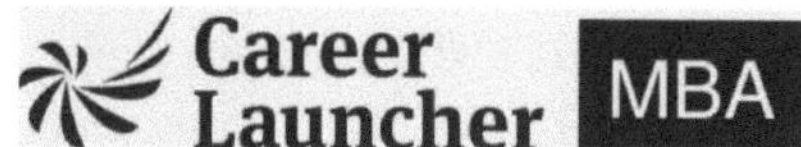

(D) Earth:

It is the fifth largest planet in the solar system. It is the third closest planet to the sun. Its shape is oblate spheroid, like a ball which is flattened at the poles.

Important facts about Earth:

(i)   Mean distance from the Sun: 1,49,407,000 km.

(ii) Time taken by Earth to revolve around the Sun: 365 days, 5 hours, 48 minutes and 45.51 seconds.

(iii) Time taken by Earth for rotating on its own axis: 23 hours 56 minutes and 4.09 seconds.

(iv) Earth is covered 70% by water and 30% by land.

Movements of Earth:

(i) **Revolution:** The Earth revolves around the Sun in an elliptical orbit. One complete revolution is called a year and this revolution of Earth causes change of seasons.

(ii) **Rotation:** Earth rotates on its own imaginary axis also, simultaneously revolving around the Sun. It moves from west to east. This causes day and night.

Notes:

Duration of days and nights is equal at the equator.

(E) Eclipses:

An eclipse is an astronomical event that occurs when an astronomical object is temporarily obscured, either by passing into the shadow of another body pass between it and the viewer.

(i) **Solar eclipse:** It occurs when the Moon comes between the Sun and the Earth, and this causes hindrance in Sun's light, when viewed from the Earth.

(ii) **Lunar eclipse:** When the Earth comes between the Moon and the Sun, the shadow cast by the Earth on the Moon causes lunar eclipse.

(F) Atmosphere:

The Earth is surrounded by a gaseous cover called the atmosphere. There are many gases in the atmosphere like Oxygen, Nitrogen, Carbon Dioxide, Helium, Argon, Xenon, etc. The maximum percentage of gas present in the atmosphere is Nitrogen and that comprises 78.09%.

Atmosphere is divided mainly into four layers:

(i)   **Troposphere:** It is the nearest layer to the Earth's surface and is up to 15 km of height from the Earth's surface.

(ii) **Stratosphere:** From the end of 15 km of troposphere, stratosphere is present till 50 km of the atmosphere.

(iii) **Mesosphere:** It lies between 50 km and 80 km above the surface of the Earth.

(iv) **Ionosphere:** It lies above the mesosphere and extends from 80 km to 400 km above the Earth's surface. Radio communication takes place because of this layer.

Note:

Ozone Layer: The ozone layer is situated in the stratosphere belt of earth's atmosphere. The basic Ozone gas structure consists of three oxygen atoms. Ozone gas is present in the stratosphere in the form of a layer, which extends from 12 km to 30 km above the earth's surface. The main function of Ozone is that it protects mankind from harmful radiations which comes from outer space i.e.; Ultra Violet radiations (UV- radiations) from the Sun. Now-a-days this Ozone layer is getting depleted which can cause skin cancer and damage vegetation. The main reason behind the depletion of Ozone layer is pollution and pollutants present in the atmosphere like Chlorofluorocarbons (CFC's, also known as Freons), which comes from refrigeration systems, aerosols, air conditioners and solvents.

To minimize the Ozone layer depletion the governments of many countries are now replacing the CFC's with simple hydrocarbons.

(G) Continents:

It is defined as any of the world's main continuous expanses of land (Europe, Asia, Africa, North and South America, Australia, Antarctica)

The surface of the Earth is made up of big land masses which are divided into seven continents. The seven continents are as follows:

(i) Asia: The largest continent (covers approximately. 30 per cent of the world land and hosts 59 per cent of the world population)

(ii) Africa: (The largest desert—Sahara—is there.)

(iii) North America

(iv) South America

(v) Antarctica: Covered with ice (coldest)

(vi) Europe (Comprises of western most peninsula of Eurasia)

(vii) Oceania (Australia): The smallest continent (The only continent with capital. i.e., Canberra)

Note:

Antarctica and Oceania are island continents.

(H) Oceans:

(i) There are five oceans on the Earth: (i) Pacific, (ii) Atlantic, (iii) Indian, (iv) Arctic, (v) Antarctic. Pacific being the largest, occupies 35.25% of the Earth's surface.

(ii) South China Sea has the maximum area among all the seas of the world.

(I) Rocks:

These are naturally occurring solid aggregate of one or more minerals or mineraloids.

These form the crust of the Earth. They are classified into three broad categories:

(i) Igneous rocks: It is the product of cooled solidified magma/lava and it constitutes 90% of the Earth's crust.

(ii) Metamorphic rocks: Original igneous or sedimentary rocks when subject to change due to pressure or temperature, metamorphose into metamorphic rocks, i.e. slate, marble, etc.

(iii) Sedimentary rocks: As the name suggests, these rocks are formed from the sedimentary deposits on the ocean beds, i.e. gypsum, limestone, etc.

(J) Important Mountain Ranges and Mountain Peaks of the World:

(i) Mountain ranges:

Name	Continent
Himalaya-Karakoram	Asia
Rockies	North America
Alps	Europe
Andes	South America

(ii) Mountain peaks:

Name	Continent	Height (In metres)
Everest	Asia	8848
K2 (Godwin Austen)	Asia	8,610
Kanchenjunga	Asia	8,590
Lhotse	Asia	8,500
Makalu 1	Asia	8,470
Dhaulagiri	Asia	8,170
Nanga Parbat	Asia	8,130
Nanda Devi	Asia	7,820

Note:

Everest is the highest mountain peak of the world, situated in Nepal and extended to Tibet and K2 is India's highest mountain peak, but it is situated in POK. Therefore, Kanchanjunga is the highest peak within India.

(K) Important Water bodies of the World:

(i) Lakes (Natural):

Name	Location
Caspian (also called the Caspian Sea)	Iran, Azerbaijan, Russia, Turkmenistan, Kazakhstan
Superior (largest fresh water lake of North America)	USA/Canada
Victoria	Kenya and Tanzania
Baikal (deepest lake of the world)	Russia
Titicaca (highest lake of the world)	South America

(ii) Canals (Shipping):

1. **Panama Canal:** It links the Pacific and the Atlantic Ocean. It is located in Central America and is 58 kilometres long.
2. **Suez Canal:** It links the Red Sea and the Mediterranean Sea. It is in Egypt and is 169 kilometres long.
3. **Kiel Canal:** It lies between Baltic Sea and North Sea ports. It is in Germany and is 98 kilometres long.

Note:

Angel Waterfall which is in Venezuela, is the highest waterfall in the world having a height of about 979 metres.

(iii) Important Rivers of the world:

Name	Length (km)	Country/Continent
Nile	6,690	Egypt, Africa
Amazon	6,570	Brazil, South America
Mississippi-Missouri	6,020	USA, North America
Yangtze-Kiang	5,980	China, Asia
Hwang Ho	4,840	China, Asia
Niger	4,800	Nigeria, Africa
Congo	4,800	Zaire, Africa
Murray	3,720	Australia
Volga	3,700	Russia, Asia
Indus	3,180	India and Pakistan, Asia
Brahmaputra	2,960	India, Asia
Danube	2,820	Austria, Hungary and Yugoslavia, Europe

Note:

The longest river in the world is Nile (6,690 km). The largest river of the world (in terms of volume of water it carries) is Amazon river.

(L)   New names of certain cities and countries

	Old Names	New Names
1	Abyssinia	Ethiopia
2	Baroda	Vadodara
3	Burma	Myanmar
4	Calicut	Kozhikode
5	Congo	Zaire
6	Constantinople	Istanbul
7	Dacca	Dhacca
8	Formosa	Taiwan
9	Gold Coast	Ghana
10	Irish Free State (Eire)	Ireland
11	Kampuchea	Cambodia
12	Mesopotamia	Iraq
13	Panjim	Panaji
14	Peking	Beijing
15	Siam	Thailand
16	South Rhodesia	Zimbabwe
17	Trivendrum	Thiruvanthapuram
18	Rangoon	Yangoon
19	Madras	Chennai
20	Calcutta	Kolkata
21	Pondichery	Puduchery
22	Bangalore	Bengaluru

(M)   Important world cities on river banks

	City	River
1	London	Thames
2	Rome	Tiber
3	Paris	Siene
4	Vienna	Danube
5	Budapest	Danube
6	Belgrade	Danube
7	Baghdad	Tigiris

(N)   Important Indian Cities On river banks

City	River
Delhi	Yamuna
Agra	Yamuna
Kolkata	Hoogly
Kanpur	Ganga
Allahabad	Ganga and Yamuna
Nasik	Godavari
Indore	Narmada
Lucknow	Gomti
Srinagar	Jhelum

Country	Capital	Currency	Continent
Afghanistan	Kabul	Afghani	Asia
Algeria	Algiers	Algerian Dinar	Africa
Angola	Luanda	New Kwanza	Africa
Argentina	Buenos Aires	Peso	South America
Australia	Canberra	Australian Dollar	Australia
***Austria**	Vienna	Schilling/Euro	Europe
Azerbaijan	Baku	Manat	Europe
Bahrain	Manama	Bahrain Dinar	Asia
Bangladesh	Dhaka	Taka	Asia
Barbados	Bridgetown	Barbados Dollar	North America
***Belgium**	Brussels	Belgian Franc	Europe
Bermuda	Hamilton	Bermuda Dollar	North America
Bhutan	Thimphu	Ngultrum	Asia
Bolivia	La Paz (administrative) Surce (legal)	Boliviano	South America
Bosnia and Herzegovina	Sarajevo	Convertible Mark	Europe
Botswana	Gaborone	Pula	Africa
Brazil	Brasilia	Cruzeiro Real	South America
Bulgaria	Sofia	Lev	Europe
Burundi	Bujumbura	Burundi Franc	Africa
Cambodia	Phnom Penh	Riel	Asia
Cameroon	Yaounde	CFA Franc	Africa
Canada	Ottawa	Canadian Dollar	North America
Chad	N'djamena	CFA Franc	Africa
Chile	Santiago	Chilean Peso	South America
China	Beijing (Peking)	Renminbi Yuan	Asia
Colombia	Bogota	Colombian Peso	South America
Democratic Republic of Congo	Kinshasa	Zaire	Africa
Costa Rica	San Jose	Costa Rican Colon	North America
Cote d'Ivoire	Yamoussoukro	CFA Franc	Africa
Croatia	Zagreb	Kuna	Europe
Cuba	Havana	Cuban Peso	North America
***Cyprus**	Nicosia	Cyprus Pound/Euro	Europe
Czech Republic	Prague	Koruna	Europe
Denmark	Copenhagen	Danish Krone	Europe

Country	Capital	Currency	Continent
Ecuador	Quito	Sucre	South America
Egypt	Cairo	Egyptian Pound	Africa
El Salvador	San Salvador	Colon	North America
Ethiopia	Addis Ababa	Ethiopian Birr	Africa
East Timor	Dili	US Dollar	Asia
Fiji	Suva	Fijian Dollar	Australia
*Finland	Helsinki	Markka/Euro	Europe
*France	Paris	French Franc/Euro	Europe
Gambia, The	Banjul	Dalasi	Africa
Georgia	Tbilisi	Lari	Europe
*Germany	Berlin	Deutsche Mark/Euro	Europe
Ghana	Accra	Cedi	Africa
*Greece	Athens (Athinai)	Drachma/Euro	Europe
Guatemala	Guatemala City	Quetzal	North America
Guyana	Georgetown	Guyana Dollar	South America
Haiti	Port-au-Prince	Gourde	North America
Hungary	Budapest	Forint	Europe
Iceland	Reykjavik	Krona	Europe
India	New Delhi	Indian Rupee	Asia
Indonesia	Jakarta	Indonesian Rupiah	Asia
Iran	Teheran	Iranian Rial	Asia
Iraq	Baghdad	Iraqi Dinar	Asia
*Ireland	Dublin	Irish Pound/Punt/Euro	Europe
Republic of Israel	Jerusalem	New Israeli Shekel	Asia
*Italy	Rome	Italian Lira	Europe
Jamaica	Kingston	Jamaican Dollar	North America
Japan	Tokyo	Yen	Asia
Jordan	Amman	Jordan Dinar	Asia
Kenya	Nairobi	Kenyan Shilling	Africa
Korea, North	Pyongyang	Won	Asia
Korea, South	Seoul	Won	Asia
Kuwait	Kuwait City	Kuwaiti Dinar	Asia
Laos	Vientiane	Kip	Asia
Lebanon	Beirut	Lebanese Pound/Livre	Asia
Libya	Tripoli	Libyan Dinar	Africa
*Luxemburg	Luxemburg	Luxemburgish Franc/Euro	Europe

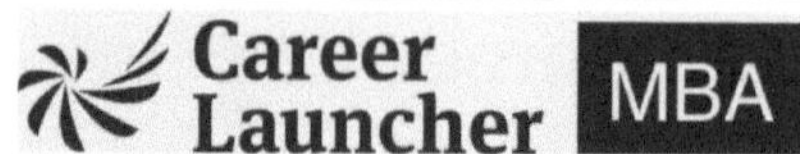

Country	Capital	Currency	Continent
Malaysia	Kuala Lumpur	Malaysian Dollar/Ringgit	Asia
Maldives	Male	Rufiyaa	Asia
Mauritius	Port Louis	Mauritian Rupee	Asia
Mongolia	Ulanbaatar	Tugrik	Asia
Morocco	Rabat	Moroccan Dirham	Africa
Myanmar (Burma)	Naypyidaw	Kyat	Asia
Namibia	Windhoek	Namibian Dollar	Africa
Nepal	Kathmandu	Nepalese Rupee	Asia
*Netherlands	Amsterdam	Guilder	Europe
New Zealand	Wellington	New Zealand Dollar	Oceania
Nigeria	Abuja	Naira	Africa
Norway	Oslo	Norwegian Krone	Europe
Oman	Muscat	Omani Rial	Asia
Pakistan	Islamabad	Pakistan Rupee	Asia
Peru	Lima	New Sol	South America
Philippines	Manila	Philippine Peso	Asia
Poland	Warsaw	Zloty	Europe
*Portugal	Lisbon	Escudo	Europe
Qatar	Doha	Qatar Riyal	Asia
Romania	Bucharest	Leu	Europe
Russia	Moscow	Rouble	Asia/Europe
Rwanda	Kigali	Rwanda Franc	Africa
Saudi Arabia	Riyadh	Soudi Arabian Riyal	Asia
Seychelles	Victoria	Seychelles Rupee	Africa
Singapore	Singapore City	Singapore Dollar/Ringgit	Asia
Slovak Republic	Bratislava	Slovak Koruna	Europe
South Africa	Cape Town (Legislative) Pretoria (Administrative) Bloemfontein (Judicial)	Rand	Africa
South Sudan	Juba	South Sudanese Pound	Africa
*Spain	Madrid	Peseta	Europe
Sri Lanka	Sri-Jayawardenapura (since 1983); former capital, Colombo	Rupee	Asia
Sudan, The	Khartoum	Sudanese Dinar	Africa
Suriname	Paramaribo	Suriname Guilder Florin	South America
Swaziland	Mbabane	Lilangeni	Africa

Country	Capital	Currency	Continent
Sweden	Stockholm	Swedish Krona	Europe
Switzerland	Berne	Swiss Franc	Europe
Syria	Damascus	Syrian Pound	Asia
Taiwan	Taipei	New Taiwan Dollar	Asia
Tanzania	Dodoma (formerly Dar es Salam)	Tanzanian Shilling	Africa
Thailand	Bangkok	Baht	Asia
Tunisia	Tunis	Dinar	Africa
Turkey	Ankara	Tunisian Lira	Asia
Uganda	Kampala	Uganda Shilling	Africa
Ukraine, The	Kiev	Hryvna	Europe
United Arab Emirates (UAE)	Abu Dhabi	United Arab Emirates	Asia
United Kingdom (UK)	London	Pound Sterling	Europe
United States of America	Washington, DC	US Dollar	North America
Uruguay	Montevideo	New Uruguayan Peso	South America
Uzbekistan	Tashkent	Som	Asia
Venezuela	Caracas	Bolivar	South America
Vietnam	Hanoi	Dong	Asia
Yemen	Sana (Political) Aden (Commercial)	Yemeni Riyal	Asia
Yugoslavia	Belgrade (Serbia)	Yugoslav Dinar	Europe
Zambia	Lusaka	Kwacha	Africa
Zimbabwe	Harare	Zimbabwe Dollar	Africa

Note:

The asterisk mark above represents the member states of European Union that participate in Euro. Please note that Euro is the official currency of 19 out of 27 member states of the European Union as on January 2017. In addition to the above 13 countries (marked as bold) 6 more countries viz. Malta, Slovakia, Slovenia, Estonia, Latvia and Lithuania are part of Eurozone.

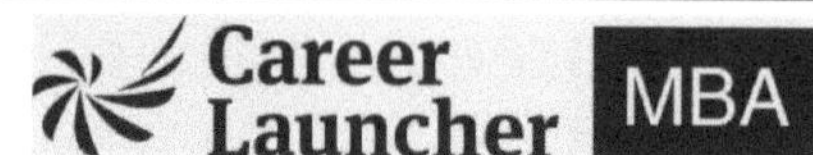

Country	Name of the Parliament
Afghanistan	Shura
Argentina	National Congress
Australia	The Parliament of the Commonwealth of Australia
Bahamas	General Assembly
Bangladesh	Jatiyo Sangsad
Bhutan	Tshogdu
Brazil	National Congress
Bulgaria	Narodno Sabranieye(National Assembly)
Myanmar	Pyithu Hluttaw
Cambodia	National Assembly
Canada	Parliament of Canada
China (Mainland)	National People's Congress
China (National)	Li fa Yuan (Legislative Yuan)
Colombia	Congress of the Republic
Cuba	National Assembly of People's Power
Denmark	Folketinget
Ethiopia	Shergo
Egypt	Consultative Council and People's Assembly
Finland	Eduskusta/Riksdagen
France	Parlement
Germany (United)	Bundestag (Lower House) Bundestrat (Upper House)
Greenland	Landstinget
Hungary	National Assembly
Iceland	Althingi
India	Sansad [Lok Sabha (Lower House) and Rajya Sabha (Upper House)]
Indonesia	People's Consultative Assembly and House of Representatives

Country	Name of the Parliament
Iran	Majles
Iraq	National Assembly
Israel	The Knesset
Japan	The Diet
Laos	National Assembly
Libya	General People's Congress
Maldives	Majlis
Mongolia	Great Hural
Nepal	Sansad
Netherlands, The	Staten-Generaal
New Zealand	House of Representatives
Norway	Stortinget
Papua New Guinea	National Parliament
Poland	Sejm
South Africa	House of Assembly
Spain	Cortes Generales (General Courts)
Surinam	Staten
Sweden	Riksdagen
United Kingdom (UK)	Parliament (House of Commons and House of Lords)
United States	Congress (House of Representatives and Senate)

Geographical Facts of India

(A) Geographical Location

India lies in the Asian continent and Northern Hemisphere between parallels of latitude 8° 4' and 37° 6' North and between the meridians of longitude 68° 7' and 97° 25' East.

1. In the **west,** India shares its boundary with Pakistan.
2. In the **south,** Sri Lanka is India's neighbouring country.
3. In the **north,** Nepal and China are the neighbouring countries.
4. In the **east,** Bangladesh and Myanmar are the two major countries which surround India.

In south-east of India, there is Bay of Bengal, in south-west it is Arabian Sea and in south, it is the Indian Ocean and in the north, it is surrounded by the Himalayan range of mountains.

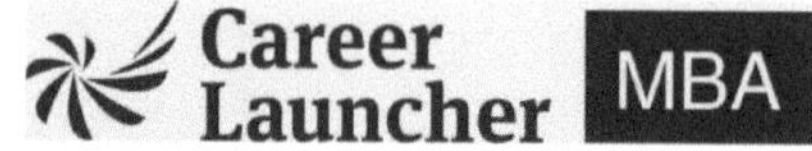

<u>Important dimensions of India</u>

1. **India covers 2.4 per cent of the Earth's surface.**
2. Total land area of India is 32,87,263 sq.km.
3. Distance from east to west is 2,933 km.
4. Distance from north to south is 3,214 km.
5. **The total length of the coastline of the mainland, Lakshadweep Islands and Andaman and Nicobar Islands, is 7,516.6 km. The coastline of only mainland is about 6300 km.**

(B) Important Geographical Structures of India

Major rivers of India: The longest Indian river is Ganga, its length is 2,640 km. The other major rivers of India are Indus (has five major tributaries: Sutlej, Chenab, Jhelum, Ravi and Beas), Brahmaputra, Godavari, Krishna, Narmada, Tapti, Cauvery, Damodar, Mahanadi and Periyar.

Notes:

The world's largest delta, (in West Bengal) Sundarban, is made by Brahmaputra and Ganga.

Mountains: They are Himalayas **(highest mountains in the world and one of the youngest moutain ranges),** Vindhyas, Satpura, Sahyadri, Aravallis (one of the oldest mountain ranges of the world), Patkai (Purvanchal or Eastern mountains) and the Eastern Ghats.

(C) Soil: The following table shows various types of soils and related information

Types of soil	Major areas of presence
Black soils:	Most suitable for cotton cultivation and is found majorly in the Maharashtra, Andhra Pradesh, Tamil Nadu, Madhya Pradesh (Western), Gujarat
Laterite soils:	Originated from weathering, mainly present in Andhra Pradesh, Deccan, Eastern Ghats, laterite rocks Tamil Nadu, Mysore
Alluvial soils:	Very fertile soil, covering Haryana, West Bengal, Punjab, Bihar, UP. approximately **25%** of all the Indian soil
Red soils:	Good for cultivating **coarse grains**, mainly present in Madhya Pradesh, Andhra Pradesh, Odisha **and pulses** because of high iron content

(D) Agriculture

Agriculture in India: More than 50 percent of the area of the country is under the cultivation and **about 64% of the Indian population is engaged in agriculture.**

There are two major crop seasons in India, viz.:
1. **Rabi**
2. **Kharif**

Rabi: It is **sown in October or December** and **harvested in April or May.** Major crops are: **barely, wheat, peas, gram and mustard.**

Kharif: It is **sown in June or July** and **harvested in September or October.** Major crops are: **bajra, cotton, jowar, rice and jute.**

<u>**Some important facts about Indian agriculture**</u>

1. **Green Revolution** White Revolution was launched in India in **1967-68** for **improving agricultural productivity.**
2. **Operation Flood/ White Revolution** was initiated in **1970** and mainly aimed at **improving the milk production** in India.
3. **Yellow Revolution** for improving oil seed production.
4. **Blue Revolution** for fishries

(E) Forests: The total forest and tree cover is 80.20 million hectare, which is 24.4% percent of the total geographical area of India. (as per Forest Survey Report 2017). The target as per the national forest policy is to cover 33% of area by forests.

Important National Parks, Wildlife Sanctuaries and Biosphere Reserves of India

Name	Location
Bandipur National Park	Border of Karnataka and Tamil Nadu
Jim Corbett National Park	Nainital, Uttaranchal
Dachigam Sanctuary	Dachigam, Kashmir
Ghana Bird Sanctuary	Bharatpur, Rajasthan
Gir National Park	Junagadh, Gujarat
Kanha National Park	Chhattisgarh
Kaziranga National Park	Jorhat, Assam
Periyar Sanctuary	Idukki, Kerala
Ranthambore Tiger Sanctuary	Sawai Madhopur, Rajasthan
Sariska Sanctuary	Alwar, Rajasthan
Sharavathy Sanctuary	Shimoga, Karnataka
Similipal Tiger Sanctuary	Mayurbhanj, Odisha
Sonai Rupai Sanctuary	Tezpur, Assam
Sunderbans Tiger Reserve	South 24 Parganas, West Bengal
Tungabhadra Sanctuary	Bellary, Karnataka
Wild Ass Sanctuary	Little Rann of Kutch, Gujarat
Bharatpur Bird Sanctuary	Bharatpur, Rajasthan
Jaldapara Bird Sanctuary	Kuch Bihar District, West Bangal

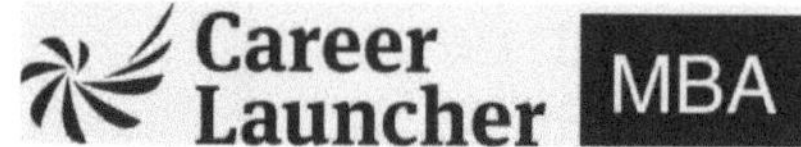

Biosphere Reserves of India : In total there are 15 Biosphere Reserver of India which are as follows.

S. No.	Name of the Biosphere reserve	Location	State
1	Great Rann of Kutch	Part of Kutch, Rajkot and Surendranagar District	Gujarat
2	Gulf of Mannar	Indian part of Gulf of Mannar between India and Sri Lanka	Tamil Nadu
3	Sunderbans	Part of delta of Ganges and Barahamaputra river system	West Bengal
4	Nanda Devi	Parts of Chamoli District, Pithoragarh District & Almora District	Uttarakhand
5	Nilgiri Biosphere Reserve	Part of Wynad, Nagarhole, Bandipur and Mudumalai, Nilambur, Silent Valley and Siruvani Hills	Tamil Nadu, Kerala and Karnataka
6	Dehang Debang	Part of Siang and Debang valley	Arunachal Pradesh
7	Pachmarhi Biosphere Reserve	Parts of Betul District, Hoshangabad District and Chhindwara District	Madhya Pradesh
8	Simlipal	Part of Mayurbhanj district	Odisha
9	Achanakamar - Amarkantak	Part of Annupur, Dindori and Bilaspur districts	Madhya Pradesh Chattisgarh
10	Manas	Part of Kokrajhar, Bongaigaon, Barpeta, Nalbari, Kamrup and Darrang District	Assam
11	Kanchanjunga	Parts of Kanchanjunga Hills	Sikkim
12	Agasthyamalai Biosphere Reserve	Neyyar, Peppara and Shenduruny Wildlife Sanctuary and their adjoining areas	Kerala
13	Great Nicobar Biosphere Reserve	Southern most islands of Andaman and Nicobar Islands	Andaman and Nicobar Islands
14	Nokrek	Part of Garo Hills	Meghalaya
15	Dibru-Saikhowa	Part of Dibrugarh District and Tinsukia District	Assam
16	Cold Desert	Pin Valley National park and surrounding; Chandratal Wildlife Sanctuary	Himachal Pradesh
17	Seshachalam Hills	Seshachalam Hill Ranger covering parts of Chittoor and Kadapa District	Andhra Pradesh

Cotton Textile	Most important industry in terms of employment and production of export goods. In Maharashtra (Mumbai, Sholapur, Pune, Kolhapur, Satara, Wardha, Hajipur), Gujarat (Ahmedabad, Vododara, Rajkot, Surat, Bhavnagar), Tamil Nadu (Coimbatore-Manchester of South India). Tamil Nadu has the largest number of cotton textile mills in India.
Silk Textile	The location of silk industry is governed by two factors- prevalence of sericulture practices and availability of skilled labour. Karnataka is the leading producer, followed by West Bengal, Bihar, etc.
Woollen Textile	In Punjab (Dhariwal, Amritsar, Ludhiana, Ferozpur), Maharashtra (Mumbai), UP (Kanpur, Mirzapur, Agra, Tanakpur), etc.
Jute	India manufactures the largest quantity of jute goods in the world. Mainly located in West Bengal, followed by Andhra Pradesh, Bihar, UP, MP.
Iron and Steel	Located near the sources of raw materials and fuel (coal). In Jamshedpur (Jharkhand), Durgapur, Burnpur (W.B.), Bhadrawati (Karnataka), Bokaro (Jharkhand), Rourkela (Odisha), Bhilai (Chhatisgarh), Salem (T.N.), Vishakhapatnam (A.P.).
Aluminium Smelting	Located mainly near the sources of raw materials, means of transport and cheap electricity. In Hirakud, Koraput (Odisha), Renukoot (UP), Korba (MP), Ratnagiri (Maharashtra), Mettur (TN), Alwaye.
Copper Smelting	In Khetri, Alwar, Jhunjhunu (Rajasthan), Singhbhum (Jharkhand), Agnigundala (A.P.).
Heavy Machinery	In Ranchi, Vishakapatnam, Durgapur, Tiruchirapalli, Mumbai, Naini.
Machine Tools Industry	It forms the basis for the manufacturing of industrial, defence equipments, automobiles, railway engines and electrical machinery. In Bangalore, Pinjore (Haryana), Kalamassery (Kerala), Hyderabad, Secunderabad, Srinagar, Ajmer.
Heavy Electrical Equipments	Power generation equipments. In Bhopal, Tiruchirapalli, Jammu, Ramchandrapuram (Hyderabad), Hardwar, Bangalore and Jagdishpur (UP).
Railway Equipments	Locomotives: In Chittaranjan (WB), Varanasi, Jamshedpur, Bhopal. Coaches: Perambur (TN), Kapurthala (Punjab), also at Bangalore and Kolkata.
Ship Building	Hindustan Shipyard at Vishakhapatnam, Cochin Shipyard, Mumbai (Mazgaon Dock) and Kolkata (Garden Reach Workshop). For Indian Navy, only at Mazgaon.
Cycles	In Mumbai, Asansol, Sonepat, Delhi, Chennai, Jalandhar and Ludhiana.
Tractors	At Faridabad, Pinjore, Delhi, Mumbai, Chennai.
Fertilizers	The location of fertilizer industry is closely related to petro-chemicals. About 70% of the plants producing nitrogenous fertilizers use naphtha as raw material. Naphtha is a by-product of oil refineries. Phosphate plants are dependent on mineral phosphate found in UP and MP. Now natural gas based fertilize plants are also being set up. The Fertilizer Corporation of India (FCL) was set up in 1961. National Fertilizer Limited (NFL) was set up in 1974. In Sindri (Bihar), Nangal, Trombay, Gorakhpur Durgapur, Namrup, Cochin, Rourkela, Neyveli, Varanasi Vadodara, Vishakhapattnam, Kota and Kanpur.
Pharmaceuticals and Drugs	Antibiotics are prepared at Pimpri and Rishikesh. The Indian Drugs and Pharmaceuticals Limited has 5 plants at Hyderabad Rishikesh, Chennai, Gurgaon and Muzaffarpur. A number of other units are concentrated in Mumbai, Baroda, Delhi, Kolkata and Kanpur.
Pesticides	Delhi and Alwaye
Sugar Industry	UP, Maharashtra, AP, TN, Karnataka and Bihar.
Aircraft	Hindustan Aeronautics India Ltd. was formed by merging two aircraft factories at Bangaluru and Kanpur. Four other factories are at Nasik, Hyderabad, Koraput (Odisha), Lucknow.
Rubber Industry	Bareilly (UP), Baroda (Gujarat)- Synthetic Rubber Units, Mumbai, Ahmedabad, Amritsar- Reclaimed Rubber Units.

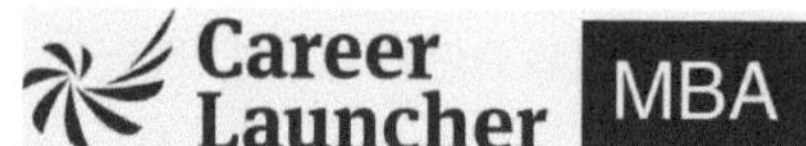

Barauni Refinery (IOC)

Guwahati Refinery (IOC)

Mathura Refinery (IOC)

Bongaigaon Refinery (IOC)

Manali Refinery (IOC)

Jamnagar Refinery (Reliance Petroleum)

Kochi Refinery (Kochi Refineries Ltd)

Numaligarh Refinery (NRL)

Mangalore Refinery (MRPL)

Tatipaka Refinery (ONGC)

Essar Refinery (Essar)

////////////////////////////////Nuclear Power Stations////////////////////////////////

Tarapur	Maharashtra
Kalpakkam	Tamil Nadu, called Indira Gandhi Nuclear Power Station
Narora	UP
Rawatbhata	Kota, Rajasthan
Kaiga	Karnataka
Kakrapara	Gujarat
Kundnkulam (TN)	Under construction with the assistance of Russia.

////////////////////////////////Major Thermal Power Plants////////////////////////////////

Power Plant	State	Power Plant	State
Neyveli	Tamil Nadu	Talcher	Odisha
Korba	Chhattisgarh	Farakka	West Bengal
Obra	UP	Satpura	MP
Haduaganj	UP	Ramagundam	Telangana
Rihand	UP	Vindhyanchal	MP
Singrauli	UP	Bokaro	Jharkhand
Parichha	UP		

////////////////////////////////Ultra Mega Power Plants////////////////////////////////

Power Plant	State
Mundra	Gujarat
Sasan	Madhya Pradesh

General Knowledge

3

Constitution of India

You should pay special attention to this section – not only because it is critical for the entrance examination, but also because this is information that every young citizen should have! This section starts off with a short description of how our Constitution was framed, and then moves on to an introduction of the various features of the Constitution in some detail.

The Indian Constitution is the largest ever written legal document in the world. It took exactly **2 years, 11 months and 17 days for the Constituent Assembly to complete the text of the Constitution** from the date of its first meeting, December 9, 1946 to its last meeting on November 26, 1949. Initially, it contained 395 **Articles and 8 Schedules** and after fifty-six years it has 395 Articles (**444 workable Articles** comprising clauses and sub-clauses) and **12 Schedules**.

The Creation of Our Constitution

The **Cabinet Commission** (1946) comprised three Labour Party Cabinet members – Lord Pethick Lawrence, Sir Stafford Cripps and A.V. Alexander, who recommended the formation of an interim government and the creation of a constitution. The **interim government** was set-up under **Pandit Jawahar Lal Nehru**, and a **Constituent Assembly** was formed from amongst the elected members of the Legislative Assemblies. Each member was a representative of one million people (1 : 10,00,000). **Sir Sachchidananda Sinha**, the eldest, was the first chairman of the assembly. **Doctor Rajendra Prasad** was, however, elected permanent Chairman later. On August 29, 1947 the Assembly appointed a Drafting Committee under the Chairmanship of **Dr. B.R. Ambedkar**, and the Constitutional Advisor, **B.N. Rau**, created the draft Constitution of India. After three readings by the Constituent Assembly, the draft of the Constitution was finally approved, adopted and signed by **284 members** on **November 26, 1949**. Accordingly, **November 26** is observed as **Law Day**. The clauses of citizenship, Parliament and elections were implemented at the time of adoption of the Constitution, whereas the rest of the clauses were made effective from **January 26, 1950**, the date of enforcement and commencement of the Constitution, and the day India became a republic, our **Republic Day**. This day was chosen because the resolution of 'Purna Swaraj', or complete independence, had been adopted at the Lahore Session of the Indian National Congress on **January 26, 1929**.

It is also important to note that the Constituent Assembly adopted the **National Flag** on July 22, 1947, whereas the **state emblem**, which shows three lions, a galloping horse, a bull and chakra in print (taken from the capital of Ashoka's Sarnath pillar which has four lions carved, facing outwards, back to back), was adopted by the Government of India on January 26, 1950.

The words '**Satyameva Jayate**' ("*Truth alone will prevail*") have been adopted from the **Mundaka Upanishad**.

The **National Anthem** was adopted by the Constituent Assembly on January 24, 1950. It is actually the first stanza of the *Jana Gana Mana*, originally composed by **Rabindranath Tagore**, which actually contains five stanzas. The playing time for the National Anthem is fifty-two seconds, however, its shorter version can be completed in twenty seconds.

The **National Calendar** is based on the Shaka Era, starting with 1st Chaitra (equivalent to March 22nd in the Gregorian calendar), and was adopted by the Government of India on March 22, 1957.

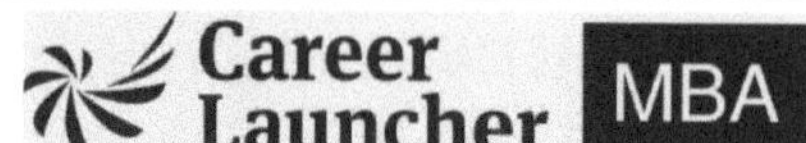

The Sources of Our Constitution

The framers of the Indian Constitution referred to various provisions of the existing Constitutions of the world, weighed their merits, and applied them according to their suitability to our country. The major sources of the Constitution of India are as under:

1. **The Government of India Act, 1935**, the Centre / State List System, Federal Set-up, centre-state autonomies (federal set-up).
2. **The British Constitution:** Parliamentary Privileges, Unitary Citizenship, and the Rule of Law.
3. **The Australian Constitution:** Preamble, Concurrent List, Freedom of trade and commerce.
4. **The American Constitution:** Fundamental Rights, Judicial Review, and Impeachment of the President.
5. **The Japanese Constitution:** The Procedure established by the Law.
6. **The South African Constitution:** The Amendment clauses.
7. **The Irish Constitution:** The Directive Principles, Nominations to Rajya Sabha (The Council of States).
8. **The Russian Constitution:** The Fundamental Duties.
9. **The Canadian Constitution:** The Federal structure.
10. **The German Constitution:** The Emergency Provisions.

The Preamble

The Preamble reflects the philosophy of our Constitution. Though it is not enforceable in a court, yet it serves its utility, as it reflects the objectives and interpretation of the Constitution. The notable characteristics of our Preamble are as under:

1. India is a **Sovereign, Socialist, Secular and Democratic Republic**. **Sovereign** means that India is an independent country, competent to decide its political destiny as it feels correct. The government works for the welfare of its people (a '**welfare state**'), and its economy is based on a **Socialistic Pattern**, where the Public (controlled by the Government) and Private (controlled by private individuals) Sectors are allowed to work together. **Secularism** signifies that the government has no religion of its own, but respects all religions equally, and that choice of religion does not disqualify its citizens on any basis. A **Democratic** set-up implies the selection of the government by the people, through universal adult franchise, where the will of the people is respected. Likewise, this element of democracy is not only restricted to politics, but also to the economy and society. Finally, it is a **Republic**, wherein the people select all the important heads of government, directly or indirectly, and these offices are not occupied on a hereditary basis.
2. The inspiration for the ideology of **Liberty, Equality** and **Fraternity** is drawn from the French Revolution (1789). The Preamble embodies the noble concepts of
   Justice in social, economic and political aspects,
   Liberty of thought, expression, belief, faith and worship,
   Equality of status and opportunity, and
   Fraternity, assuring dignity, unity and integrity to all citizens of this nation.
3. The Preamble also declares that the Constituent Assembly adopted and enacted the Constitution on November 26, 1949 in pursuance of the above objectives.

The Preamble to the Constitution has been amended once, by the 42nd Amendment to the Constitution (1976). The two changes that were made were: (a) the words 'Socialist' and 'Secular' were added to the sentence '...constitute India into a SOVEREIGN *SOCIALIST SECULAR* DEMOCRATIC REPUBLIC and to secure to all its citizens...', and (b) the words ' and integrity' were added in the sentence 'FRATERNITY assuring the dignity of the individual and the unity **and integrity** of the Nation.'

The reason why the word 'Socialist' was added was to give voice to the philosophy of 'socialism' in the Constitution, which aims at elimination of inequality in income and status and standard of life, which might also be used by the courts to lean more heavily in favour of nationalism and State ownership of industry.

The word Secular would mean that the State should have no religion of its own. It also meant that no political party should espouse a particular religion. Some authors are of the opinion that this was a redundant change, since the Fundamental Right to freedom of religion is guaranteed in the Constitution anyway.

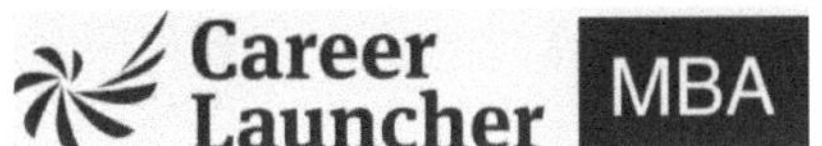

The Union and The States

The Union is referred to as 'India, that is **Bharat'** and its members are currently **29 states** (with Andhra Pradesh re-organisation Act 2014 Andhra Pradesh has been bifurcated into Telangana and Seemandhra).

There are **7 union territories**, of which Delhi and Pondicherry has its own Legislative Assembly having its own Chief Minister – the rest of the Union Territories are governed by Administrators / Lt. Governors appointed by the President of India.

In 1961, **Goa** was liberated from Portuguese control.

Sikkim first became an associate state, and later a regular state in 1975.

Under **Article 3** of the Constitution, the Parliament may, by law, form a new state by altering the boundaries of the existing state(s).   It can also increase or decrease the area of states and can also change the name of a state through a simple majority.

It is important to know that *vide* the Government of India's notification dated January 15, 1976 an **Exclusive Economic Zone (EEZ)** of India in ocean waters has been created up to a distance of 200 nautical miles from the coastline.

Citizenship

Only Indian citizens can contest the posts of the President, Vice President, Governor of a State, Judge of the Supreme Court / High Court, Attorney-General, member of Parliament / Legislatures in the States. It may be noted that our Constitution has not intended any comprehensive law on citizenship. The detailed laws are framed by the Parliament in the **Citizenship Act, 1950** wherein citizenship can be acquired:
1.   by birth,
2.   by descent,
3.   by registration
4.   by naturalisation and
5.   by incorporation of an external territory.

In the same act, citizenship can be lost
(i)   through renunciation (voluntary act),
(ii)   through termination (on acquiring of citizenship of another nation),
(iii)   through Deprivation (in case of fraud and disloyal cases).
The Constitution recognises **Single Citizenship** (Dual Citizenship is not yet recognised under the Constitution). **Domicile** is not defined in the Constitution, but a permanent home can be inferred where a person resides with an intention to continue to do so for future periods. Persons born after the commencement of the Constitution are not covered under this principle (**Article 5**).

Based on the recommendations of the **Singhvi Committee**, the Government has considered the extension of Dual Citizenship to NRIs living in 16 countries.

Our Federal Structure

The presence of the government at a single level makes for a unitary constitution, whereas more than one level makes it a federation. In the Indian Constitution, the presence of the government is at three different levels, Centre, State and Local. In ordinary situations, each level enjoys its own autonomy but in cases of emergency, the Centre prevails. Therefore, truly speaking, India has a **Quasi-Federal** structure.

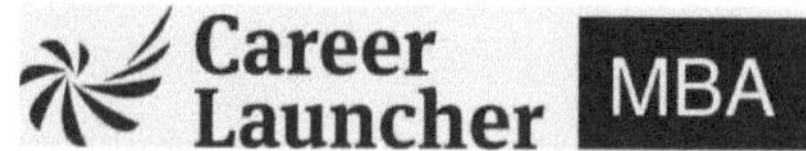

In order to avoid any confusion in the area and workings of the Centre and the States, the framers of the Constitution chalked out detailed guidelines, which are incorporated in **the Seventh Schedule to the Constitution** in the form of the **List System**. Some of the important provisions relating to the Centre and States are stated below:

Central List	State List	Concurrent List
• Defence	• Law and Order	• Criminal Law under IPC
• CBI	• Police and Prison	• Criminal Procedure-CPC
• UNO	• Local Government	• Preventive Detention
• War and peace	• Inland water	• Marriage and Divorce
• Citizenship	• Burials and cremations	• Contracts
• Extradition	• Agriculture	• Partnerships and Agency
• Railways	• Cattle and Fisheries	• Actionable wrongs
• Pilgrimages abroad	• Pilgrimages in India	• Bankruptcy/Insolvency
• Ports and Light houses	• Gas and Gas works	• Civil Procedure
• Airways	• Tax on entry	• Contempt of Court
• National Highways	• Vehicle Tax	• Forest
• Patents	• Animal and Boat Tax	• Trade Unions
• Labour safety	• Tolls	• Economics and Planning
• Opium	• Capitation Taxes	• Legal Professions
• Supreme Court	• Betting and Gambling	• Factories/Boilers
• Interstate migration	• Entertainment Tax	• Jurisdiction/powers of
• Income Tax	• Profession Tax	• All courts
		(Except the Supreme Court)
• Customs	• Offences against Laws	• Education
• Corporation Tax	stated in this list.	
• Currency and coinage		• Mines
• RBI		
• Foreign Loans		
• Banking and Insurance		
• Stock Markets		
• Offences against Laws stated in this list.		

Three tiers of village panchayats have been introduced on the recommendations of the **Balwant Rai Mehta Committee**, 1956 (a) at the village level (b) at the block Level and (c) at the district level. Accordingly, the **Local Governments at rural panchayats** and **urban bodies** were added through the 73rd and 74th Constitutional amendments (1992). Their detailed powers and responsibilities are contained in **Articles 243 to 243ZC of the Constitution. Schedules XI and XII** to the Constitution have been included for Panchayats and Municipalities respectively. Up to one-third of the seats of Local governments have been reserved for women. **The duration of office is for 5 years.**

It is important to note that these provisions are not applicable to the states of Meghalaya, Mizoram, Nagaland and Delhi.

Nagore District in Rajasthan was the pioneer in introducing the Panchayati Raj system, which it did way back in 1957.

Fundamental Rights (FRs')

The Fundamental Rights ('**FRs**') are set out in **Part III** of our Constitution, and are the basic and natural rights of citizens. Some of these rights are also given to non-citizens living in the territory of India. These rights can be protected through the courts, and any law that violates the FRs can be declared null and void (**Article 13**). This also establishes the supremacy of the Constitution and the scope of judicial review. Under the "doctrine of severability", that portion of any law, which stands against the spirit of the FRs, can be struck down, and if such a portion is vital to the law and is not 'severable' from that law, the entire law can be struck down.

It is also important to note that the fundamental rights cannot be terminated or waived voluntarily by an individual. If a person wants to die, for example, it is not permitted, and is thus unlawful. Remember the case of Venketesh, the ailing muscular dystrophy patient who was on a life support system for a long time and wanted to donate his organs to others? The doctors refused to do so because such an act could only be performed when he was dead. Thus his mother requested the court to allow his son to die so that he may fulfil his wishes, but the court disallowed the plea.

The FRs can be broadly divided into the following categories:

1. **The Right to Equality**
    (a) Equality and Equal Protection before law (**Article 14**).
    (b) No discrimination on the basis of religion, race, sex, or place of birth (**Article 15**).
    (c) Equal opportunities in case of employment (**Article 16**).
    (d) Social Equality-banning untouchability (**Article 17**).
    (e) Abolition of royal titles (**Article 18**).

The concepts of equality and equal protection under the law are applicable to all persons in similar circumstances, and those in different circumstances, unequally, (simply put, equals are treated as equals, and persons in unequal situations are treated unequally, e.g., reservation for castes that have been oppressed for centuries), but this cannot be done arbitrarily by the state. The concept is similar, for example, to the concept of differential treatment between a non-criminal and a criminal. It is important to note that the applicability of every law need not be the same, and that there can be distinctions, but such distinctions should be reasonable and should not be based on the classification of religion, race, sex, and place of birth. However, in some cases these categories can further be relaxed, as was done in the case of **Article 15**, which is affirmative to women. Also, any legislation, which gives power to the executive to select cases for special treatment, without indicating the policy for the same, or by arbitrary action or discretion, can be declared void.

It should be noted that the government has also taken some steps towards '**positive discrimination**' to benefit the SCs / STs and other underprivileged sections, through reserving jobs in certain sectors (the Supreme Court's decision in the 1993 case of **Indira Sawhney**, on the **Mandal Commission Report** issue). In fact, reservation for such purposes cannot exceed 50%, and if there is a single post, then reservation is not applicable to it, as that would amount to 100% reservation. There can be reservation within reservations, but the allotment of quota of seats (in courses) for candidates to be selected from various organisations / institutions / government departments (which are sources for filling up positions) is not covered under 'reservation'. Special provisions, measures and programmes are not considered to be void in the case of women and children, and this exception is even extended to criminal laws (pregnant women, sexual harassment to women, children below 14 years etc).

Article 16 is the extension of **Article 14**. Thus, non-arbitrariness is a part of the concept of equality, such as, relaxation in the minimum marks / eligibility can be granted by the employer for SC/ST categories but such relaxation cannot be arbitrary; rather it should be consistent with the eligibility criteria.

One of the social evils carried from the ancient past to the current period is untouchability, wherein *sudras* were given the title of *nirvasit* (socially boycotted). Gandhiji called them the children of God, or *Harijans*. The Constitution bans untouchability.

Titles earned on the basis of merit, such as academic, military or state awards (National Awards, such as the *Bharat Ratna, Padma Vibhushan, Padma Bhushan, Padma Shree*), are permitted, but not hereditary titles.

2. **Right to Freedom**
    Six core Freedoms
    (a) of Speech and Expression, (b) of free Assembly, (c) of Association, (d) of Movement, (e) of Settlement and (f) of Profession, occupation, trade and business (**Article 19(1)**), and (g) to hold, acquire, dispose property (this last freedom was omitted through the 44th amendment to the Constitution, in 1978).
    (b) Freedom against Ex-post Facto Laws, double jeopardy and protection against self-incrimination (**Article 20**).
    (c) Freedom of life and personal liberty (**Article 21**).
    (d) Freedom against arrest / detention in selected cases (**Article 22**).

The six core freedoms set out above are guaranteed only to citizens, and are not absolute. Some limitations are imposed in order to arrive at a balance between personal liberty and social control, as specified in **Articles 19(2) to 19(6)**. These freedoms are restricted in matters of   (a) defamation, (b) contempt of court, (c) decency / morality, (d)

security of the state, (e) friendly relations with foreign countries, (f) incitement of an offence, (g) maintenance of public order and (h) maintenance of the sovereignty and integrity of India. One instance of the restriction of a core freedom could be: a person suffering from some communicable disease can be banned from moving around freely on medical grounds.

A ban on the slaughter of bulls below sixteen years of age can be considered reasonable, but a blanket ban on bull slaughter is unreasonable. The Government cannot reject any lower bid (in the case of tenders for Government projects) in favour of higher bids arbitrarily. If done so, proper reasons should be given.

It is important to note that the Press and Media, also referred as the Fourth Estate, (a term that derives from French political history, and which now means one of the pillars of democracy) in India enjoy their freedom under **Article 19(1)(a)** whereas, **censorship** of the press can be evoked under **Article 19(2)** of the Constitution.

All people living within India are protected against the operation of **ex-post facto criminal legislation**, i.e., laws that declare any activity or action as unlawful and punishable, with retrospective effect. This means that an individual cannot be punished for an action or activity committed in the past when there was no law prohibiting that action, which in current times is considered unlawful. Furthermore, a person cannot be subjected to a penalty greater than that which was in force at the time of commission of the act charged as an offence. (**Article 20(1)**)

Further, no person may be prosecuted and punished for the same offence more than once (the '**rule against Double Jeopardy**') (**Article 20(2)**) nor can a person accused of any offence be compelled to be a witness against himself. (**Article 20(3)**)

Freedom of life and liberty is one of the most vital features of the FRs, as this cannot be suspended even in the periods of emergency. This concept has been inspired by Great Britain's **Magna Carta** (1215 A.D), a charter of rights. This personal liberty is subject to the 'procedure established by law'. This expression is further extended, so that no person can be arrested / detained without substantial reason. The arrested / detained person must necessarily be informed of the reason for his confinement, he must be permitted to seek legal help, and must be produced before the nearest magistrate within twenty-four hours of his detention. In the case of '**Preventive Detention**', however, where arrest / detention is made for the security of the nation, for defence, for foreign affairs, for maintenance of essential services, etc., the detention can even be without trial, but the period of custody in such cases is limited to three months. Here, the accused is prevented from committing the proposed wrongs. It is different from '**Punitive Detention**', where the accused is prosecuted for the wrong that he has already committed.

It may also be noted that the term '**Procedure established by Law**' used in **Article 21** gives the judiciary scope to crack down on all rules that are unreasonable, unfair and unjust, and therefore, invalid. This phrase, if read with **Articles 39(a)** and **22**, has a wide scope, with the inclusion of the implication of free legal aid to a poor prisoner, giving the prisoner a fair chance of leading a normal life. If jail authorities arbitrarily deny or deprive the detenu the opportunity to see / talk to / interview his relatives or lawyer, such an action would also be invalid. Due to this wide, positive interpretation, several other rights have been sheltered under the canopy of this Article: say for example, if a detained person is suffering from some disease and is not able to pay for his treatment, then the state should carry out his treatment, and that too, without delay. Likewise, issues linked with traffic control, pertaining to public safety, ban on smoking in public places, telephone tapping (except under special permission), water and pollution-free environment etc., are all protected from arbitrariness under the scope of the phrase 'procedure established by law'.

Recently, free and compulsory education to all children of the age group of six to fourteen years has also been added to the Constitution *vide* the **Constitution (86th Amendment) Act, 2002 (Article 21(A))**.

3.   Right against Exploitation
    (a) Prohibition of traffic in human beings and forced labour (**Article 23**)
    (b) Prohibition of employment of children in hazardous employment (**Article 24**)

These two articles were created against the backdrop of massive poverty, unemployment, illiteracy and ignorance of the rural population, where *begar* and human trafficking still continues. The age-old social evil of *Devdasis* is also covered within the ambit of human trafficking. The Supreme Court has already issued detailed guidelines on the issue of child labour in the case of ***Bandhua Mukti Morcha* v. *Union of India*,** (AIR 1997 SC 2218). Children below the age of 14 years cannot be engaged to work in a factory, mine or at any hazardous places of employment. Directions were given to set up a child rehabilitation welfare fund for child labour, and any offending employer must pay Rs.2,000/- as a penalty into the fund. The apex court has also given directions related to the education, health,

and nutrition of child labourers, and to check the spread of child prostitution under a PIL (Public Interest Litigation) (*Vishaljeet* v. *Union of India*, in 1990).

4. Right to Freedom of Religion

    (a) Freedom of Conscience and free profession (**Article 25**)
    (b) Freedom to manage religious affairs (**Article 26**)
    (c) Freedom as to payment of taxes for promotion of any particular religion (**Article 27**)
    (d) Freedom as to attendance at religious instructions in certain educational institutions (**Article 28**) In order that they may satisfy their spiritual requirements as well as its outward expressions, all persons living in India are allowed to carry out their religious obligations, rituals and ceremonies in a peaceful and harmonious manner. It may be kept in mind that services by priests are secular, and thus come under the purview of state regulation (*Bhuri Nath* v. *State of J&K,* 1997).

Religion is a matter of faith, and the principles associated with religion are essential parts of it; nevertheless, in the case of disputes, the Courts are competent to examine them. If use of voice-amplifiers and loudspeakers, drum-beating etc, is a part of a religious practice, they are permissible, but only up to the extent where the rights of others are not adversely affected.

As the State is secular, it can neither force its people to pay taxes for the welfare of a particular religion, nor can it permit religious instructions in any educational institution, which is wholly funded through government funds.

Every religious group can establish, maintain and acquire property in the name of religion, subject to the interests of public order, morality and in accordance with the law. No one can be forced to pay any taxes, the proceeds of which are specifically appropriated towards the payment of expenses for the promotion or upkeep of any specific religion or religious purpose.

It is important to note that the right to freedom of religion is actually the foundation of secularism in India.

5. Cultural and Educational Rights

    (a) Right of Minorities to protect their language, script or culture (**Article 29**)
    (b) Right of Minorities to establish and maintain their Educational Institutions (**Article 30**)

The above provisions are an assurance to the section of citizens who are part of any minority, towards the preservation of their ethnic, linguistic or cultural heritage. As pointed out earlier in the section on the Right to Equality, religion cannot be considered a disqualification for any opportunity; therefore, a minority-run educational institution may reserve up to 50% of its seats for students from its community. If the government seeks to acquire such institutions, it would have to pay compensation to the concerned minority. **It is important to note** that such rights are not absolutely free, and state restrictions may be imposed if such institutes are not administered in the proper manner by the minority agency.

6. Right to Constitutional Remedies

Obviously, it is all very well to talk about the various rights that the Constitution affords us – however, we must have a means of enforcing them! This section discusses the writs of *habeas corpus, mandamus, prohibition, certiorari* and *quo-warranto* as remedies for the enforcement of the FRs stated in Part III of the Constitution.

The term 'prerogative writs' comes from English law, since these writs originated as a part of the King's unquestionable authority of superintendence to ensure the observance of the rules of law by the King's officers and tribunals.

Dr. B.R. Ambedkar called these writs the '*very soul of the Constitution*'. Through these 'prerogative writs', the judiciary can declare any arbitrary action or law of the Executive or of the Legislature null and void, if such action of law goes against the spirit of the FRs. These writs can be issued by the Supreme Court as well as by High Courts.

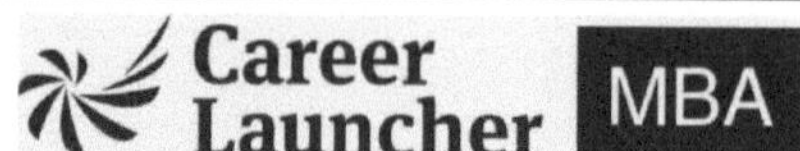

The latter have wider powers in issuing of these writs. The Supreme Court has the power to issue these writs in order to enforce the FRs (**Article 32**), but the High Courts may issue these writs not only in order to enforce the FRs, but also in those cases where an ordinary legal right has been violated (**Article 226**).

Habeas corpus: It literally means, 'to have a body'. By this writ, the court ensures the physical appearance of the detained person and enquires about the reason for his detention. If sufficient grounds for detention are not reported, the detenu can be set free. However, this writ cannot be issued in cases where the imprisoned person is arrested on proven guilt, or on the charge of contempt of court.

Mandamus: It literally means 'we command'. It is issued against a person who, despite having legal rights, fails to perform his duties in the capacity of his holding a position of public office. The officers, government and subordinate / inferior courts refusing to perform their jurisdiction are covered under this writ. This writ, however, cannot be issued against the President, Governors of States, or against private, individual parties.

Prohibition: Here, the Supreme Court / High Courts issue writs to their subordinate/inferior courts to check or discontinue such proceedings as are not within their jurisdiction.

Prohibition commands 'rightful inactivity', whereas Mandamus commands 'rightful activity'.

Certiorari: It literally means 'to quash' a decision taken by a lower / subordinate / inferior court / tribunal in a matter in which it was not competent to give its verdict, and has thereby violated the limits of its jurisdiction. *As Prohibition is issued in the proceedings stage, Certiorari is issued at a verdict stage.* Both these writs can be issued to subordinate / inferior courts / tribunals.

Quo-warranto: This writ can be issued in those cases where the court wants to enquire about the legality or claim of an individual for holding a public office. If the same is found faulty, the person is ousted from the office. The prime objective of this writ is to safeguard public offices from unlawful claimants.

Finally, it may be noted that the FRs stated in Articles 15, 16, 19 and 30 are for citizens only and those stated in Articles 14, 20, 21, 23, 25, 27 and 28 are for both, citizens and non-citizens, living in India.

A short note on the Right to Property

There have been several amendments on this issue, *viz*, the 1st amendment (1951), the 4th amendment (1955), the 17th amendment (1964), the 25th amendment (1971), the 42nd amendment (1976) and the 44th amendment (1978). The effect of all these amendments on the Right to Property has been the reduction in status of this right from a FR to a **Constitutional Right**, covered under **Article 300(A)**; thus, **Article 19 (1)(f)** has accordingly been repealed. The basic objective behind the state acquiring personal properties shows its superiority over the individual's right, i.e. the **Doctrine of Eminence**. This was also necessary for the successful implementation of the Land Reforms. The **Ninth Schedule to the Constitution** has also been added for this purpose.

Remember that there is a distinction between a **Fundamental Right** and a **Constitutional Right**. Since the Right to Property is no longer a FR, the Supreme Court can no longer issue any writ on this regard; the High Courts can, however, look into these matters on the same footing as any other ordinary suit. Since this is a legal right, in the event that the Government acquires any private property, it will have to do so in accordance with the law, and it will then have to pay compensation for the same.

A short note on the Right to Privacy

The **Supreme Court** (SC) ruled that privacy is a fundamental right because it is intrinsic to the right to life. "Right to Privacy is an integral part of Right to Life and Personal Liberty guaranteed in Article 21 of the Constitution", the SC's nine-judge bench ruled unanimously. It added that the right to privacy is intrinsic to the entire fundamental rights chapter of the Constitution.

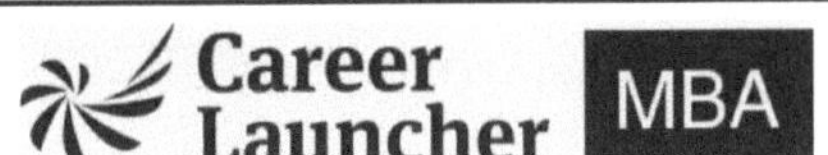

Article 370 scrapped, Jammu and Kashmir loses its special status, divided into two UTs

- The Union Government scrapped Article 370 of the Constitution that grants special status to Jammu and Kashmir, with an order saying "it shall come into force at once". The abrogation follows the Centre introducing the Jammu and Kashmir Reorganization Bill in Parliament.
- Union Home Minister Amit Shah earlier moved the Rajya Sabha, announcing the government has decided to repeal Article 370. Shah also said the government has decided to bifurcate the state into two Union Territories – Jammu and Kashmir with a legislature similar to Puducherry, and Ladakh without one like Chandigarh was passed with a two-thirds majority of the members present in Rajya Sabha.
- The scrapping of Article 370 will have far-reaching repercussions on the restive state as the abrogation suspends the clause that allowed all laws to be first be ratified by the state assembly, which currently stands dissolved.
- President Ram Nath Kovind has exercised his power under Clause 1 of Article 370. The presidential order has done away sections under Article 35A, which provides special privileges to "permanent residents" of the state while defining the term "permanent residents".
- Under Article 370 there is a provision that the President may by public notification declare that this article shall cease to be operative from such date as he may specify.
- Article 370 laid down that except for matters related to defence, foreign affairs, communications and issues specified in the Instrument of Accession of Jammu and Kashmir, Parliament needs the state government's ratification for all other laws. So far, residents of the state lived under a separate set of laws, including those related to citizenship, ownership of property and fundamental rights. Jammu and Kashmir will now be governed by the laws applicable to other Indian citizens.

Directive Principles (DPSP)

The **Directive Principles of State Policy (DPSP)**, as the name suggests, are guidelines to the Government in order that it may better carry out its duty of governance. It is expected that the Government should strive to achieve them, and thus become a 'welfare state'. It may be noted that a huge amount of effort and resources are required to fulfil these objectives, and since the government has a shortage of funds, these are not expected to be put in force immediately: it is expected that these will be taken up and implemented by the Government in the course of time. Therefore, the non-implementation of any DPSP cannot be challenged in the Courts.

DPSP are categorised into ideologies, policy orientation and certain rights of the citizens, which cannot be challenged in the courts. The ambit of the DPs runs from **Article 36** to **Article 51** in **Part IV** of our Constitution.

Some of the noted principles are stated as under:

(A) **DPSP as ideologies for the Government:**
1. Securing a social order through social, economic and political justice along with minimising inequalities: **Articles 38(1) and (2)**.
2. Striving towards an equitable distribution pattern of resources: **Articles 39(b) and (c)**.
3. Securing decent living standards and social and cultural opportunities to all: **Article 43**.
4. Working towards better health of the masses through improved nutrition: **Article 47**.
5. Promoting international peace and amity: **Article 51**.

(B) **DPSP as policy orientation for the Government:**
1. Development of Village Panchayats towards self-government: **Article 40**.
2. Development of cottage industries: **Article 43**.
3. Securing a uniform civil code: **Article 44**.
4. Providing free and compulsory primary education: **Article 45**.
5. Protecting the weaker sections against exploitation: **Article 46**.
6. Working towards the modernisation of agriculture and animal husbandry: **Article 48**.
7. Protecting and maintaining historical sites / monuments: **Article 49**.
8. Separating the Judiciary from the Executive: **Article 50**.

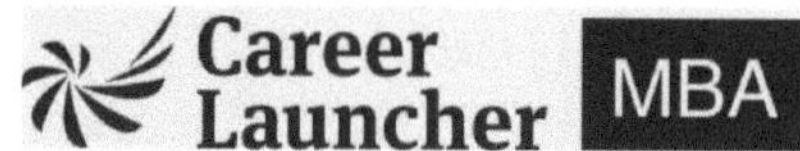

(C)   **DPs as non-justiciable rights (to citizens):**
   1. Provision of equal means of livelihood, equal pay for equal work and the right against economic exploitation: **Articles 39 (a)**, **(d)**, **(e)** and **(f)**.
   2. Providing equal opportunities for justice and free legal aid: **Article 39(A)**.
   3. Right to work and government assistance in unemployment, illness and old age: **Article 41**.
   4. Provision of maternity leave: **Article 42**.
   5. Participation of workers in management: **Article 43**.
   6. Providing free and compulsory education to children: **Article 45**.

Apart from Part IV, there are some more directives stated in our Constitution, such as- instruction in mother tongue to children at their primary level of education (**Article 350 A**), promotion of Hindi (**Article 351**) and considerations in appointments in case of SC/ST candidates (**Article 335**).

Fundamental Duties

On the basis of the recommendations of the **Swarn Singh Committee**, ten Fundamental Duties have been added to the Constitution in **Article 51-A** (**Part IV-A** of the Constitution) through the 42nd Amendment to the Constitution (1976). These are not enforceable in the courts unless and until specific laws in this regard are violated (remember the recent controversy regarding the use of the national flag by sportspersons on their equipment?)

These duties are:
1. To abide by the Constitution and respect the National flag and the National Anthem;
2. To cherish and follow the noble ideas which inspired our national struggle for freedom;
3. To uphold and protect the sovereignty and the integrity of India;
4. To defend the country and render national service when called upon to do so;
5. To promote harmony and the spirit of common brotherhood amongst all the people of India transcending religious, linguistic and regional or sectional diversities and to renounce practices derogatory to the dignity of women;
6. To value and preserve the rich heritage of our composite culture;
7. To protect and improve the natural environment including forests and rivers;
8. To develop the scientific temper, humanism and the spirit of inquiry and reform;
9. To safeguard public property and abjure violence; and
10. To strive towards excellence in all spheres of individual and collective activity so that the nation constantly rises to higher levels of endeavour and achievement.

Emergency Provisions

These provisions are contained in **Part XVII of the Constitution**. It is generally assumed that due to the distribution of powers and responsibilities, a Federal form of government is a weak government. However, this may not be completely correct in the case of India, because the Union is vested with wider and mightier powers, both economically and politically, compared to those of the States. Emergency provisions are powerful examples of this, as the President can proclaim the implementation of these provisions for the entire nation, or even for a part thereof. Needless to say, the President is a part of the Union Executive. During periods of declaration of Emergency, our federal set-up is converted into a unitary system, and all rules and regulations are issued by the Parliament (which is the Union legislature). *Other than the FRs stated in Articles 20 and 21, all the other FRs remain suspended during the period of the Emergency.*

The duration of the Emergency Proclamation is initially for a period of **two months**, and if the Parliament fails to extend the term of the Emergency within that period, the period is extended automatically for **one month**, but if the Parliament extends the period of the Emergency within that period, it can do so for another period of **six months**, and for another period of **six months** thereafter. The Election Commission has to certify the difficulty in holding general elections in the event that the period of Emergency is sought to be extended beyond a period of one year on the grounds of a Constitutional breakdown. This can be done for a maximum period of **three years**.

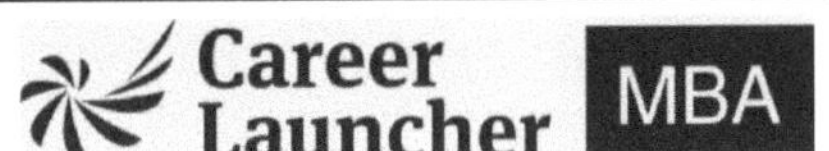

There are three types of Emergencies recognised by the Constitution. They are as under:

1. In those cases where the security of India is threatened by reasons of a war or external aggression or internal armed rebellion (**Article 352**). This may also be termed a '**National Emergency**'. The President can impose such emergencies even before the actual crisis has broken. The duration of the first of such proclamations was from October 26, 1962 to January 10, 1968 in view of the Chinese aggression against the territory of the nation.

2. In those cases where the Constitutional machinery has failed in the States (**Article 356**). It is the duty of the Union to see to the smooth functioning of the Constitutional machinery, as laid down in **Article 355**; this Article, therefore can be used as a sort of a 'Yellow card', as a warning to the erratic State. Based upon the report of the Governor of the State concerned or otherwise, the President can impose such an emergency. The concerned State's Legislature is suspended, and executive authority is vested in the President (except for those powers that are vested in the High Courts). That is why such a situation is also called '**President's rule in the State**'. The duration of the first of such proclamations was from June 20, 1951 to April 17, 1952 in Punjab.

   Here's an interesting fact: Which State do you think has had President's rule imposed on it the maximum number of times? Bihar? Wrong! The answer is Uttar Pradesh and Kerala (nine times each until 2001), followed by Punjab (8 times).

   After its decision in the case of *S.R. Bommai* v. *Union of India*, (1994) the Supreme Court has held the view that the courts possess the power of judicial review enabling them to look into the substantial grounds / relevancy / *mala fide* intentions behind such proclamations of a state of Emergency.

3. In those cases where the financial ability / credit worthiness of the nation is threatened (**Article 360**). In such cases, the President can declare a reduction (partially or wholly) in the salaries and allowances of the Government employees, including the judges of the Supreme Court and the High Courts. Thus far, this sort of an Emergency has not been evoked in India.

Amendment Procedures

Article 368 sets out the procedure for the amendment of the Constitution, but a differentiation has been made in it depending upon the nature of provisions to be amended.

(a) For amendments of a general nature, the bill seeking amendment has to be passed in each house of Parliament by a **simple majority** (more than 50%) of the total membership of the concerned house, and by a majority of not less than two-thirds of the members of that house present and voting.

(b) Where a bill seeks amendment in the federal set up, *viz* President's election, powers of the Union and the States, the 7th Schedule's List System, number of Rajya Sabha members, or the powers or composition of the Supreme Court or the high Courts, **Article 368** itself requires a **special majority**, and a ratification by at least one-half of the States.

(c) There are some **basic features** in our Constitution which cannot be altered, such as the objectives of the Preamble, federalism, secularism, unity and integrity of the nation, socio-economic justice, balance between Fundamental Rights and Directive Principles, Supreme Court and judicial review, etc.

This last exception to the scope of amendments to the Constitution is known as the '**Basic Structure**' doctrine, and was laid down in the historic case of ***Kesavananda Bharti* v. *Union of India* in** 1973. This case is famous for having the largest bench strength till date: thirteen judges of the Supreme Court were called upon to decide whether the Government could carry out any changes to the Constitution it wished, and by a narrow majority of seven judges to six, the Supreme Court held that some parts of the Constitution formed its 'Basic Structure', and that these could not be touched! The fact that the unity and integrity of our nation is placed on such a high pedestal, and is so well protected, therefore, would not have been possible if only one judge on that Bench had decided in a different manner!

After the 24th amendment to the Constitution in 1971, it has now become obligatory for the President to give his assent to an ordinary bill (governed by **Article 111**) for amendment in the Constitution that has been passed by Parliament. A joint session of both Houses of Parliament (**Article 108**) for the purposes of making an amendment

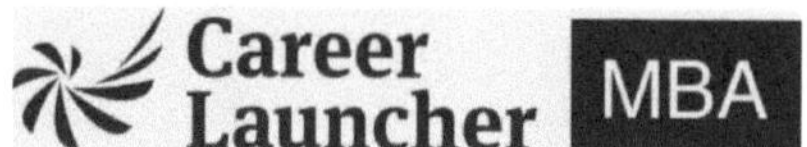

to the Constitution is not permissible. Parliament may amend any part of the Constitution, but any amendment causing drastic changes to the basic features of the Constitution can be termed as null and void by the Courts.

The **42nd Amendment** to the Constitution, 1976 is often referred as the '**Mini Constitution**' as it practically revised large chunks of the original Constitution. It introduced changes in the Preamble, included Fundamental Duties, and amended fifty-two Articles, as well as the Seventh Schedule. It reduced the scope of judicial review to a great extent, and the ideologies of the Directive Principles were heavily loaded against the Fundamental Rights by expanding the scope of **Article 31** on the lines of the **Doctrine of Eminence** (Do you remember the meaning of this doctrine? If not, go back to the section on the Right of Property, and refresh your memory!) Subsequently, the **43rd and 44th Amendments**, made in 1977, repealed many provisions added through the 42nd Amendment.

The Judicial System Under the Constitution

Part V of the Constitution fleshes out the theory, and the professed ideal of the framers of the Constitution, of the division of power between the three branches of government, the Executive, the Legislature, and the Judiciary. This Part, therefore, sets out the structure, powers, and functioning of the three branches of government. The Supreme Court is described as the apex institution in the Indian judicial system. ***Despite the federal set-up of the government, our judiciary is single and integrated.***

There is uniformity in the designation of officials engaged in civil and criminal sides. *Nyaya Pachayats / Panchayat Courts / Gram Katchery / Panchayat Adalats* function at the grassroots level. The following is a broad sketch of our judicial structure:

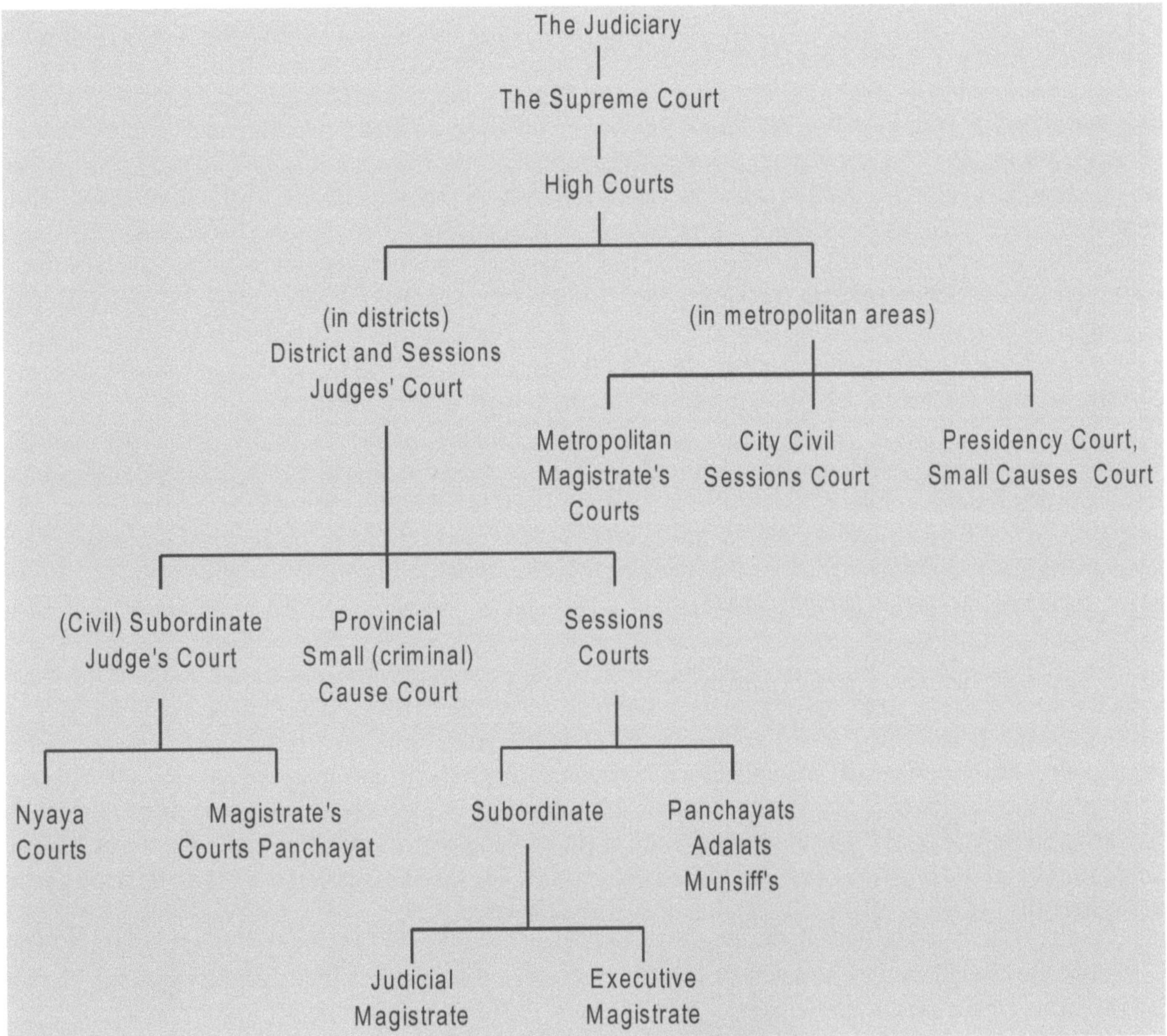

```
                                The Judiciary
                                      |
                              The Supreme Court
                                      |
                                 High Courts
                    ______________________|______________________
                   |                                             |
            (in districts)                            (in metropolitan areas)
         District and Sessions                ____________________|____________________
            Judges' Court                    |                    |                    |
                   |                    Metropolitan          City Civil        Presidency Court,
                   |                    Magistrate's        Sessions Court      Small Causes  Court
                   |                      Courts
        ___________|___________                       _________|_________
       |           |           |                     |                   |
  (Civil)      Provincial   Sessions             Subordinate         Panchayats
 Subordinate   Small         Courts                                   Adalats
 Judge's Court (criminal)                                             Munsiff's
               Cause Court
       |                                     ________|________
   ____|____                                |                 |
  |         |                           Judicial          Executive
 Nyaya   Magistrate's                  Magistrate         Magistrate
 Courts  Courts Panchayat
```


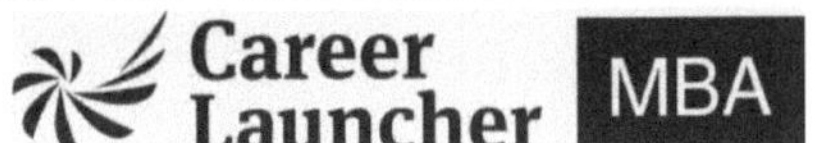

The Supreme Court

The provision for a Supreme Court is made in **Article 124**, wherein the total number of judges is set out at 30, including the Chief Justice of India (i.e., 30 +1). Parliament is competent to make laws pertaining to the Constitution, organisation, powers and jurisdiction of the Supreme Court. It is a **Federal Court**, vested with original and exclusive jurisdiction to deal with disputes between the Union and the State(s), or between the States (**Article 131**). It may be noted that the parties involved here must be the units of the Federation, i.e., the Union or the State(s). It also acts as the final **Appellate Tribunal** to hear those civil cases where the High Court concerned certifies the involvement of a substantial issue of law of general importance and the decision of Supreme Court is needed (**Article 133**). As regards criminal cases, an appeal will lie with the Supreme Court as a matter of right- especially in cases of the awarding of a death sentence by the lower court (**Article 134**). The Supreme Court may in its discretion grant **special leave to appeal (Article 136)** against any judgment, decree determination, sentence or order in any cause or matter passed or made by any court or tribunal (except a military court or tribunal) in India. **Article 136** marks the widest expression in appeals. Under its **Advisory Jurisdiction**, the Supreme Court also gives its opinions on issues of public importance sought by the President of India. The Supreme Court, however, can also decline to express its opinions if it considers them superfluous or unnecessary (**Article 143**). Finally, the Supreme Court can also issue writs to cure any ills against the FRs (**Article 32**).

High Court

Each State can have its own High Court (**Article 214**). The Bombay, Madras and Calcutta High Courts were established in the Presidency towns in 1862, under Charters of the ruling British Government and are the oldest, whereas the Ranchi High Court (Jharkand), the Bilaspur High Court (Chhatisgarh) and the Nainital High Court (Uttranchal) were created in 2000, and are the youngest. ***Today, there are 24 High Courts and 17 additional benches functioning in the territory of India.*** Parliament can also establish a 'common' High Court for two or more states (**Article 231**). The jurisdiction of a High Court prevails over the state(s) or Union Territories concerned, such as Bombay High Court's extended territorial jurisdiction over Maharastra, Dadra and Nagar Haveli, Goa, and Daman and Diu, and that of Calcutta High Court's over West Bengal, and Andaman and Nicobar Islands. The High Courts can issue writs (**Article 226**). The High Court has to judicially and administratively superintend the tribunals working within its jurisdiction (**Article 227**). The High Courts too accept *Public Interest Litigation* (**PIL**) (**Article 226**).

Appointment and Removal of the Supreme Court / High Court Judges

The President of India appoints the judges of the Supreme Court on the advice of his Council of Ministers. The President consults with the judges of the Supreme Court and the High Courts when appointing the Chief Justice of India (the **CJI**). In 1993, a nine-judge bench of the Supreme Court prescribed that the senior-most judge should be appointed as the CJI. While appointing the other judges of the Supreme Court, the concurrence of the CJI is required in addition to the above criterion (**Article 124 (1)**).

A judge of the Supreme Court should be (1) an Indian citizen (2) either a distinguished jurist or should have worked as a High Court judge for 5 years, or should have been an Advocate of a High Court for a minimum of 10 years (**Article 124(3)**). His tenure would be till his obtaining the age of 65 years or his own resignation or his removal by the President on proven misbehaviour / incompetence, through impeachment, or through death. In 1991-93, such an impeachment motion was brought against the Supreme Court Judge R. Ramaswamy, but was unsuccessful. **As on July 2009 the basic salary of Chief Justice of India is Rs. 100000 per month. The basic salary of SC Judges and Chief Justice of the high courts is Rs. 90000 per month. The basic salary of the high court judges is Rs. 80000 per month.**

The Chief Justice of a High Court is appointed by the President of India in consultation with the Chief Justice of India, the Chief Justice of the State concerned, and the Governor of the State concerned.

A judge of a High Court should (1) be an Indian citizen (2) have worked for 10 years as an advocate of a High Court (**Article 217 (2)**) or have held a judicial office in India for a minimum period of 10 years. His tenure would be until he attains the age of 62 years or his own resignation or his removal by the President of India in the same manner as applicable to a judge of the Supreme Court.

Judges of the Supreme Court, the High Courts, and all other persons appointed to any official post in the Government, are said to hold office '**at the pleasure of the President**'.

It is important to note that Justice Hiralal J. Kania was the first Chief Justice of India, and Justice P. Sathashivam is the current Chief Justice of India.

Justice Fatima Bibi was the first woman judge of the Supreme Court. Currently, there are 31 judges of the Supreme Court.

The first woman Chief Justice of a High Court was Justice Leela Seth, of the Himachal Pradesh High Court.

The National Judicial Academy, an academy registered under the Societies Registration Act, 1860, was established in 1993 in Bhopal.

The nineteenth Law Commission was chaired by **Mr. Justice P. V. Reddi**, (2009-2012).

Justice A.P. Shah, former Chief Justice, Delhi High Court is the current **Chairman of the Twentieth Law Commission of India**.

21st Law Commission

Former Supreme Court judge Balbir Singh Chauhan was appointed Chairman of the 21st Law Commission, a post lying vacant since last September. Justice Chauhan (66) is currently heading the Cauvery River Water Disputes Tribunal. A judge of the Supreme Court from May 2009 to July 2014, he also served as the Chief Justice of Odisha High Court from July 2008 to May 2009. One of the key issues pending before the law panel is a call on amending the Indian Penal Code amid allegations of abuse and arbitrary use of the law. The Law Ministry had urged the Commission to study the usage of the provisions of Section 124A (Sedition) of the IPC. The Commission is reconstituted every three years and is usually headed by a retired Supreme Court judge or former Chief Justice of a high court. The panel will have to look at the issue of revamp of the criminal justice system and recommend a bail law to ensure uniformity in the procedure of granting the relief.

The President

The President is the first citizen of India, and heads the Union. He is an integral part of the Parliament along with the Lok Sabha and the Rajya Sabha (Parliament = President + LS +RS). In order to be **elected** as the President of India, a person must:
(a)   Be an Indian citizen;
(b)   Have completed 35 years of age;
(c)   Be qualified for election as a member of the Lok Sabha; and
(d)   Must not hold any office of profit under the Government of India / State Government/ Local Government (**Article 58**).

The President is indirectly elected by the people of India, in accordance with the system of proportional representation through the **single transferable voting system**, by an electoral college comprising of (a) elected members of the Lok Sabha and the Rajya Sabha, and (b) the elected members of the Legislative Assemblies of the States and those from Delhi and Pondicherry (UT). The **duration** of his office is for a period of 5 years. He may seek re-election.

The President **can be removed** from office if he (a) dies, (b) resigns, (c) is removed through the process of impeachment, or (d) on the expiry of his tenure. In case of the death of the President, the Vice-President will assume the position until a new President is elected. In the case of completion of his tenure, the President can continue in office until such time as the new President takes charge. In case of his inability to exercise his duties on grounds of illness, or during his visits abroad, etc., the Vice-President discharges the functions of his office.

The Constitution has vested **wide powers** in the President, such as:

1. **Administrative Powers:** He can appoint the Prime Minister, the other Union Ministers, the Attorney General, the Comptroller and Auditor General, the Judges of the Supreme Court and the High Courts, the Governors of the States, the members of the Finance Commission, the members of the Union Public Service Commission and joint commissions for two or more States, the Chief Election Commissioner and the Election Commissioners, officers for official languages and linguistic minorities, and for the welfare of the Scheduled Castes / Schedules Tribes.

2. **Legislative Powers:** He exercises these powers on ministerial advice. He can summon, prorogue and dissolve the Lok Sabha and joint parliamentary sessions. He can nominate 2 Anglo-Indians to the Lok Sabha and 12 persons to the Rajya Sabha.

3. **Judicial Powers:** He has powers to grant pardons, reprieves, respite, suspensions, remissions or commutations in respect of sentences of courts martial, punishment for an offence against the law or in even in cases of death sentence. Pardoning powers of the President are set out in **Article 72 of the Constitution.**

4. **Military Powers:** He is the supreme commander of our Armed Forces, but these functions are to be carried out according to the law. He can declare war or peace, with the consultation of Council of Minister.

5. **Diplomatic Powers:** He represents India internationally as the Head of State. He can appoint Indian representatives in foreign countries and receives foreign diplomatic representatives.

6. **Other Powers:** He has a mixture of absolute, suspensive and pocket vetoes.

List of Indian Presidents

S.No	Name	Period
1	Dr. Rajendra Prasad	January 30, 1950 to May 13, 1962
2	Sarvepalli Radhakrishnan	May 13, 1962 to May 13, 1967
3	Zakir Hussain	May 13, 1967 to May 3, 1969
4	Varahagiri Venkata Giri	May 3, 1969 to July 20, 1969
5	Muhammad Hidayatullah	July 20, 1969 to August 24, 1969
6	Varahagiri Venkata Giri	August 24, 1969 to August 24, 1974
7	Fakhruddin Ali Ahmed	August 24, 1974 to February 11, 1977
8	Basappa Danappa Jatti	February 11, 1977 to July 25, 1977
9	Neelam Sanjiva Reddy	July 25, 1977 to July 25, 1982
10	Giani Zail Singh	July 25, 1982 to July 25, 1987
11	Ramaswamy Venkataraman	July 25, 1987 to July 25, 1992
12	Shankar Dayal Sharma	July 25, 1992 to July 25, 1997
13	Kocheril Raman Narayanan	July 25, 1997 to July 25, 2002
14	A. P. J. Abdul Kalam	July 25, 2002 to July 25, 2007
15	Smt. Pratibha Devisingh Patil	July 25, 2007 to July 25, 2012
16	Shri Pranab Mukherjee	July 25, 2012 to July 25, 2017
17	Shri Ram Nath Kovind	July 25, 2017 to till date

Vice President

The Vice President acts as the *ex officio* Chairman of the Rajya Sabha. The following are a few basic facts about the Vice President that you should keep in mind:

1. He is elected by the elected members of the Lok Sabha and the Rajya Sabha only.
2. He is elected through the same system as applies to the President.

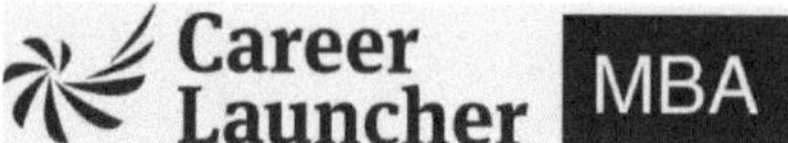

3. Requisite qualifications for appointment as Vice President are the same as apply to the office of the President, except for his qualification for election to the Rajya Sabha.
4. The term of office of the Vice President is for 5 years or less. He is eligible for re-election.
5. The Vice President can be removed either by resignation addressed to the President or may be removed by resolution of the Rajya Sabha passed by a majority, and agreed to by the Lok Sabha.
6. If the post of President is vacant, the Vice President carries out all his functions and then receives the salary of the President. For that period he is not the *ex officio* Chairman of the Rajya Sabha.
7. The Supreme Court is competent to deal with disputes over the election of the President and Vice President.

List of Indian Vice Presidents

Dr Sarvepalli Radhakrishnan	1952-1962
Dr Zakir Hussain	1962-1967
Varahagiri Venkata Giri	1967-1969
Gopal Swarup Pathak	1969-1974
B. D. Jatti	1974-1979
Mohammed Hidayatullah	1979-1984
R. Venkataraman	1984-1987
Dr Shankar Dayal Sharma	1987-1992
K. R. Narayanan	1992-1997
Krishna Kant	1997 -2002
Bhairon Singh Shekhawat	2002-2007
M. H. Ansari	2007-2012
M. H. Ansari	2012-2017
Muppavarapu Venkaiah Naidu	2017-till date

The Council of Ministers

Though "no specific number" has been specified for the council of ministers, they can be appointed as per need. While the President selects the Prime Minster, the council of ministers is appointed on the advice of the Prime Minster. Further, there is no specified classification of this council into Cabinet, State, and Deputy Ministers. Their salary is determined by the Parliament. It is ultimately the Cabinet Ministers who shape government policies. Ministers can be either from the Lok Sabha or the Rajya Sabha. Even a person who is not a Member of Parliament can be a minister, provided he becomes a member of either of the Houses within a period of six months from the date of his appointment. The council of ministers has "**collective responsibility**" towards the Lok Sabha, meaning thereby that they are deemed to be unanimous in supporting the government policies and also personally and morally responsible for the success and failure for any such policy.

Union Cabinet of India

The cabinet of ministers of the Government of India led by the Prime Minister of India is referred to as the Union Cabinet in India. The Prime Minister has the right to decide who he wants to include in his cabinet of ministers and what portfolio is assigned to them. The Union Cabinet is the most powerful executive body in India. The Union Cabinet has ministers of 3 types: 1) Cabinet Ministers 2) State Ministers 3) Deputy Ministers.

The Prime Minister

The Prime Minister is the head of the government in India. He should convey all decisions of the council to the President. He advises the President as regards the appointments of other ministers. The real executive power lies with the Prime Minister. The Prime Minister also acts as a chairman for non-constitutional bodies like the Niti Aayog and the National Development Council (NDC)

S.No.	Name	Period From	Period To	Political party
1	Jawahar Lal Nehru	15-Aug-47	27-May-64	Indian National Congress
2	Gulzarilal Nanda	27-May-64	9 June 1964 *	Indian National Congress
3	Lal Bahadur Shastri	9-Jun-64	11-Jan-66	Indian National Congress
4	Gulzarilal Nanda	11-Jan-66	24 January 1966 *	Indian National Congress
5	Indira Gandhi	24-Jan-66	24-Mar-77	Indian National Congress
6	Morarji Desai	24-Mar-77	28-Jul-79	Janata Party
7	Charan Singh	28-Jul-79	14-Jan-80	Janata Party
8	Indira Gandhi	14-Jan-80	31-Oct-84	Indian National Congress
9	Rajiv Gandhi	31-Oct-84	2-Dec-89	Indian National Congress (Indira)
10	Vishwanath Pratap Singh	2-Dec-89	10-Nov-90	Janata Dal
11	Chandra Shekhar	10-Nov-90	21-Jun-91	Samajwadi Janata Party
12	P. V. Narasimha Rao	21-Jun-91	16-May-96	Indian National Congress
13	Atal Bihari Vajpayee	16-May-96	1-Jun-96	Bharatiya Janata Party
14	H. D. Deve Gowda	1-Jun-96	21-Apr-97	Janata Dal
15	Inder Kumar Gujral	21-Apr-97	19-Mar-98	Janata Dal
16	Atal Bihari Vajpayee	19-Mar-98	22-May-04	Bharatiya Janata Party
17	Dr. Manmohan Singh	22-May-04	26-May-14	Indian National Congress
18	Narendra Damodardas Modi	26-May-14	Incumbent	Bharatiya Janata Party

It is important to note that Gulzari Lal Nanda was the acting Prime Minister on two occasions, the first from May 27, 1964 to June 9, 1964 and secondly, from January 11, 1966 to January 24, 1966 upon the deaths of Jawaharlal Nehru and Lal Bahadur Shastri, the then Prime Ministers, respectively.

The Union Legislature

In India, the Union legislature, known as, the Parliament, consists of the President, the Lok Sabha, and the Rajya Sabha. The Constitution has adopted a "Parliamentary system" of government, which necessarily implies harmony between the legislature and the executive. The function of the Parliament is to provide a cabinet, to make laws, and to suggest and allow ways and means for expenditure and revenue and many more.

Though the President is a part of the legislature, he does not sit in the Parliament except for the purpose of delivering his opening address. The composition of the Lok Sabha and the Rajya Sabha is as under:-

1. House of the People (Lok Sabha)
- Presided over by a Speaker
  He certifies a bill as a Money Bill (**Article 110**). He also presides over the joint Sessions.
- **Strength: 552** members of which-
  (a) Not more than **530** are representatives from the States.
  (b) Not more than **20** representatives of Union Territories.
  (c) Not more than **2** nominated Anglo Indians
- **Term:** Normally for **5** years, but can be dissolved earlier also and can be extended during Emergency.

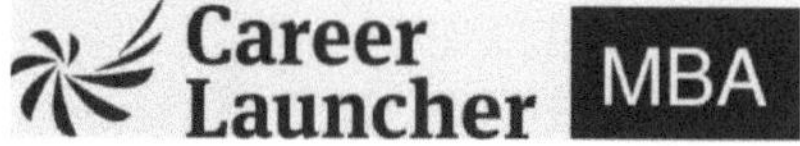

- **Election:** Directly elected by the people, through universal adult franchise (the voting age has been reduced from 21 to 18 years by the **61st Amendment to the Constitution in 1989**.)
- **Qualification:** For membership
  (a) He / She must be a citizen of India.
  (b) He / She must be not less than 25 years of age.
  Additional qualifications:
  (a) He/She should not hold any office of profit under the government.
  (b) He / She should not be of unsound mind.
  (c) He / She should not be declared insolvent.
  (d) He / She should not be disqualified under any law.

2. Council of the States (Rajya Sabha)

- Presided over by a chairman (Vice President acts as ex-officio chairman). RS cannot be dissolved.
- **Strength:** not more than **250** members of which-
  (a) Not more than **238** States and Union Territories representatives.
  (b) **12** nominated by the president.
  Term: 6 years. It is not subject to dissolution. One-third of its members retire every second year.
- **Election:** By the elected Members of the State Legislatures.
- **Qualification:** for membership-
  (a) He / She must be a citizen of India.
  (b) He / She must be not less than 30 years of age.
- **Additional** qualifications: (Same as Lok Sabha)

The State Executive

Part VI of the Constitution deals with the executive, which is uniform for all State governments.

The Governor (Article 155)

The Governor is the head of the State executive. He has discretionary powers as well as special responsibilities, especially in the affairs of the North-Eastern States. A Governor can look after the affairs of two or more States. A Governor is appointed by the President for a period of 5 years, and can be re-appointed. The Governor has the following powers-

(a) **Executive powers:** He appoints the council of ministers, the Advocate General, and the members of the State Public Service Commission, and the High Court Judges can be appointed on his suggestion; he also nominates one Anglo-Indian member to the State Legislature. The Governor also has veto powers.

(b) **Legislative powers:** Like the President, the Governor addresses, sends messages, summons, prorogues and dissolves the State legislature.

(c) **Judicial Powers:** He has the power to grant pardons, reprieves, respites or remission of punishment or to suspend, remit or commute punishments for an offence against the law, other than in cases of courts martial and death sentences (**Article 161**).

The Council of Ministers (Article 163) and the Chief Minister

The Governor appoints the council of ministers in each State on the advice of the Chief Minister. The ministers are jointly and severally responsible to the legislature.

Though there is no prescribed qualification provided for the appointment of a Chief Minister, he should be qualified for election to the legislative assembly. His appointment is to be made by the Governor (**Article 164(A)**).

It is important to note that Smt. Sucheta Kriplani and **Smt. Sarojini Naidu** were the country's first woman Chief Minister and Governor, respectively. They were appointed in Uttar Pradesh.

The 97th Amendment to the Constitution has now laid down the rule that the council of ministers is to be restricted to 15% of the sanctioned strength of the state legislature assembly.

Important Articles in Indian Constitution and their areas of concern

S.No.	Articles	Area of conern
1	Article 3	Citizenship
2	Article 21	Right to life
3	Article 32	Right to constitutional remedies
4	Article 44	Uniform civil code
5	Article 51A	Fundamental duties
6	Article 61	Impeachment of president
7	Article 110	Definition of money bill
8	Articel 123	Ordinance making powers of president
9	Article 324	Establishment of election commission of India
10	Article 300A	Right to property
11	Article 280	Finance commission
12	Article 352	National emergency
13	Article 356	Emergency in states
14	Article 360	Financial emergency
15	Article 368	Amendment of Constitution

List of Schedules in the Constitution of India and their areas of function.

Schedule	Area of function
First	All the States and Union Territories of India
Second	Salaries and allowances of the President, Governor, Chief Justice, Judges of High Court and Supreme Court and CAG
Third	Prescriptions regarding forms of affirmations and oaths for the new entrants to the public offices
Fouth	Allocation of seats in Rajya Sabha to each Union Territory and State
Fifth	Provisions to the control of administration of scheduled areas
Sixth	Administrative provisions for tribal areas in Meghalaya, Mizoram and Assam
Seventh	Three lists of subjects and powers to be looked after by the State and the Union, i.e. : (1) Union list, containing the subjects of national importance, railway, defence, income tax, etc. (2) State list contains locally important subjects. (3) Concurrent list contains subjects under the authority of the Parliament and the State Legislature
Eighth	Deals with 18 (now 22) officially recognized regional languages by the Constitution.
Ninth	Contains acts and regulations dealing with abolition of zamindari system and land reforms of the State Legislatures. **The provisions of this schedule cannot be challanged in Supreme Court.**
Tenth	Contains provisions for the disqualification of members on the grounds of defection.
Eleventh	Deals with implementation of schemes needed for social justice and economic development at the rural levels.
Twelfth	Deals with municipal committees and their categorizations.

Note:

Originally, there were eight schedules. Later, four more schedules were added to it, taking the total tally of schedules to twelve.

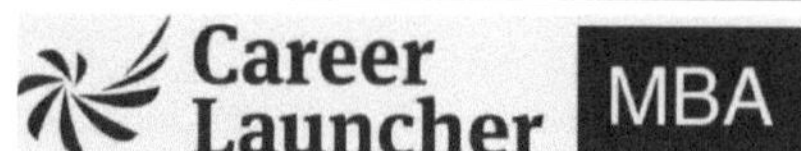

Here is a quick look at the most important Amendments to the Constitution so far. You should know this list well, since a few questions are often from this area!

1st Amendment (1951): Schedule IX added, in order to save land reforms laws from judicial review. A nine-judge bench of the Supreme Court has now been asked to lay down the guidelines for the inclusion of any law in this Schedule. This has been caused due to the efforts on the parts of some States to include their reservation policy implementation laws in the Schedule.

42nd Amendment (1976): This amendment was also called the "Mini Constitution", as it is the largest amendment ever. Some of the changes it introduced are:
➢ The Preamble was amended to include the words 'Secular', 'Socialist' and 'integrity'.
➢ 'Fundamental Duties' added in Article 51A.
➢ The new Directive Principles in Articles 39A, 43A and 48A were added.

44th Amendment (1978): The Right to Property (Article 31) was abolished from the chapter of Fundamental Rights, and included under Article 300A, to remain a constitutional right.

61st Amendment (1989): Voting Age reduced from 21 to 18 years.

73rd and 74th Amendments (1992): Provisions relating to Panchayats and Municipalities revived, and Schedules XI and XII added.

84th Amendment (2000): Three new states, Chhattishgarh, Uttaranchal and Jharkhand created.

86th Amendment (2002): The Right to Education was made a Fundamental Right under the new Article 21A. A new Fundamental Duty was added under Article 51A(k), relating to a Parent's fundamental duty to ensure that his child is not prevented from enjoying free and compulsory education up to the age of Fourteen. Article 45 of the Directive Principles was also amended, and it now provides that early childhood care (up to the age of Six) shall be the responsibility of the state.

91st Amendment (2003): Anti-defection law, *i.e.* disqualification of a Member of Parliament or a Legislative Assembly on the ground of defection. The strength of the Council of Ministers in the Union Government, as well as in any State Government, is now restricted to not more than 15% of total membership.

92nd Amendment (2003): VIII Schedule amended to include four new languages, *i.e.,* Bodo, Dogri, Maithili and Santhali.

93rd Amendment (2005): Article 15 amended to include a new clause empowering the Government to make laws to provide reservations to the socially and educationally backward classes in all educational institutions, including private institutions, but not in minority educational institutions.

94th Amendment Act (2006): Freed Bihar from the obligation of having a tribal welfare minister and extended the same provision to Jharkhand and Chattisgarh. This provision will now be applicable to the newly formed states and Madhya Pradesh and Odisha, where it has already been in force (Article 164(1)).

95th Amendment Act (2010): The extend the reservation of seats for SC's and ST's in the Lok Sabha and States assemblies from sixty to seventy years (Article 334)

96th Amendment Act (2011): Substituted "Odia" for "Oriya" (Schedule 8)

97th Amendment Act (2012): Amended article 19 and Part IX B. Added words "or cooperative societies" after the word "or unious" in article 19(1)(c) and inserted article 43B and added Part IX B.

98th Amendment Act (2013): Inserted article 371J in the constitutional and empowered Governor of Karnataka to take steps to develop Hyderabad-Karnataka Region.

100th Amendment Act (2015): Land Boundary Agreement (LBA) Treaty between India and Bangladesh.

101 Amendment Act (2017): This amendment act introduced a national Goods and Services Tax in India from 1ˢᵗ July 2017.

Part–I (Article 1 – 4)
- Deals with territory of India formation of new States, alterations, names of existing states.

Part – II (Art. 5 – 11)
- Deals with various rights of citizenship.

Part–III (Art. 12 – 35)
- Deals with fundamental rights of Indian citizens.
- [Art. 31- dealing with the right to property was deleted by 44th amendment]

Part – IV (Art. 36 – 51)
- Deals with Directive Principles of State Policy.

Part – IV-A (Art. 51A)
- Added by 42nd amendment in 1976. Contains the duties of the citizens.

Part – V (Art. 52 – 151)
- Deals with govt. at the Union Level. (Duties & function of PM, Ministers, President, Attorney General, Parliament - Lok Sabha & Rajya Sabha, Comptroller & Auditor General).

Part – VI (Art. 152 – 237)
- Deals with govt. at State Level.
- [Art-152 exempts J&K from the category of ordinary states].
- [Duties & functions of Chief Minister & his ministers, Governor, State legislature, High Court, Advocate General of the State].

Part – VII (Art. 238)
- Deals with States, was replaced in 1956 by the 7th amendment.

Part – VIII (Art. 239 – 241)
- Deals with Union Territories.

Part – IX
- Consists of 2 parts:
  1. Added by 73rd amendment in 1992. Contains a new schedule 'SCHEDULE ELEVEN'. It contains 29 subjects related to Panchayati Raj. (They have been given administrative powers).
  2. Added by 74th amendment in 1992. Contains a new schedule 'SCHEDULE TWELVE'. It contains 18 subjects related to Municipalities. (They have been given administrative powers).

Part – X (Art. 244, 244A)
- Deals with Scheduled & Tribal Areas.

Part – XI (Art. 245-263)
- Deals with relations between the Union and States.

Part – XII (Art. 264-300A)
- Consists of articles on finance, property , contracts and suits.

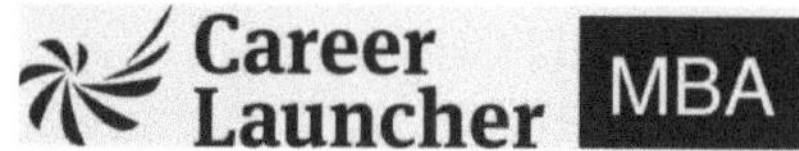

Science

(A) Various Important Branches of Science

Name of science	Related to
Acoustics	Sound and sound waves
Aeronautics	Activities of flying
Agronomy	Production of crops and soil management
Anatomy	Dissectional learning of animal and human body
Anthropology	Origin, cultural and physical development of man
Archaeology	Study of material remains of past as proofs
Astronautics	Space vehicles and travelling in space
Astronomy	Planets (the heavenly bodies)
Biology	Science of living organisms
Botany	Plants
Cardiology	Heart and related diseases
Ceramics	Manufacturing of clay objects
Cetology	Aquatic mammals, especially the whales
Cosmology	Universe
Cryogenics	Studying effects of low temperature
Cytology	Structure and function of cells
Dactylogy	Study of fingerprints
Dermatology	Skin
Dietetics	Diet and nutrition
Ecology	Organisms and environment relationship
Entomology	Insects
Endocrinology	Endocrine glands
Etymology	Origin and history of words
Genetics	Heredity and its laws
Geology	Earth's (chemical and physical) structure
Gerontology	Ageing process, problems and diseases
Gynaecology	Female diseases of reproductive system
Haematology	Blood and related disorders
Histology	Tissues
Immunology	Body's immune system
Morphology	External structure of living organisms
Mycology	Fungi and fungal diseases
Nephrology	Kidney
Obstetrics	Pregnancy, child birth and their follow up
Ornithology	Birds
Orthopaedics	Human skeletal system
Osteology	Study of bones

Name of science	Related to
Paediatrics	Child diseases
Palaeontology	Fossils and ancient life-forms
Pathology	Mechanisms and manifestation of diseases
Pharmacology	Drugs and their effects on the body
Physiology	Life processes of various organs of living beings
Psychiatry	Mental disorders
Semiology	Sign language and signs
Seismology	Earthquakes
Theology	Religions
Toxicology	Toxic substances and poisons
Zoology	Animal life
Zymology	Fermentation process

(B) Important Units of Measurement

Name of the unit	Used to measure
Ampere	Electric current
Angstrom	Wavelength of light
Bar	Atmospheric pressure
Calorie	Quantity of heat
Candela	Luminous intensity
Celsius	Temperature
Coulomb	Electric charge
Decibel	Sound level
Dyne	Force
Erg	Work
Fahrenheit	Temperature (commonly used by doctors to measure body temperature)
Fathom	Depth of water
Faraday	Electric charge (used in electrolysis) = 96,500 coulomb
Gauss	Magnetic induction/Magnetic flux density
Henry	Inductance
Hertz	Frequency
Horsepower	Power
Joule	Work or Energy
Kelvin	Temperature (SI unit)
Light year	Distance, (Distance light travels in one year at a speed of 2,97,600 km)
Newton	Force (SI unit)
Ohm	Electrical resistance
Pascal	Pressure
Poise	Viscosity
Volt	Electrical potential
Watt	Power

(C) Medical Discoveries

Discovery	Discovered by
Penicillin	Alexander Fleming
Aspirin	Felix Hoffmann
Blood circulation	William Harvey
Blood group	K. Landsteiner
Cholera	Robert Koch
Electro cardiogram (ECG)	Williem Einthoven
Heart transplant surgery	Christian Barnard
Malaria germs	A. Laveran
Ultrasound	Ian Donald

(D) Important Scientific Inventions

Invention	Inventor
Aeroplane	Wright Brothers
Bicycle	K. Macmillan
Centigrade scale	A. Celsius
Computer	Charles Babbage
Diesel engine	Rudolf Diesel
Dynamite	Alfred Nobel
Dynamo	Michael Faraday
Electric lamp	Thomas Alva Edison
Fountain pen	L.E. Waterman
Gramophone	Thomas Alva Edison
Jet engine	Sir Frank Whittle
Microphone	David Hughes
Microscope	Z. Jansen
Radium	Marie and Pierre Curie
Safety lamp	Sir Humphery Davy
Safety pin	William Hurst
Sewing machine	B. Thimmonnier
Shorthand (modern)	Sir Isaac Pitman
Steam engine (piston)	Thomas Newcome
Steam engine (condenser)	James Watt
Telegraph code	Samuel F.B. Morse
Telephone	Alexander Graham Bell
Telescope	Hans Lippershey
Television	John Logie Baird
Thermometer	Galileo Galilei
X-ray	Wilhelm Roentgen

(E)   Scientific Instruments

Name of instrument	Function
Ammeter	Used for measuring strength of electric current
Barometer	Used for measuring atmospheric pressure
Calorimeter	Used for measuring quantities of heat
Cardiograph (ECG)	Used for measuring movements of the heart; recorded on a cardiograph
Dynamo	Converts mechanical energy into electrical energy
Electroencephalograph (EEG)	Records and interprets the electrical waves of the brain
Electrometer	Used for measuring very small, potential difference in electric currents
Endoscope	Examines internal organs of the body and can be used for minor surgical procedures
Fathometer	Used for measuring depth of the ocean
Galvanometer	Used for measuring the electric current
Hydrometer	Used for measuring the relative density of liquids
Hygrometer	Used for measuring the level of humidity in the atmosphere
Kymograph	Graphically records physiological movements (e.g. blood pressure/heartbeat)
Lactometer	Used for measuring the relative density of milk to determine the purity (fat content)
Manometer	Used for measuring the pressure of gases
Micrometer	Measures distances/angles
Microscope	Used for obtaining a magnified view of small objects
Periscope	Used for viewing objects above sea level (used in submarines)
Polygraph	Used for recording changes simultaneously in physiological processes such as heart beat, blood pressure and respiration; also used as a lie detector
Pyrometer	Used for measuring very high temperature
Salinometer	Used for determining the salinity of solutions
Sextant	Used by navigators to find the latitude of a place by measuring the elevation above the horizon of the sun or another star; also measures the height of distant objects
Sphygmomanometer	Used for measuring blood pressure
Stethoscope	Used by doctors to hear and analyze heart and lung sounds
Tacheometer	Used for measuring distances and elevations and bearings during survey
Telescope	Used for viewing distant objects in space
Transponder	Used to receive a signal and transmit a reply immediately
Viscometer	Used for measuring the viscosity of liquid
Voltmeter	Used to measure electric potential difference between two points
Wattmeter	Used for measuring the power of an electric circuit

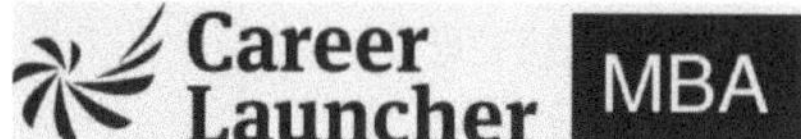

(F)   Important Vaccines

Vaccine	Discovered by
Smallpox	Edward Jenner
Cholera, Rabies Vaccine	Louis Pasteur
TB vaccine	Leon Calmette and Camille Guerin
Polio vaccine	Jonas E. Salk

(G)   Important Information About the Human Body

Blood: It is a red, viscous fluid which circulates in the human body. It is basically a connective tissue which is contained in the blood vessels. A healthy man possesses on an **average, 5 litres of blood in the body.**

Composition: It is made up of two chief constituents:

(a) **Plasma (fluid),** constitutes the **major part** while (b) **Blood cells (solid),** which constitutes the **minor** part.

The blood cell corpuscles are of two types: **(1) RBC (2) WBC.** The RBC is **red blood corpuscles** which contains **a pigment called hemoglobin which is responsible for the red colour of the blood. Iron is the element which is present in the hemoglobin. The WBC are white blood corpuscles** which are primarily responsible for **combating with the infection of the body or they** fight with the foreign harmful organisms of the body.

Blood groups: They are of four types, viz.

(i) **A-type**

(ii) **B-type**

(iii) **AB-type**

(iv) **O-type**

AB - type is called **universal recipient** as it can receive all the four types (mentioned above) of blood and **O-type** is called as **universal donor** as it can be given to any of the four types of blood groups (mentioned above).

Bones:

(i)   There are **206 bones** in the **skeletal system of an adult.**

(ii)   The **largest bone** is **femur** present in **the thigh.**

(iii)   The **shortest bone** is the **stirrup** which is **present in the middle ear.**

Other important facts about the various organs of the human body:

1.   The **largest organ** of the human body is **skin.**

2.   Heart is responsible for regulating the circulation of blood in the body. The heart beat of adult males **is 72 beats per minute.**

3.   **Liver is the largest gland** of the human body. It is concerned with the digestion of the food intake.

4.   Two kidneys are responsible for the filtering of nitrogenous waste of the body and throw it all in the form of urine.

5.   **Pituitary gland** is called **the master gland as it** influences the growth and metabolism by controlling the other ductless glands, viz. thymus, thyroid, adrenal, prostrate, pancreas and gonads.

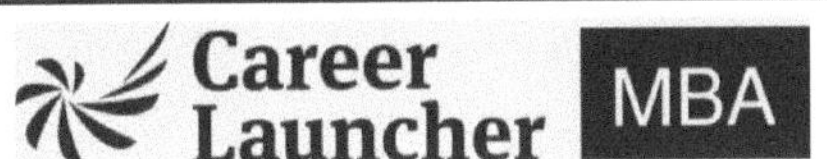

(H)   Vitamins, Their Sources and Diseases Caused Due to Their Deficiencies

Name of the vitamin	Main source	Disease caused due to their deficiencies
Vitamin A	Milk, carrot, egg, animal fat, etc.	**Night blindness**
Vitamin B$_1$ (Thiamine)	Cereals, pulses, carrots	**Beriberi**
Vitamin B$_2$ (Riboflavin)	Liver, kidney, milk	Chilosis, dermatitis
Vitamin B$_6$ (Pyridoxine	Yeast, cereals, liver	Anaemia
Niacin (Nicotinic acid)	Peas, tomato, eggs	Polyneuritis
Folic Acid	Green leafy vegetables, meat, egg	Anaemia
Pantothenic Acid	Kidney, meat, yeast	Dermatitis
Vit. B$_{12}$ (Cyanocobalamin)	Milk, liver, meat	Pernicious anaemia
Vitamin C (Ascorbic acid)	Lemons, milk, oranges, fresh fruits and vegetables	**Scurvy,** sore mouth and gums bleeding
Vitamin D (Calciferol)	Dairy products, sun rays, eggs, oily fish, milk	Many diseases of the bones, rickets in children, **osteomalacia**
Vitamin E (Tocopherol)	Milk, soyabeens, egg yolk	**Interferes with reproduction and causes abortion and menstrual irregularities**
Vitamin K (Menadione)	Fish, peas and green vegetables	Causes the **delayed clotting of blood**

(I)   Other Diseases of the Human Body

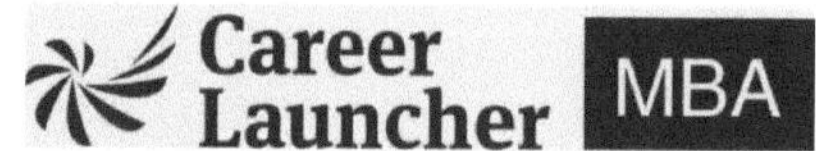

General Knowledge

Name of the disease	Caused by	Affected part of the human body
Anaemia	Deficiency of haemoglobin	
AIDS (acquired immuno deficiency syndrome)	Virus	Weakness in the immune system of the body
Asthma	Allergens	Lungs
Diabetes	Less production of insulin hormone which causes an increase in the sugar level of the blood	Pancreas and blood
Diphtheria	Bacteria	Throat
Glaucoma	High pressure in the eyes	Eyes
Goitre	Deficiency of iodine	Throat
Hepatitis	Virus (mainly)	Jaundice
Malaria	Plasmodium	
Polio	Virus	Legs
Rheumatism	Streptococcus bacteria in children	Joints
Tonsillitis	Bacterial and viral infection	Glands in throat
Tuberculosis	Bacteria	Lungs

(J) Major Enzymes in the human digestive system

Body part	Enzyme	Action
1. Mouth	Salivary amylase (Ptyalin, acidic medium)	Converts starch into disaccahrides
2. Stomach	Pepsin and Renin (Acidic medium)	They act on proteins
3. Intestine	Lipase, Trypsin, Carbohydrases (Medium is now basic)	Lipase converts fats into fatty acid and glycerol. Trypsin converts proteins into amino acids and carbohydrases converts monosaccharides into glucose.

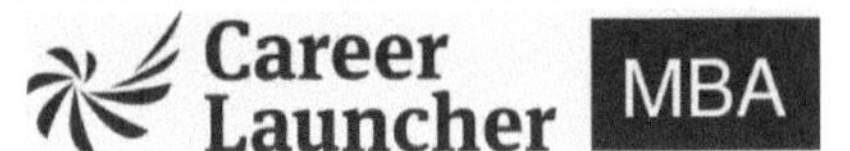

Sports

(A) Major Sports Festivals of the World

(a) **The Olympics:** This is the world's most prestigious, international sports festival. These Games originated in the ancient city of **Greece.**

Modern Olympic Games: Frenchman Baron Pierre de Coubertin is called the father of modern Olympic Games which **started in 1896, in Athens.** These Games are held every four years, since then. The Winter Olympic Games **were started separately** in **1924 in France.**

Some important facts about Olympic Games:
  (i) **The first Modern Olympic Games were held at Athens, capital of Greece in 1896.**
  (ii) India has never hosted the Olympic Games in its history.
  (iii) The last Olympic Games were held **in 2012 at London in Britain capital** and were the **30th edition** of the Games.
  (iv) The Olympic flag is white in colour and has the emblem five rings, embedded at the centre of the flag.
  (v) The emblem is made up of **five intertwined rings** having different colours **which represent the five continents of the world.**
  (vi) The Olympic motto is **'Citius, Altius, Furtius' which means swifter, higher, stronger.**
(b) **Commonwealth Games:** They were held first in 1930 at Canada. They are also held every four years, midway between the Olympic Games.
(c) **Asian Games:** It is a sports festival of Asian countries. J.L. Nehru was instrumental in giving shape to Asian Games. **First Asian Games were held at New Delhi in 1951** and since then, these games have been taking place every four years.
(d) **World Cup:** Almost all the sporting events has world cup generally conducted with an interval of every four years.

The 2016 Summer Olympics

The 2016 Summer Olympics is officially known as the Games of the XXXI Olympiad and commonly known as Rio 2016, was a major international multi-sport event held in Rio de Janeiro, Brazil, from 5 August to 21 August 2016.

More than 11,000 athletes from 207 National Olympic Committees, including first time entrants Kosovo, South Sudan, and the Refugee Olympic Team, took part. With 306 sets of medals, the games featured 28 Olympic sports, including rugby sevens and golf, which were added to the Olympic program in 2009. These sporting events took place at 33 venues in the host city, and at five in São Paulo, Belo Horizonte, Salvador, Brasília, and Manaus.

These were the first Summer Olympic Games under the IOC presidency of Thomas Bach. The host city Rio de Janeiro was announced at the 121st IOC Session in Copenhagen, Denmark, on 2 October 2009. Rio became the first South American city to host the Summer Olympics. These were the first games to be held in a Portuguese-speaking country, the first to be held entirely in the host country's winter, the first since 1968 to be held in Latin America, and the first since 2000 to be held in the Southern Hemisphere.

The United States topped the medal table for the fifth time in the past six Summer Olympics, winning the most golds (46) and most medals overall (121). Great Britain finished second and became the first country in the history of the modern Olympics to increase its tally of medals in the subsequent games after being the host nation. China finished third. Host country Brazil won seven gold medals, its most at any single Summer Olympics, finishing in thirteenth place. Fiji, Jordan, Kosovo, Puerto Rico, Singapore, Tajikistan, and Vietnam each won their first gold medals, as did the group of Independent Olympic Athletes (from Kuwait). The United States won its 1,000th Olympic gold medal in this edition.

South Asian Games — 2016

The 2016 South Asian Games, officially the XII South Asian Games, is a major multi-sport event which took place from 5 February to 16 February 2016 in Guwahati and Shillong, India. A total of 2,672 athletes competed in 226 events over 22 sports. Indian Prime Minister Narendra Modi inaugurated the 2016 South Asian Games in Guwahati on 5 February 2016. The sporting giant of the region, India continued its dominance in the game's medal tally with a staggering 308 medals including 188 gold medals.

Winter Olympics — 2018

The 2018 Winter Olympics, officially known as the XXIII Olympic Winter Games and commonly known as PyeongChang 2018, is a major international multi-sport event took place from 9 to 25 February 2018, in PyeongChang, South Korea. It was the second winter Olympics held on mainland Asia, after Sochi, Russia. The statistic reflects the medal count of the Winter Olympic Games in PyeongChang in 2018. Norway topped the table, finishing the Games with a total of 39 medals - 14 gold, 14 silver, and 11 bronze.

(B)   **Important International Cups, Trophies and Associated Sports Disciplines**

Name of the cup/trophy	Associated sports
Davis Cup(Men)/Federation Cup(Women)	Lawn tennis
Wimbledon Trophy	Lawn tennis
Australian Open,	Lawn tennis
US Open, French Open	Lawn tennis
Derby	Horse racing
Merdeka	**Football**
Thomas Cup (Men)	Badminton
Uber Cup (Women)	Badminton
Yonex Cup	Badminton
Walker Cup	Golf
Ryder Cup	**Golf**
Canada Cup	Golf
William Jones Cup	Basketball
Champions Trophy	Hockey
Champions League	Football
Sultan Azlan Shah Cup	Hockey

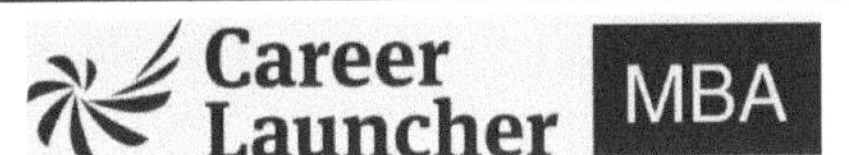

(C)   Important National Cups, Trophies and Associated Sports Disciplines

Name of the cup/trophy	Associated sports
Duleep Trophy	Cricket
Shish Mahal Trophy	Cricket
Ranji Trophy (National Title)	Cricket
Vijay Hazare Trophy	Cricket(50 Overs)
Irani Trophy	Cricket
Durand Cup	Football
Santosh Memorial Trophy	Football(School Championship)
Subroto Cup	Football
Rovers Cup	Football
Sanjay Gold Cup	Football
Nizam Gold Cup	Football
Dr. B.C. Roy Trophy (National Junior Championship)	Football
Rangaswami Cup (National Title)	Hockey
Lady Ratan Tata Trophy (Women's)	Hockey
Nehru Trophy	Hockey
Aga Khan Gold Cup	Hockey
Beighton Cup	Hockey
Guru Nanak Championship (All - India Women)	Hockey
Dhyan Chand Trophy	Hockey
Murugappa Gold Cup	Hockey
Ezar Cup	Polo

(D)   Important Terms Associated with Various Sports Disciplines

Sports	Terms associated with sports disciplines
Badminton	Luv, deuce, drop, smash, double touch
Basketball	Pivot, dribble, basket, block, held ball
Billiards	Spider, baulk, cue, scratch, cannon
Boxing	Hook, rounds, punch, jab, countdown, knock-outs, all the weights, (flyweight, middleweight, heavyweight, etc.)
Bridge	Tricks, trump, suite, little slam, rubber
Chess	Knight, king, Sicilian defence, move, gambit, checkmate, rook, stalemate, queen, bishop, pawn
Cricket	Gully, hat-trick, pull, beamer, hook, googly, flick, follow-on, maiden, declare
Golf	Tee, birdie, club, course, Iron, eagle, links, caddie, putt, hole, Bogey, Fore, Niblic
Hockey	Centre, penalty-stroke, free-hit, foul, carry, stick, corner, dribble, trapping
Table tennis	Deuce, drop, spin, smash, let
Tennis	Grand slam, lob, ace, passing shot, top-spin, forehand, crosscourt, deuce, down the line, slice
Volleyball	Heave, serve, blocking, point, doubling

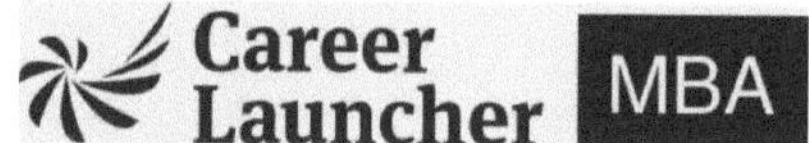

6

Culture of India

///Indian Culture///

Indian culture is one of the oldest known cultures to humanity. Although it is very difficult to cater the unique and vast cultural heritage of India but still an attempt has been made to cover some of the most important relevant areas of Indian culture.

The important sections are as follows:
A. Literature
B. Dance
C. Music
D. Architecture

A. Literature

The literature of India is one of the oldest literature in the world. Here is the collection of some of the famous works of Indian literature.

S.No.	Book	Author
1	Ramayana	Valmiki
2	Mahabharata	Ved Vyas
3	Ramcharit Manas	Tulsidas
4	Ashtadhyayi	Panini
5	Abhigyan Shakuntalam	Kalidas
6	Meghdoot	Kalidas
7	Vikmovarshiyam	Kalidas
8	Ritusamhar	Kalidas
9	Mrichchkatika	Shudraka
10	Ratnavali	Harsha Vardhan
11	Geetgovinda	Jayadeva
12	Arthashastra	Vishnugupt / Chanakya
13	Kamasutra	Vatsyayan
14	Svapnavasavdattam	Bhaasa
15	Manusmriti	Manu
16	Ananda Math / Kapal Kundala	Bankim Chandra Chatterjee
17	Devdas	Sharat Chandra Chatterjee
18	Gitanjali	Rabindranath Tagore
19	Gita Rahasya	B. G. Tilak
20	Harsha Charita	Banabhatta
21	Kadambari	Banabhatta
22	Kamayani	Jai Shankar Prasad
23	Mudra Rakshas	Vishakhadutta
24	Panchatantra	Vishnu Sharma
25	Satyartha Prakash	Swami Dayananda Saraswati
26	Mitakshara	Vignaneshwara
27	Godan	Premchand
28	Sooryakanthi	G Sankara Kurup

B. Dance

Important and famous dances of India:
Broadly the dance forms can be classified into two types, viz. classical dance and folk dance.

(i)   Important and famous classical dances of India:

1. **Kathakali, Mohiniattam, Chakiarkoothu, Ottum Thulal:** These are the famous dance forms that belongs to Kerala. Pallavi Krishnan and Bharti Shivaji are the famous exponents of Mohiniattam form of dance. Madavoor Vasudevan Nair is a famous exponent of Kathakali form of dance.
2. **Bharatnatyam:** This is a famous dance form that belongs to Tamil Nadu. The famous exponents of this dance form are Yamini Krishnamurty, Padma Subramanyam, Mallika Sarabhai.
3. **Kuchipudi:** This dance form belongs to Andhra Pradesh. The famous exponents of this dance form are Raja and Radha Reddy (duo), Yamini Krishnamurty, Mallika Sarabhai.
4. **Odissi:** This dance form belongs to Odisha. The famous exponents of this dance form are late Kelucharan Mahapatra, Sonal Mansingh.
5. **Kathak:** This is a dance form that belongs to Uttar Pradesh. The famous exponents of this dance form are Birjoo Maharaj, Uma Sharma.
6. **Manipuri:** This is a famous dance form of Manipur.
7. **Yakshagana:** This is a famous dance form of Karnataka.

(ii)   Important Folk Dances of India:

1. **Chhou Nach and Ghambira:** Folk dances form of West Bengal.
2. **Kolattam:** Folk dance form that belongs to Kerala.
3. **Bhangara:** Folk dance form of Punjab.
4. **Nautanki:** Folk dance form of Uttar Pradesh.
5. **Dandya Ras and Garba:** Folk dances forms of Gujarat.
6. **Tamasha:** Folk dance form of Maharashtra.
7. **Fagun and Jata Jatin:** Folk dances forms of Bihar.
8. **Macha:** This is a folk dance form of Madhya Pradesh.
9. **Ankia Nat and Bihu:** Folk dances forms of Assam.

C. Music

(i)   Famous and Important music artists of India and their associated disciplines

1.   **Pt. Bhimsen Joshi:** Hindustani Vocalist
2.   **Pt. Jasraj:** Hindustani Vocalist
3.   **Late M. S. Subbulakshmi:** Famous Carnatic Vocalist
4.   **Allauddin Khan:** Hindustani Vocalist
5.   **Bade Gulam Ali Khan:** Hindustani Vocalist
6.   **Basavraj Rajguru:** Hindustani Vocalist
7.   **Dr. M. Balmuralikrishna:** Carnatic Vocalist
8.   **D. K. Pattamal:** Carnatic Vocalist
9.   **K. J. Yesudas:** Carnatic Vocalist
10. **Late Gangubai Hangal:** Hindustani Vocalist
11. **Parveen Sultana:** Hindustani Vocalist
12. **Rajan and Sajan Mishra:** Hindustani Vocalist

13. **Kishori Amonkar:** Hindustani Vocalist

14. **Pt. Ravi Shankar:** Sitar

15. **Pt. Aajya Chakraborty:** Hindustani Vocalist

16. **Ustad Ali Akbar Khan:** Sarod

17. **Ustad Amjal Ali Khan:** Sarod

18. **Pt. Hari Prasad Chaurasiya:** Flute

(ii) Famous and important musical instrumentalists of India

Musical Instrument	Artist
Sitar	Pandit Ravi Shankar, Debu Chaudhury, Annapurna Devi, Anoushka Shankar
Flute	Pt. Hari Prasad Chourasiya, Jayantha Bannerjee
Violin	N. Rajam, P. L. Pawar
Sarod	Amjad Ali Kihan, Ali Akbar Khan, Aman and Ayan Ali Bangish, Sharan Rani.
Shehnai	Bismillah Khan, Shailesh Bhagat, Anant Lal
Tabla	Shafat Ahmed Khan, Kishan Maharaj, Late Allah Rakha, Ustad Zakir Hussain
Santoor	Bhajan Sopori, Shiv Kumar Sharma
Others	
(a) Mohan Veena	Vishwa Mohan Bhatt
(b) Sarangi	Ram Narayan

D. Architecture

India has a very rich architectural legacy as a result of which we have so many marvellous architectural monuments in India. Mughal architecture and Dravidian architecture are to name a few.

Given below is the list of the architectural monuments.

Important and famous architectural marvels of India

1. **Bhimbetka Caves:** Located in Madhya Pradesh at the edge of Vindhyachal hills, rock shelters of Bhimbetka are believed to be the place where earliest known traces of human life have been found in India. The interesting features of Bhimbetka include rock shelters, caves and the rock paintings of Bhimbetka.

2. **Taj Mahal:** Built by the Mughal emperor Shah Jahan in the memory of his wife Mumtaz Mahal, this is a marvellous piece of Islamic architecture in India and is one of the finest buildings of the world. Taj Mahal is located in Agra, a town in Uttar Pradesh on the banks of the river Yamuna.

3. **Konark Temple:** Built in the 13th century by King Narsimhadeva, this temple is dedicated to the Lord Sun. This temple is located in Odisha and is the epitome of the Oriya temple architecture.

4. **Mahabodhi Temple:** This is a famous Bodh temple located at Bodh Gaya in Bihar. This is the place where the founder of Buddhism, Gautam Buddha, attained enlightenment.

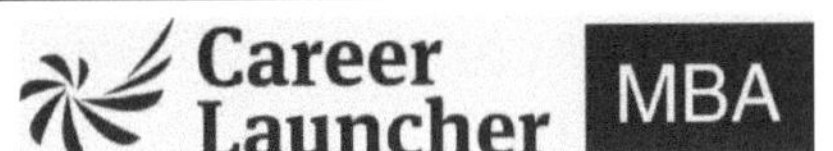

5. **Fatehpur Sikri:** This city of historical importance was built by the great Mughal emperor Akbar in 1569 in the honour of Muslim saint Sheikh Salim Chishti at a place near Agra in Uttar Pradesh.

6. **Khajuraho Temples:** This temple is situated in Madhya Pradesh. Built by the Chandela dynasty rulers, these temples are the wonderful work of medieval temple architecture.

7. **Mahabalipuram:** The temple is located in Tamil Nadu. These group of monuments including the temples were built by the Pallava Dynasty rulers and is considered as an exceptional work of Dravidian architecture. The monuments are mostly rock cut and monolithic.

8. **Qutub Minar:** Situated in New Delhi, this minaret is a wonder of Islamic architecture. Started by Qutub-ud-din-Aibak, this minaret was completed by Firoz Shah Tughlaq. The height of the tower is 72.5 metres.

9. **Humayun's Tomb:** This tomb of Humayun was built by Humayun's wife, Haji Begham. The Humayun's tomb also encompasses the tomb of Babur. The tomb located in New Delhi is an excellent piece of work of Mughal architecture.

10. **Ellora Caves:** The Ellora caves was built between 6th to 10th century. It is known for magnificent work of rock cut architecture, comprising of Jain, Buddhist, Hindu temples and monasteries. These caves are located in Maharashtra.

11. **Ajanta Caves:** Situated in Maharashtra, these caves have lot of dwelling halls, also known as Viharas.

12. **Brihadeshwara Temple:** Located in Tamil Nadu, this temple was built by Rajraja – I of Chola dynasty, around 10th century. The main god of this temple is Lord Shiva. This temple is a very good example of Dravidian architecture.

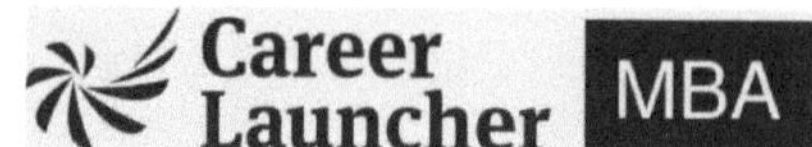

7

Miscellaneous General Knowledge

///////////////////////////////////////**Important International Organizations**///////////////////////////////////////

Major International Organizations of the World are as follows:

(A) United Nations

United Nations is world's largest organization which was **formed on October 24, 1945.** Since then **October 24 is celebrated as the United Nations Day.** The main objective of the United Nations is to make the world a better place to live in by maintaining peace and security all over the world. There are **193 members** at present in the UN and **South Sudan** is the last entrant. The organisation headquartered at New York has got **five countries** as the **permanent members** in its security council. **They are China, UK, USA, Russia and France**; Besides this they have 10 non-permanent members.

1. **Structure of the Organization:** The following principle bodies of United Nations Organization.
    (i) **General Assembly:** It is **headquartered at New York.** Its members are all member states of the United Nations Organization (UNO).
    (ii) **Security Council: Headquartered at New York,** it has **five permanent members** (mentioned earlier) who enjoy veto power and 10 non-permanent elected members. The non-permanent elected members are elected by the General Assembly and retire on rotation, every two years. The main function is to look after the international peace and security.
    (iii) **The Economic and Social Council: Headquartered at New York,** it consists of **representatives of 54 member countries** elected by two-third majority in the General Assembly. It functions in international economic, social and culture-related matters.
    (iv) **Trusteeship Council: Headquartered at New York,** it looks after the interests of inhabitants of territories which are not yet fully self-governing and are governed by any administrating country. The Trusteeship Council suspended its operations on 1 November 1994, a month after the independence of Palau, the last remaining United Nations trust territory.
    (v) **United Nations Human Rights Council,** the Human Rights Council is an inter-governmental body within the United Nations system responsible for strengthening the promotion and protection of human rights around the globe and for addressing situations of human rights violations and make recommendations on them. It has the ability to discuss all thematic human rights issues and situations that require its attention throughout the year. It meets at the UN Office at Geneva. The Council is made up of 47 United Nations Member States which are elected by the UN General Assembly. The Human Rights Council replaced the former United Nations Commission on Human Rights.
    (vi) **International Court of Justice: Headquarted at the Peace Palace The Hague, in Holland,** it consists of 15 judges elected by General Assembly and Security Council for a term of nine years. Its function is to give legal advice on legal matters to the bodies and special agencies of the UNO and considers the legal disputes which are brought before it. Ronny Abraham is the current President of International Court of Justice.

Note:

Four persons from India have been elected as Judges of International Court of Justice till date. They are:
1. Sir Benegal Rau (1952-53)
2. Dr. Negendra Singh (1985-88)
3. R. S. Pathak (1989-91)
4. Dalveer Bhandari (2012- till date)

(vii) **Secretariat:** It is headed by the Secretary - General who is the Chief Administrative Officer of the UNO and supervises the activities of UNO. **The Secretary - General is appointed by the General Assembly on the recommendation of the Security Council.** The term is of five years and can be re-elected after the expiry of the term.

2. **Secretary - General of UNO:**
    (i) **First Secretary - General was Trygve Lie, from Norway.**
    (ii) **The current Secretary-General of UN is António Guterres, appointed by the General Assembly on 13 October 2016.**

3. **Official languages of the UNO:** They are **six** in number, viz.:
    (i) **English**   (ii) **Chinese**   (iii) **French**
    (iv) **Spanish**   (v) **Russian**   (vi) **Arabic**

4. **Important agencies related to United Nations Organization:**

Name of the organization	Headquartered at
International Labour Organization (ILO)	Geneva
International Atomic Energy Agency (IAEA)	Vienna
United Nations Education, Scientific and Cultural Organization (UNESCO)	Paris
World Metrological Organization (WMO)	Geneva
World Health Organization (WHO)	Geneva
Food and Agricultural Organization (FAO)	Rome
United Nations Development Programme (UNDP)	New York
General Agreement on Tariffs and Trade (GATT) [Now known as World Trade Organization (WTO)]	Geneva
United Nations International Children's Emergency Fund (UNICEF)	New York
International Development Association (IDA)	Washington DC
United Nations Environment Programme (UNEP)	Nairobi
International Monetary Fund (IMF)	Washington DC
United Nations Fund for Population Activities (UNFPA)	New York
United Nations Conference on Trade and Development (UNCTAD)	Geneva

(B) North Atlantic Treaty Organization (NATO)

Primarily concerned with the individual as well as collective security of the member nations, many countries signed the Treaty which gave birth to NATO on 4, April 1949. **The organization is headquartered at Brussels in Belgium and** it has currently 29 members. In 1949, there were 12 founding members of the Alliance: Belgium, Canada, Denmark, France, Iceland, Italy, Luxembourg, the Netherlands, Norway, Portugal, the United Kingdom and the United States. The other member countries are: Greece and Turkey (1952), Germany (1955), Spain (1982), the Czech Republic, Hungary and Poland (1999), Bulgaria, Estonia, Latvia, Lithuania, Romania, Slovakia and Slovenia (2004), Albania and Croatia (2009), and Montenegro (2017). **The present secretary general of NATO is Jens Stoltenberg (Norway) (from October 2014).**

(C) South Asian Association for Regional Cooperation (SAARC)

It was formed on December 8, 1985, at Dhaka but the idea for the organization was first mooted by the former President of Bangladesh Zia-ur-Rahman. **There are eight members in the organization,** i.e. (i) **Nepal,** (ii) **Bangladesh,** (iii) **Sri Lanka,** (iv) **Maldives,** (v) **Bhutan,** (vi) **Pakistan** and (vii) **India** (viii) **Afghanistan** (the latest member). **The Secretariat of SAARC is at Kathmandu (Nepal). The current Secretary General of SAARC is H.E. Mr. Amjad Hussain B. Sial from Pakistan.**

(D) The Commonwealth

This is an association of independent states which originated in 1947and formally made up the British Empire. The symbolic head of the Commonwealth is the British monarch, Queen Elizabeth II. At present, there are over 50 countries which are the members of the Commonwealth. **Patricia Janet Scotland** was elected the **6th Secretary-General of the Commonwealth of Nations** at the 2015 Commonwealth Heads of Government Meeting and took office April 1, 2016. She is the first and current woman Secretary General Commonwealth. **The former Secretary -General was Kamalesh Sharma.**

(E) Group of 77

The Group of 77 (G-77) was established on 15 June 1964 by seventy-seven developing countries signatories of the "Joint Declaration of the Seventy-Seven Developing Countries" issued at the end of the first session of the United Nations Conference on Trade and Development (UNCTAD) in Geneva. Although the members of the G-77 have increased to 134 countries, the original name was retained due to its historic significance.

(F) Organization of Petroleum Exporting Countries (OPEC)

For controlling the production and pricing of crude oil, OPEC was established on September 14, 1960 by Republic of Iran, Iraq, Kuwait, Saudi Arabia and Venezuela. **It is headquartered at Vienna, Austria** was founded in Baghdad, Iraq, with the signing of an agreement in September 1960 by five countries namely Islamic Republic of Iran, Iraq, Kuwait, Saudi Arabia and Venezuela. They were to become the Founder Members of the Organization. These countries were later joined by Qatar (1961), Indonesia (1962), Libya (1962), the United Arab Emirates (1967), Algeria (1969), Nigeria (1971), Ecuador (1973), Gabon (1975) and Angola (2007). Ecuador suspended its membership in December 1992, but rejoined OPEC in October 2007. Indonesia suspended its membership in January 2009, reactivated it again in January 2016, but decided to suspend its membership once more at the 171st Meeting of the OPEC Conference on 30 November 2016. Gabon terminated its membership in January 1995. However, it rejoined the Organization in July 2016. **Currently, the Organization has a total of 14 Member Countries. HE Mohammad Sanusi Barkindo** was officially appointed as the Secretary General of the OPEC for a three-year term at OPEC's 169th Meeting of the Conference on 2 June 2016 in Vienna.

(G) Non-Aligned Movement (NAM)

The concept of Non-Aligned Movement was developed by Pt. Jawahar Lal Nehru, the first Prime Minister of Independent India. The former members of this movement were.
President of Egypt – G.A. Nasser
President of Indonesia – Dr. Sukarno
President of former Yugoslavia – Marshal Tito
Established in 1961 in Belgrade. As of 2018 it has 125 members and 25 observer countries. Nicolas Maduro is current Secretary General of NAM.

(H) Other important organizations

Organization	Year of establishment	Headquartered at
***SEATO** (South East Asia Treaty Organization)	September 4, 1954	Bangkok in Thailand
OAU (Organization of African Union)	May 25, 1963	Adis Ababa in Ethiopia
ASEAN (Association of South East Asian Nations)	August 9, 1967	Jakarta in Indonesia

*** Please note that SEATO was dissolved on June 30, 1977.**

(I) World Trade Organization (WTO)

By replacing General Agreement on Tariffs and Trade (GATT), **it came into existence on January 1, 1995.** It is the third important Economic Organization after the World Bank and International Monetary Fund and **it can settle trade disputes between nations and encourages the principle of free trade to sectors such as agriculture and services, etc. India was one of the founding members of WTO.**
The present strength of WTO is 161 members (as on July 25, 2018), headquartered at Geneva it is headed by Director General Roberto Azevedo (Brazil).

(J) The Group of 15 (G-15)

It is an economic grouping of 15 nations of the world which are Third World nations and was formed in 1989 in Non-Aligned Movement (NAM) summit at Belgrade.

(K) Amnesty International

It was established by a **British lawyer Peter Berenson on May 28, 1961** in **London** which is its headquarters also. It is primarily concerned with the investigation in the violations of human rights. It has more than 11 lakhs members in about 150 countries throughout the world.

(L) Interpole

The current Secretary General is Kim Jong Yang, unanimously elected at the 83rd INTERPOL General Assembly session in Monaco, November 2014. It is world largest International Police Organization, with 190 member countries. It has seven regional offices across the world, and a representative office at the united Nations in New York and at European Union in Brussels. It's an international organization of police commissions of the member countries which are about 150 in number and was established in 1923. **Its headquarters are at Lyons, France.**

(M) European Union (EU)

It is a group of European countries which got united to become strong — politically and economically, so that war would not be a threat any more. This organization came into existence after Second World War, in 1957, having its **headquarters at Brussels, Belgium. At present, there are 28 members in the European Union and the membership is open to any European country. The headquarters of EU is at Brussels in Belgium. Jean-claude Juncker is the 12th President of the European Commission (as in October 2015). Donald Franciszek Tusk is current President of European Council. Ursula Gertrud von der Leyen is a German politician and the President-elect of the European Commission. On 2 July 2019, von der Leyen was proposed by the European Council as the candidate for the office of President of the European Commission. She was elected by the European Parliament on 16 July. She is the first woman to become President of the European Commission. Charles Michel has been Prime Minister of Belgium since 2014 and is the President-elect of the European Council. On 23 June 2016 citizens of the United Kingdom (UK) voted to leave the European Union (EU).** On 29 March 2017 the UK formally notified the European Council of its intention to leave the EU by triggering of Article 50 of the Lisbon Treaty. **For the time being, the United Kingdom remains a full member of the EU until the final Brexit date, 31 October 2019.**

(N) Organization of Islamic Conference (OIC)

It is head quartered at Jeddah, Saudi Arabia. Having 57 muslim countries as members, it was established after a historical summit on September 25, 1969. It aims to promote Islamic co-operation and solidarity. **Dr. Yousef bin Ahmad Al-Othaimeen is the current secretary-general of the Organisation of Islamic Cooperation (OIC), since November 2016.**

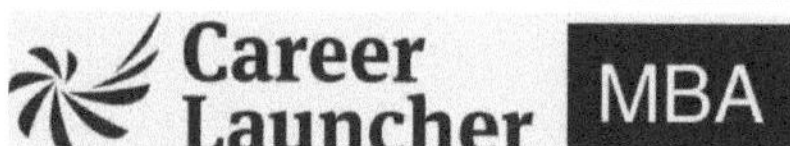

(O) Red Cross

Formed by **Swiss businessman J.H. Durant in 1863,** it is the pioneering organization in providing medical aid throughout the world. **Red Cross Day is celebrated on May 8;** its symbol is red cross on a white background. **This organization has received Nobel Prize on three occasions.** The International Committee of the Red Cross (ICRC) is a private humanitarian institution founded in 1863 in Geneva, Switzerland, by Henry Dunant and Gustave Moynier. Its 25-member committee has a unique authority under international humanitarian law to protect the life and dignity of the victims of international and internal armed conflicts. The ICRC was awarded the Nobel Peace Prize on three occasions (in 1917, 1944 and 1963). The ICRC is governed by an Assembly, an Assembly Council (a subsidiary body with certain delegated powers) and a Directorate (the executive body). Both the Assembly, with up to 25 co-opted members of Swiss nationality, and the Assembly Council are chaired by Peter Maurer, who has been President of the ICRC since 1 July 2012. He is assisted by a Vice-President, Christine Beerli. The Directorate, with five members, is chaired by the Director-General, Mr. Yves Daccord.

(P) The Group of Eight (G-8)

It is basically a group of eight countries (as the name indicates). These are world's richest industrialized nations, i.e. **Italy, Canada, USA, UK, Japan, Germany, France and Russia.** The forum primarily works to resolve issues of either mutual concern or of global concern. **The G8 reformatted as G7 from 2014 due to Russia's suspension.** It was an inter-governmental political forum from 1997 until 2014, with the participation of the major industrialized countries in the world that viewed themselves as democracies.

(Q) Medicin Sans Frontieres (MSF)

It was formed in 1971 by a small group of French doctors who believed that all people have the right to medical care. It is a private, non-profit organization. This organization is also known as Doctors without Borders. This delivers emergency aid to the needy. This organization won the Nobel Peace Prize for the year 1999.

(R) World Bank

Established as a result of Bretton Woords Conference in 1944 with the objective of assisting the member nations in their reconstruction and development. The bank is headquartered at Washington D.C. World Bank as an International Financial Institution comprises of only two instititutions (a) International Bank for Reconstruction and Development. (b) International Development Association. **Its present President is David Malpass.**

(S) International Monetary Fund (IMF)

It provides loans to member nations to tide over their balance of payment (lack of foreign exchange to pay for imports) problems. It is headquartered in Washington D.C. It is also called the twin organisation of World Bank. Both of them are popularly referred to as **Bretton Wood Twins. This organization has 189 members.** On 2 July 2019, **Christine Lagarde** was nominated by the European Council to succeed Mario Draghi as President of the European Central Bank on 1 November 2019. After consultations with the European Parliament, Lagarde is expected to become the first woman in the position of President of the European Central Bank. After going on leave, Lagarde formally submitted her resignation as MD of IMF on 16 July 2019, to take effect 12 September 2019. **David Lipton is the current acting Managing Director of IMF.**

(T) World Social Forum (WSF)

World social forum was started in Porto Alegre in Brazil. It is an antiglobalization movement, and its annual meets are held parallel to the annual sessions of World Economic Forum (at Davos).

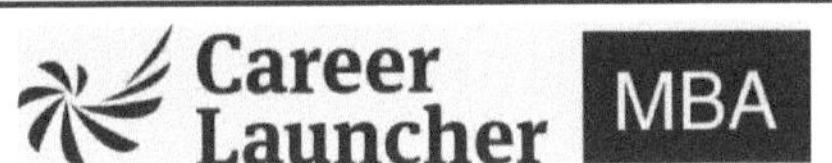

1. United Nations Secretary General: António Guterres
2. President of the International Court of Justice: Ronny Abraham
3. Director-General of International Labor Organization (ILO): Guy Ryder
4. Director-General of Food & Agriculture Organization (FAO): Jose Graziano da Silva
5. Director-General of World Health Organization (WHO): Dr. Adhanom Ghebreyesus
6. Head of United Nations Children's Fund (UNICEF): Henrietta H. Fore
7. United Nations High Commissioner for Refugees (UNHCR): Flippo Grandi
8. Director-General of United Nations Educational Scientific and Cultural Organization (UNESCO): Audrey Azoulay
9. President of the World Bank (WB): David Malpass
10. Managing Director the International Monetary Fund (IMF): David Lipton (Acting)
11. Director-General of World Trade Organization (WTO): Robert Azevedo
12. Head International Atomic Energy Agency (IAEA): Yukiya Amano
13. Secretary-General of the Non Aligned Movement (NAM): Nicolas Maduro
14. Secretary-General of South Asian Association for Regional Co-operation (SAARC): H.E.Mr. Amjad Hussain B.Sial
15. Head of the Commonwealth of Nations: Queen Elizabeth-II
16. Secretary General of the Commonwealth of Nations: Patricia Scotland
17. Secretary General of Amnesty International: Salil Shetty
18. Secretary-General of Organization for Economic Co-operation and Development (OECD): Jose Angel Gurria
19. Secretary General of Organization of Petroleum Exporting countries (OPEC): HE Mohammad Sanusi Barkindo
20. President of European Commission: Jean-Claude-Juncker
21. President International Olympic Committee (IOC): Thomas Bach
22. Chairman of International Cricket Council (ICC): Shashank Manohar
23. Chief Executive Officer of International Cricket Council: Manu Sawhney
24. President of FIFA: Gianni infantino
25. Chairman of Federal Reserve Bank of America: Jerome Powell
26. President of the Asian Development Bank (ADB): Takehiko Nakao

The Nobel Prizes 2018

The Nobel Prize in Physics 2018: The Nobel Prize in Physics 2018 was awarded "for groundbreaking inventions in the field of laser physics" with one half to Arthur Ashkin "for the optical tweezers and their application to biological systems", the other half jointly to Gérard Mourou and Donna Strickland "for their method of generating high-intensity, ultra-short optical pulses".

The Nobel Prize in Chemistry 2018: The Royal Swedish Academy of Sciences has decided to award the Nobel Prize in Chemistry 2018 with one half to Frances H. Arnold California Institute of Technology, Pasadena, USA *"for the directed evolution of enzymes"* and the other half jointly to George P. Smith

University of Missouri, Columbia, USA and Sir Gregory P. Winter MRC Laboratory of Molecular Biology, Cambridge, UK *"for the phage display of peptides and antibodies".*

The Nobel Prize in Physiology or Medicine 2018: The Nobel Prize in Physiology or Medicine 2018 was awarded jointly to James P. Allison and Tasuku Honjo "for their discovery of cancer therapy by inhibition of negative immune regulation."

The Nobel Prize in Literature 2018: The Swedish Academy, which organizes the Nobel Prize in Literature, announced that it will not award the 2018 honor due to sex abuse allegations that have raised turmoil among the academy members and cast critical light upon the prestigious annual award.

Career Launcher MBA

General Knowledge

The Nobel Peace Prize 2018: The Norwegian Nobel Committee has decided to award the Nobel Peace Prize for 2018 to Denis Mukwege and Nadia Murad for their efforts to end the use of sexual violence as a weapon of war and armed conflict. Both laureates have made a crucial contribution to focusing attention on, and combating, such war crimes. Denis Mukwege is the helper who has devoted his life to defending these victims.

New Academy prize in literature: Guadeloupean novelist Maryse Condé has been announced as the winner of the New Academy prize in literature, a one-off award intended to fill the void left by the cancellation of this year's scandal-dogged Nobel Prize for literature.

The Nobel Prizes 2017

The Nobel Prize in Physics 2017:
The Nobel Prize in Physics 2017 was divided; one half awarded to **Rainer Weiss**, the other half jointly to **Barry C. Barish and Kip S. Thorne** for *"decisive contributions to the LIGO detector and the observation of gravitational waves"*.

The Nobel Prize in Chemistry 2017:
Jacques Dubochet, Joachim Frank and Richard Henderson for "developing cryo-electron microscopy for the high-resolution structure determination of biomolecules in solution".

The Nobel Prize in Physiology or Medicine 2017:
Jeffrey C. Hall, Michael Rosbash and Michael W. Young for "their discoveries of molecular mechanisms controlling the circadian rhythm".

The Nobel Prize in Literature 2017:
The Nobel Prize in Literature 2017 was awarded to **Kazuo Ishiguro** "who, in novels of great emotional force, has uncovered the abyss beneath our illusory sense of connection with the world".

The Nobel Peace Prize 2017:
The Nobel Peace Prize 2017 was awarded to **International Campaign to Abolish Nuclear Weapons (ICAN)** "for its work to draw attention to the catastrophic humanitarian consequences of any use of nuclear weapons and for its ground-breaking efforts to achieve a treaty-based prohibition of such weapons".

The Sveriges Riksbank Prize in Economic Sciences 2017:
The Sveriges Riksbank Prize in Economic Sciences in Memory of Alfred Nobel 2017 was awarded to Richard H. Thaler "for his contributions to behavioural economics".

Pulitzer Prizes 2018

Journalism:
Public Service: The New York Times for reporting led by Jodi Kantor and Megan Twohey, and The New Yorker, for reporting by Ronan Farrow

Breaking News Reporting: Staff of The Press Democrat, Santa Rosa, California

Investigative Reporting: Staff of The Washington Post

Explanatory Reporting: Staffs of The Arizona Republic and USA Today Network

Local Reporting: The Cincinnati Enquirer Staff

National Reporting: Staffs of The New York Times and The Washington Post

International Reporting: Clare Baldwin, Andrew R.C. Marshall and Manuel Mogato of Reuters

Feature Writing: Rachel Kaadzi Ghansah, freelance reporter, GQ

Commentary: John Archibald of Alabama Media Group, Birmingham, Alabama

Criticism: Jerry Saltz of New York magazine

Editorial writing: Andie Dominick of The Des Moines Register

Editorial cartooning: Jake Halpern, freelance writer, and Michael Sloan, freelance cartoonist, The New York Times

Breaking News Photography: Ryan Kelly of The Daily Progress, Charlottesville, Virginia

Feature Photography: Photography Staff of Reuters

Letters and Drama:

Fiction: Andrew Sean Greer won the Pulitzer Prize for Fiction

Drama: Cost of Living, by Martyna Majok won the Pulitzer Prize for Drama

History: The Gulf: The Making of an American Sea, by Jack E. Davis won the Pulitzer Prize for History

Biography: Prairie Fires: The American Dreams of Laura Ingalls Wilder, by Caroline Fraser won the Pulitzer Prize for Biography

Poetry: Half-light: Collected Poems 1965-2016, by Frank Bidart won the Pulitzer Prize for Poetry

General Non-fiction: Locking Up Our Own: Crime and Punishment in Black America, by James Forman Jr. won the Pulitzer Prize for General Non-fiction.

Music: DAMN., by Kendrick Lamar

Pulitzer Prizes 2017

Journalism:

Public Service: New York Daily News and ProPublica

Breaking News Reporting: Staff of *East Bay Times*, Oakland, CA

Investigative Reporting: Eric Eyre of *Charleston Gazette-Mail*, Charleston, WV

Explanatory Reporting: International Consortium of Investigative Journalists, McClatchy and Miami Herald

Local Reporting: The Salt Lake Tribune Staff

National Reporting: David A. Fahrenthold of *The Washington Post*

International Reporting: The New York Times Staff

Feature Writing: C. J. Chivers of *The New York Times*

Commentary: Peggy Noonan of *The Wall Street Journal*

Criticism: Hilton Als of *The New Yorker*

Editorial Writing: Art Cullen of *The Storm Lake Times*, Storm Lake, IA

Editorial Cartooning: Jim Morin of *Miami Herald*

Breaking News Photography: Daniel Berehulak, freelance photographer

Feature Photography: E. Jason Wambsgans of *Chicago Tribune*

Letters and Drama:

Fiction: The Underground Railroad, by Colson Whitehead (Doubleday)

Drama: Sweat, by Lynn Nottage

History: Blood in the Water: The Attica Prison Uprising of 1971 and Its Legacy, by Heather Ann Thompson (Pantheon)

Biography or Autobiography: The Return: Fathers, Sons and the Land in Between, by Hisham Matar (Random House)

Poetry: Olio, by Tyehimba Jess (Wave Books)

General Non-Fiction: Evicted: Poverty and Profit in the American City, by Matthew Desmond (Crown)

Music: Angel's Bone, by Du Yun

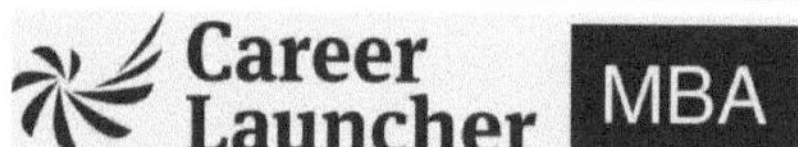

Man Booker Prize 2019

Omani author Jokha Alharthi has become the first Arabic-language writer to win the prestigious Man Booker International Prize for Celestial Bodies, a novel that deals with family connections and history in the coming-of-age account of three sisters. "Celestial Bodies evokes the forces that constrain us and those that set us free."

Man Booker Prize 2018

Olga Tokarczuk has become the first Polish writer to win the Man Booker International prize, which goes to the best work of translated fiction from anywhere in the world. **Flights** is a fragmentary novel by the Polish author Olga Tokarczuk.

Ramon Magsaysay Awards 2019

Senior Indian journalist **Ravish Kumar was awarded this year's Ramon Magsaysay Award**, regarded as the Asian version of the Nobel Prize. He is NDTV India's senior executive editor is one of India's most influential TV journalists, the award citation by the Ramon Magsaysay Award Foundation said. **The four other winners of the 2019 Ramon Magsaysay Award are Ko Swe Win from Myanmar, Angkhana Neelapaijit from Thailand, Raymundo Pujante Cayabyab from Philippines and Kim Jong-Ki from South Korea.**

Ramon Magsaysay Awards 2018

Two Indians, Bharat Vatwani and Sonam Wangchuk are among the six winners of this year's Ramon Magsaysay Award. The awards declared are regarded as the Asian version of the Nobel Prize.

Abel prize (2019)

An American professor has become the **first woman to be awarded the Abel Prize, one of the world's most prestigious international mathematics awards.** The Norwegian Academy of Science and Letters announced in Oslo that **Karen Keskulla Uhlenbeck** of the University of Texas at Austin was this year's winner of the prize, seen by many as the Nobel Prize in mathematics. The award was worth 6m Norwegian kroner ($704,000).

Abel prize (2018)

Robert Langlands was awarded the 2018 Abel Prize for the **Langlands program**, which predicts unexpected connections between different fields by the Norwegian Academy of Science and Letters and is worth 6 million Norwegian krone (about £550,000). It is considered by many to be a **maths equivalent of the Nobel Prize**, which has no prize for mathematics.

Right livelihood awards (2018)

The Right Livelihood Award 2018- known as the "Alternative Nobel" - has been given to three jailed Saudi human rights defenders and two Latin American anti-corruption crusaders.
The prize foundation says that the 1 million kronor ($113,400) cash award for 2018 was to be **shared by Abdullah al-Hamid, Mohammad Fahad al-Qahtani and Waleed Abu al-Khair** "for their visionary and courageous efforts, guided by universal human rights principles, to reform the totalitarian political system in Saudi Arabia."

World Food Prize (2018)

Drs Lawrence Haddad and **David Nabarro** have won the 2018 World Food Prize. They were rewarded for their individual but complementary global leadership in elevating child and maternal nutrition to a critical priority in the international development dialogue.

World Food Prize (2017)

Dr. Akinwumi Adesina wins the 2017 World Food Prize for his incredible work in reducing corruption in the fertilizer industry, increasing credit for smallholder farmers and expanding food production by 21 million metric tons.

Jnanpith Award (2018)

Noted English writer Amitav Ghosh has been honoured with this year's Jnanpith Award, a literary award given to an author for "outstanding contribution towards literature", Bharatiya Jnanpith announced. His most recent book, The Great Derangement; Climate Change and the Unthinkable, a work of non-fiction, was released in 2016. Ghosh is also recipient of the Padma Shri and Sahitya Akademi Award.

Jnanpith Award (2017)

Renowned **Hindi littérateur Krishna Sobti** has been awarded for the 2017 **Jnanpith Award**. She is a Hindi fiction writer and essayist, who won the Sahitya Akademi Award in 1980 for her novel Zindaginama.

Saraswati Samman (2018)

Telugu poet K Siva Reddy has been conferred the prestigious Saraswati Samman, 2018, for his collection of poems titled Pakkaki Ottigilite (Turning Aside While Lying Down). The award, instituted by the KK Birla Foundation, is given annually for an outstanding literary work written in any official Indian language and published during the preceding 10 years. It is the highest recognition in the field of Indian literature and carries a cash purse of Rs 15 lakh, apart from a citation and a plaque.

Saraswati Samman (2017)

Eminent **Gujarati poet Sitanshu Yashaschandra's poetry collection "Vakhar"** has been awarded for the Saraswati Samman for 2017 by the K K Birla Foundation.

Sahitya Akademi Yuva Puraskar – 2017

Manu S. Pillai for *The Ivory Throne* (English)

Taro Sindik for Aksharo *Ki Vinti* (Hindi)

Academy Awards or "Oscars Awards"

The 90th Academy Awards ceremony, presented by the Academy of Motion Picture Arts and Sciences (AMPAS), honored the best films of 2018 and took place at the Dolby Theatre in Hollywood, Los Angeles, California. The ceremony was held on February, 2019.

2019 Winners list:

Best Picture - *Green Book*

Best Actor in a Leading Role - Rami Malek for *Bohemian Rhapsody*

Best Actress in a Leading Role - Olivia Colman for *The Favourite*

Best Directing - Alfonso Cuarón for *Roma*

Best Supporting Actor - Mahershala Ali for *Green Book*

Best Supporting Actress - Regina King for *If Beale Street Could Talk*.

Best Original Score - Ludwig Goransson for *Black Panther*

Best Original Song - Lady Gaga, Mike Ronson, Anthony Rossomondo and Andrew Wyatt for *A Star Is Born*

Best Adapted Screenplay- Charlie Wachtel & David Rabinowitz and Kevin Willmott & Spike Lee for *Blackkklansman*

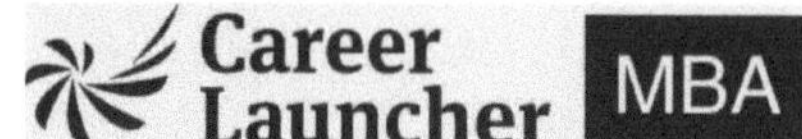

Original Screenplay - Nick Vallelonga, Brian Currie, Peter Farrelly for *Green Book*

Best Live Action Short - *Skin*

Best Visual Effects - Paul Lambert, Ian Hunter, Tristan Myles and J.D. Schwalm for *First Man*

Best Animated Short - Domee Shi and Becky Neiman-Cobb for *Bao*

Best Documentary Short - Rayka Zehtabchi and Melissa Berton for *Period. End of Sentence*

Best Animated Feature - *Spiderman: Into the Spider Verse*

Best Film Editing - John Ottman for *Bohemian Rhapsody*

Best Foreign Language - *Roma*

Best Cinematography - Alfonso Cuarón for *Roma*

Best Sound Editing - John Warhurst and Nina Hartstone for *Bohemian Rhapsody*

Best Sound Mixing - Paul Massey, Tim Cavagin and John Casali for *Bohemian Rhapsody*

Makeup & Hairstyling - *Vice*

Best Costume Design - Ruth Carter for *Black Panther*

Best Production Design - Hannah Beachler (Production Design); Jay Hart (Set Decoration) for *Black Panther*

Best Documentary Feature - *Free Solo*

2018 Winners list:

Best Picture: The Shape of Water

Best Director: Guillermo del Toro Gómez (The Shape of Water)

Best Actor: Gary Oldman (*Darkest Hour*)

Best Actress: Frances McDormand (*Three Billboards Outside Ebbing, Missouri*)

Best Foreign Language Film: *A Fantastic Woman* (Chile) in Spanish – Directed by Sebastián Lelio

Supporting Actor: Sam Rockwell, "Three Billboards Outside Ebbing, Missouri"

Supporting Actress: Allison Janney, "I, Tonya"

Original Screenplay: "Get Out"

Adapted Screenplay: "Call Me by Your Name"

Animated Feature: "Coco"

Visual Effects: "Blade Runner 2049"

Film Editing: "Dunkirk"

Animated Short: "Dear Basketball"

Live Action Short: "The Silent Child"

Documentary Short: "Heaven Is a Traffic Jam on the 405"

Score: "The Shape of Water"

Song: "Remember Me" from "Coco"

Production Design: "The Shape of Water"

Cinematography: "Blade Runner 2049"

Documentary Feature: "Icarus"

Costume Design: "Phantom Thread"

Makeup and Hairstyling: "Darkest Hour"

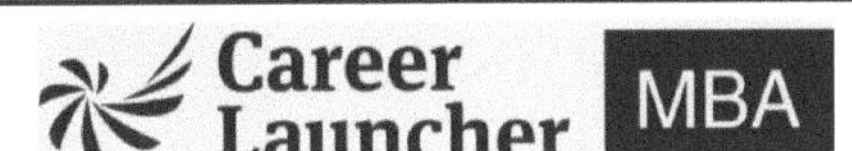

66th National Film Awards

Ayushmann Khurrana-Radhika Apte starrer Andhadhun has won the 'Best Film' award in the 66th National Film Awards announced. Aditya Dhar-directorial debut Uri: The Surgical Strike has bagged four awards - best actor, best background music, best sound design and best direction in the 66th National Film Awards 2019.

Best Actor: Ayushmann Khurrana, Andhadhun, and Vicky Kaushal, Uri

Best Actress: Keerthy Suresh for Mahanati

Best Direction: Aditya Dhar for Uri

Best Feature Film: Hellaro (Gujarati)

Best Children's Film: Sarkari. Hi. Pra. Shale Kasaragodu, Koduge

Best Film on Environment Conservation: Paani

Nargis Dutt Award for National Integration: Ondanya Eradalu

Best Popular Film Providing Wholesome Entertainment: Badhaai Ho

Jury Awards: Kedara (Bengali), Hellaro (Gujarati)

Indira Gandhi Award for Best Debut Film of A Director: Sudhakar Reddy Yakanthi for Naal

Best Female Playback singer: Bindu Mani for Mayavi Manave from Nathicharami

Best Male Playback Singer: Arijit Singh for Binte Dil from Padmaavat

Best film on social issues: Pad Man

Best music director: Padmaavat

Best Rajasthani Film: Turtle

Best Panchanga Film: In The Land Of Poisonous Women

Best Garo Film: Anna

Best Marathi Film: Bhonga

Best Tamil Film: Baram

Best Hindi Film: Andhadhun

Best Urdu Film: Hamid

Best Bengali Film: Ek Je Chhilo Raja

Best Malayalam Film: Sudani From Nigeria

Best Telugu Film: Mahanati

Best Kannada Film: Nathicharami

Best Konkani Film: Amori

Best Assamese Film: Bulbul Can Sing

Best Punjabi Film: Harjeeta

Best Gujarati Film: Reva

Dada Saheb Phalke Award

The Dadasaheb Phalke Award is India's highest award in cinema. It is presented annually at the National Film Awards ceremony by the Directorate of Film Festivals, an organisation set up by the Ministry of Information and Broadcasting. First presented in 1969, the award was introduced by the Government of India to commemorate Dadasaheb Phalke's contribution to Indian cinema.

- At the 65th National Film Awards, late actor Vinod Khanna was posthumously honoured with the Dadasaheb Phalke Award. This award is considered as the highest honour in Indian cinema and is presented annually by the Ministry of Information and Broadcasting. The award is given for a personality's "outstanding contribution to the growth and development of Indian cinema". Vinod Khanna is the 49th recipient of the Dadasaheb Phalke Award.

- Renowned filmmaker K Viswanath was given a standing ovation as he received the prestigious Dada Saheb Phalke award by President Pranab Mukherjee at the 64th National Film Awards ceremony . A prominent name not just in Telugu cinema but also in Tamil and Hindi films, Viswanath, 87, became the 48th recipient of the Phalke award, the highest recognition in Indian cinema, which includes a golden lotus, a cash prize of Rs 10 lakhs, a citation and a shawl.

- Veteran actor and director Manoj Kumar was conferred the 47th Dadasaheb Phalke Award for the year 2015. The award — conferred by the Centre for outstanding contribution to the growth and development of Indian Cinema — consists of a Swarn Kamal (Golden Lotus), a cash prize of Rs 10 lakh and a shawl.

64th Filmfare Awards (North) 2019

The 64th Vimal Filmfare Awards 2019 kicked off at the Jio Garden in BKC, Mumbai.

Best Actor (Popular): Ranbir Kapoor for *Sanju*

Best Actress (Popular): Alia Bhatt for *Raazi*

Best Film: Raazi

Critics' Award for Best Film: AndhaDhun

Critics' Award for Best Actor (Female): Neena Gupta, Badhaai Ho

Critics' Award for Best Actor (Male): Ranveer Singh, Padmaavat

Best Debut Actor (Female): Sara Ali Khan, Kedarnath

Best Debut Actor (Male): Ishaan Khatter, Beyond The Clouds

Best Director: Meghna Gulzar, Raazi

Best Debut Director: Amar Kaushik, Stree

Best Actor In A Supporting Role (Male): Gajraj Rao, Badhaai Ho and Vicky Kaushal, Sanju

Best Actor in a Supporting Role (Female): Surekha Sikri, Badhaai Ho

Best Dialogue: Akshat Ghildial, Badhaai Ho

Best Original Story: Anubhav Sinha, Mulk

Best Actor (Male) in a Short Film: Hussain Dalal, Shameless

Best Actor (Female) in a Short Film: Kirti Kulhari, Maya

People's Choice Award for Best Short Film: Plus Minus

Best Short Film (Fiction): Rogan Josh

Best Short Film (Non-Fiction): The Soccer City

Best Music Album: Padmaavat [ALSO SEE: Zee Cine Awards 2019 winners' list: Ranbir Kapoor, Deepika Padukone take top honours]

Best Playback Singer (Male): Arijit Singh for Ae Watan, Raazi

Best Playback Singer (Female): Shreya Ghoshal for Ghoomar, Padmaavat

Best Lyrics: Gulzar for Ae Watan, Raazi.

Best Lyrics: AndhaDhun

Best Background Score: Daniel George, AndhaDhun

Best Sound Design: Kunal Sharma, Tumbbad

Best Choreography: Kruti Mahesh Midya, Jyoti Tomaar for Ghoomar from Padmaavat

Best Cinematography: Pankaj Kumar, Tumbbad

Best Editing: Pooja Ladha Surti, AndhaDhun

Best Costume: Sheetal Sharma, Manto

Best Production Design: Nitin Zihani Chaudhary and Rajesh Yadav (Tumbbad)

65th Jio Filmfare Awards (South) 2018

All the members of the four South Indian film industries got together to celebrate the best of Kannada, Telugu, Tamil and Malayalam films of 2017 at the 65 th Jio Filmfare Awards (South) 2018.

Best Film: Ondu Motteya Kathe

Best Actor in a Leading Role (Female): Sruthi Hariharan for Beautiful Manasugalu

Best Actor in a Leading Role (Male): Puneeth Rajkumar for Raajakumara

Critics' Award for Best Actor (Male): Dhananjaya for Allama

Critics' Award for Best Actor (Female): Shraddha Srinath for Operation Alamelamma

Best Director: Tharun Sudhir for Chowka

Best Actor in a Supporting Role (Male): P Ravi Shankar for College Kumara

Best Actor in a Supporting Role (Female): Bhavani Prakash for Urvi

Best Playback Singer (Male): Armaan Malik for Ondu Malebillu- Chakravarthy

Best Playback Singer (Female): Anuradha Bhat for Appa I Love You- Chowka

Best Lyrics: Nagendra Prasad for Appa I Love You- Chowka

Best Music Director: Bharath BJ for Beautiful Manasugalu

Tennis Grand Slams

2018 US Open Champions

Men's Singles: Novak Djokovic

Women's Singles: Naomi Osaka

Men's Doubles: Mike Bryan /Jack Sock

Women's Doubles: Ashleigh Barty /CoCo Vandeweghe

Mixed Doubles: Bethanie Mattek-Sands /Jamie Murray

2019 Australian Open Champions

Men's Singles: Novak Djokovic

Women's Singles: Naomi Osaka

Men's Doubles: Pierre-Hugues Herbert /Nicolas Mahut

Women's Doubles: Samantha Stosur / Zhang Shuai

Mixed Doubles: Barbora Krejcikova / Rajeev Ram

2019 French Open Champions

Men's Singles: Rafael Nadal

Women's Singles: Ashleigh Barty

Men's Doubles: Kevin Krawietz / Andreas Mies

Women's Doubles: Tímea Babos /Kristina Mladenovic

Mixed Doubles: Latisha Chan / Ivan Dodig

2019 Wimbledon Champions

Men's Singles: Novak Djokovic

Women's Singles: Simona Halep

Men's Doubles: Juan Sebastian Cabal / Robert Farah

Women's Doubles: Hsieh Su-wei / Barbora Strycova

Mixed Doubles: Ivan Dodig / Latisha Chan

List of Rajiv Gandhi Khel Ratna Awardees

Year	Name of the Sportsperson(s)	Sport Discipline
1991-92	Viswanathan Anand	Chess
1992-93	Geet Sethi	Billiards
1993-94	Not Conferred* -	
1994-95	Cdr. Homi D. Motivala	(Joint) Yachting (Team Event)
1994-95	Lt. Cdr. P. K. Garg	(Joint) Yachting (Team Event)
1995-96	Karnam Malleswari	Weightlifting
1996-97	Nameirakpam Kunjarani	(Joint) Weightlifting
1996-97	Leander Paes	(Joint) Tennis
1997-98	Sachin Tendulkar	Cricket
1998-99	Jyotirmoyee Sikdar	Athletics
1999-2000	Dhanraj Pillay	Hockey
2000-01	Pullela Gopichand	Badminton
2001-02	Abhinav Bindra	Shooting
2002-03	Anjali Ved Pathak Bhagwat	(Joint) Shooting
2002-03	K. M. Beenamol	(Joint) Athletics
2003-04	Anju Bobby George	Athletics
2004-05	Lt. Col Rajyavardhan Singh Rathore	Shooting
2005-06	Pankaj Advani	Billiards and Snooker
2006-07	Manavjit Singh Sandhu	Shooting
2007-08	Mahendra Singh Dhoni	Cricket
2008-09	Mary Kom	(Joint) Boxing
2008-09	Vijender Singh	(Joint) Boxing
2008-09	Sushil Kumar	(Joint) Wrestling
2009-10	Saina Nehwal	Badminton
2010-11	Gagan Narang	Shooting
2011-12	Vijay Kumar, Yogeshwar Dutt (Joint)	Shooting, Wrestling
2012-13	Ranjan Sodhi	Shooting
2013-14	No sportsperson has been named for the prestigious award. This is the third time no sportsperson has been named since its inception of the country's heighest sporting award in 1991.	
2014-15	Ms Sania Mirza	Tennis
2015-16	P.V. Sindhu	Badminton
2015-16	Sakshi Malik	Wrestling
2015-16	Dipa Karmakar	Gymnastics
2015-16	Jitu Rai	Shooting
2016-17	Devendra Jhajharia	Athletics
2016-17	Sardara Singh	Hockey
2017-18	Mirabai Chanu	Weightlifting
2017-18	Virat Kohli	Cricket

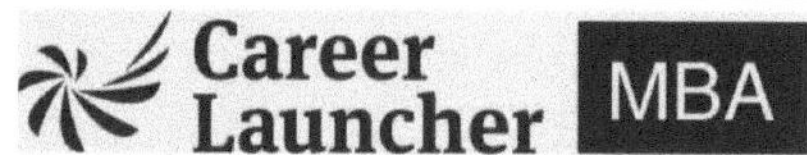

List of all Bharat Ratna awardees so far:

S.No.	Name	Birth Year	Death Year	Awarded Year	About
1	Shri Chakravarti Rajagopalachari	1878	1972	1954	Independence Activist, Last Governor General
2	Sir C.V Raman	1888	1970	1954	Physicist , Nobel Prize Winner (1930)
3	Sarvepalli Radhakrishnan	1888	1975	1954	Philosopher, India's First Vice President (1952-1962), and India's Second President (1962-1967)
4	Bhagvan Das	1869	1958	1955	Independence activist, author
5	Mokshagundam Visvesvarayya	1861	1962	1955	Civil engineer, Diwan of Mysore
6	Jawaharlal Nehru	1889	1964	1955	Independence activist, author, First Prime Minister (1947-1964)
7	Govind Ballabh Pant	1887	1961	1957	Independence activist, Chief Minister of Uttar Pradesh, Home Minister
8	Dhondo Keshav Karve	1858	1962	1958	Educator, social reformer
9	Bidhan Chandra Roy	1882	1962	1961	Physician, Chief Minister Of West Bengal
10	Purushottam Das Tandon	1882	1962	1961	Independence activist, educator
11	Rajendra Prasad	1884	1963	1962	Independence activist, jurist, First President (1950-1962)
12	Zakir Hussain	1897	1969	1963	Independence activist, Scholar, Third President (1967-1969)
13	Pandurang Vaman Kane	1880	1972	1963	Indologist and Sanskrit scholar
14	Lal Bahadur Shastri	1904	1966	1966	Posthumous, independence activist, Second Prime Minister (1964-1966)
15	Indira Gandhi	1917	1984	1971	Third Prime Minister (1980-1984)
16	V.V. Giri	1894	1980	1975	Trade unionist and Fourth President (1969)
17	K. Kamaraj	1903	1975	1976	Posthumous, independence activist, Chief Minister of Tamil Nadu State
18	Mother Teresa	1910	1997	1980	Catholic nun, founder of the Missionaries of Charity
19	Vinoba Bhave	1895	1982	1983	Posthumous, social reformer, independence activist
20	Khan Abdul Gaffar Khan	1890	1988	1987	First non-citizen, independence activist
21	M.G. Ramchandran	1917	1987	1988	Posthumous, film actor, Chief Minister of Tamil Nadu

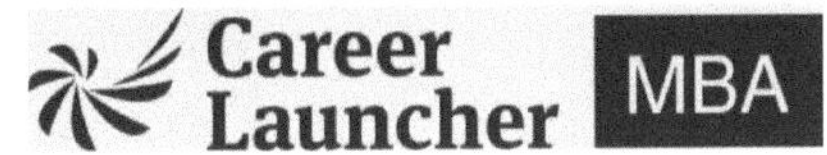

S.No.	Name	Birth Year	Death Year	Awarded Year	About
22	B.R. Ambedkar	1891	1956	1990	Posthumous, chief architect of the Indian Constitution, politician, economist, and scholar
23	Nelson Mandela	1918	2013	1990	Second non-citizen and non-Indian recipient, Leader of the Anti-Apartheid movement
24	Rajiv Gandhi	1944	1991	1991	Posthumous, Sixth Prime Minister (1984-1989)
25	Vallabhbhai Patel	1875	1950	1991	Posthumous, independence activist, first Home Minister (1947-1950)
26	Morarji Desai	1896	1995	1991	Independence activist, fourth Prime Minister (1977-1979)
27	Abul Kalam Azad	1888	1958	1992	Posthumous, independence activist, first Minister of Education
28	J. R. D. Tata	1904	1993	1992	Industrialist and philanthropist
29	Satyajit Ray	1922	1992	1992	Bengali Filmmaker
30	A.P.J. Abdul Kalam	1931	2015	1997	Aeronautical Engineer, 11th President of India
31	Gulzarilal Nanda	1898	1998	1997	Independence activist, interim Prime Minister
32	Aruna Asaf Ali	1908	1996	1997	Posthumous, independence activist
33	M.S. Subbulakshmi	1916	2004	1998	Carnatic classical singer
34	Chidambaram Subramaniam	1910	2000	1998	Independence activist, Minister of Agriculture
35	Jayaprakash Narayan	1902	1979	1999	Posthumous, independence activist and politician
36	Ravi Shankar	1920	2012	1999	Sitar Player
37	Amartya Sen	1933		1999	Economist
38	Gopinath Bardoloi	1890	1950	1999	Posthumous, independence activist, Chief Minister of Assam
39	Lata Mangeshkar	1929		2001	Playback singer
40	Bismillah Khan	1916	2006	2001	Hindustani Classical Shehnai Player
41	Bhimsen Joshi	1922	2011	2008	Hindustani Classical Singer
42	Sachin Tendulkar	1973		2013	Indian Cricketer, First Sportsman and Youngest Indian who got Bharat Ratna,
43	Prof. C.N.R Rao	1934		2013	Chemist
44	Madan Mohan Malaviya	1861	1946	2014	Educationist and politician
45	Atal Bihari Vajpayee	1924		2014	Former Prime Minister of India (1996), (1998), (1999-2004)
46	Pranab Mukherjee	1935		2019	Former President of India (2013-17)
47	Bhupen Hazarika	1926	2011	2019	Indian playback singer, lyricist, musician
48	Nanaji Deshmukh	1916	2010	2019	Social Activist

International

Date	Name of the Day
January 26	International Customs Day
March 8	International Women's Day
March 15	World Consumers' Day
March 21	World Forestry Day
March 22	World Day for Water
March 23	World Meteorological Day
April 7	World Health Day
April 17	World Haemophilia Day
April 18	World Heritage Day
April 22	World Earth Day
May 1	International Labour Day
May 3	International Press Freedom Day
May 8	World Red Cross Day
May 31	Anti-tobacco Day/World No Tobacco Day
June 5	World Environment Day
June 21	International Yoga Day
June 26	International Day against Drug Abuse and Illicit Trafficking
July 11	World Population Day
August 12	International Youth Day
September 8	World Literacy Day
September 16	World Ozone Day
September 27	World Tourism Day
October 3	World Habitat Day
October 14	World Standards Day
October 16	World Food Day
December 1	World AIDS Day
December 10	World Human Rights Day

Date	Name of the Day
January 12	National Youth Day (birth anniversary of Swami Vivekananda)
January 15	Army Day
January 23	Netaji S.C. Bose's Birth Anniversary
January 26	Republic Day
January 30	Martyr's Day (Mahatma Gandhi's Death Anniversary)
February 24	Central Excise Day
February 28	National Science Day
May 21	Antiterrorism Day (Rajiv Gandhi's Death Anniversary)
August 15	Independence Day
August 29	National Sports Day
September 5	Teachers' Day
October 2	Gandhi Jayanti/International Day for Non-Violence
October 8	Indian Air Force Day
November 14	Children's Day
December 4	Navy Day
December 23	Kisan Divas (Farmers' Day)

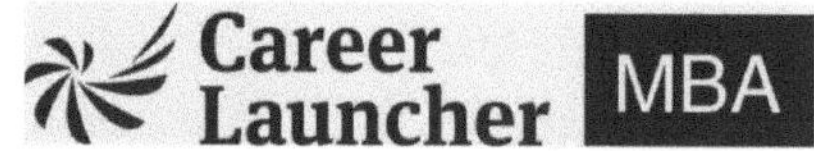

Distinctive Name	Country / Place
Bengal's Sorrow	Damodar river
Blue Mountains	Nilgiris
City of Arabian Nights	Baghdad
City of Palaces	Kolkata
City of Seven Hills/Eternal city	Rome
City of Skyscrapers /Empire city / Big Apple	New York
City of the Golden Gate	San Francisco
City of Joy	Kolkata
Commercial Capital of India	Mumbai
Dairy of Northern Europe	Denmark
Dark Continent	Africa
Forbidden City	Lhasa (Tibet)
Garden of England	Kent
Garden City of India	Bangalore
Gate of Tears	Bab-el-Mandab, Jerusalem
Gateway of India	Mumbai
Gift of the Nile	Egypt
Golden City	Johannesburg
Great White Way	Broadway (New York)
Hermit's Kingdom	Korea
Holy Land	Palestine
Island of Pearls	Bahrain
Key to the Mediterranean	Gibraltar
Land of Five Rivers	Punjab
Land of a Thousand Lakes	Finland
Land of Cakes	Scotland
Land of Kangaroos	Australia
Land of Lillies /Lady of Snow	Canada
Land of Morning Calm	Korea

Distinctive Name	Country / Place
Land of the Golden Fleece	Australia
Land of the Golden Pagoda	Myanmar
Land of the Midnight Sun	Norway
Land of the Rising Sun	Japan
Land of Thunderbolt	Bhutan
Land of White Elephants	Thailand
Manchester of South India	Coimbatore
Mother-in-Law of Europe	Denmark
Never, Never Land	Prairies (North America)
Pink City of India	Jaipur
Playground of Europe	Switzerland
Queen of the Arabian Sea	Cochin (India)
Roof of the World	Pamir (Tibet)
Sick Man of Europe	Turkey
Sorrow of China /Yellow river	River Hwang Ho
Spice Garden of India	Kerala
Sugar Bowl of the World	Cuba
Sugar Bowl of India	Uttar Pradesh
The Battlefield of Europe	Belgium
The Down Under	Australia
The Imperial City	Rome
The Promised Land	Canaan
The Saw Mill of Europe	Sweden
The Sea of Mountains	British Colombia
The Spice Island of the West	Grenada
Twin City	Budapest
Valley of Kings	Thebes
White City	Belgrade
White Man's Grave	Guinea Coast (West Africa)
Windy City	Chicago
Workshop of Europe	Belgium
World's Bread Basket	Prairies of North America

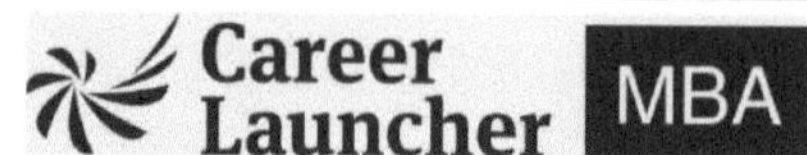

Name of the book	Author

Adventures of Sherlock Holmes	Sir Arthur Conan Doyle
Adventures of Tom Sawyer, The	Mark Twain
Ain-i-Akbari	Abul Fazal
Alchemist, The	Paulo Colelho
Alice in Wonderland	Lewis Carroll
All's Well that Ends Well	William Shakespeare
An American Tragedy	Theodore Dreiser
An Idealist View of Life	Dr S. Radhakrishnan
Anand Math	Bankim Chandra Chatterjee
Androcles and the Lion	George Bernard Shaw
Ape and Essence	A. Huxley
Apple Cart	George Bernard Shaw
Arabian Nights	Sir Richard Burton
Area of Darkness	V. S. Naipaul
Arthashastra	Kautilya
Arms and the Man	George Bernard Shaw
Around the World in Eighty Days	Jules Verne
As You Like it	William Shakespeare
Autobiography of an Unknown Indian	Nirad C. Choudhury

Babur-nama	Babur
Between the Lines	Kuldip Nayar
Bharat Bharati	Maithili Sharan Gupt
Bitter Sweet	Noel Coward
Brave New World	Aldous Huxley
Broken Wing	Sarojini Naidu
Bunch of Old Letters, A	Jawaharlal Nehru

Name of the book	Author

Name of the book	Author
Caesar and Cleopatra	George Bernard Shaw
Canterbury Tales	Geoffrey Chaucer
Chitra	Rabindranath Tagore
Comedy of Errors	William Shakespeare
Coolie	Mulk Raj Anand
Crime and Punishment	Fyodor Dostoevsky

Name of the book	Author
Das Kapital	Karl Marx
David Copperfield	Charles Dickens
Descent of Man	Charles Darwin
Dilemma of Our Time	Harold Joseph Laski
Discovery of India	Jawaharlal Nehru
Divine Life	Swami Sivananda
Doctor's Dilemma	George Bernard Shaw
Doctor Zhivago	Boris Pasternak
Don Juan	Lord Byron

Name of the book	Author
Ends and Means	Aldous Huxley

Name of the book	Author
Farewell to Arms, A	Ernest Hemingway
First Among Equals	Jeffrey Archer
For Whom the Bell Tolls	Ernest Hemingway
Freedom at Midnight	Larry Collins and Dominique Lapierre
Future Shock	Alvin Toffler

General Knowledge

Name of the book	Author

Geet Govinda	Jay Deva
Gitanjali	Rabindranath Tagore
Gita Rahasya	Bal Gangadhar Tilak
Glimpses of World History	Jawaharlal Nehru
Godan	Munshi Prem Chand
Golden Threshold	Sarojini Naidu
Golden Gate, The	Vikram Seth
Gone with the Wind	Margaret Mitchell
Gora	Rabindranath Tagore
Grammar of Politics	Harold Laski
Great Expectations	Charles Dickens
Guide, The	R K. Narayan
Gul-e-Naghma	Raghupati Sahai Firaq
Gulliver's Travels	Jonathan Swift

Hamlet	William Shakespeare
Harsha Charita	Bana Bhatt
Heat and Dust	Ruth P. Jhabwala
Hindu View of Life	Dr S. Radhakrishnan

Name of the book	Author

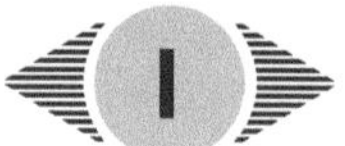

Name of the book	Author
If I am Assassinated	Z. A. Bhutto
Illiad	Homer
Importance of Being Earnest	Oscar Wilde
India Divided	Rajendra Prasad
India Wins Freedom	Maulana Abul Kalam Azad
Indian Home Rule	M. K. Gandhi
Indian Philosophy	Dr S. Radhakrishnan
Invisible Man	H. G. Wells
Iron in the Soul	Jean Paul Sartre
Ivanhoe	Walter Scott

Name of the book	Author
Judgement, The	Kuldip Nayar
Julius Caesar	William Shakespeare
Jungle Book	Rudyard Kipling

Name of the book	Author
Kadambari	Bana Bhatt
Kamasutra	Vatsyayan
Kamayani	Jai Shankar Prasad
King Lear	William Shakespeare
Kumar Sambhava	Kalidas

Name of the book	Author
Life Divine	Aurobindo Ghosh
Letters from a Father to his Daughter	Jawaharlal Nehru
Lolita	V. Nabakov
Love Story	Eric Segal

Career Launcher MBA

Name of the book	Author

Name of the book	Author
Macbeth	William Shakespeare
Mahabharata	Ved Vyas
Man and Superman	George Bernard Shaw
Man of Destiny	George Bernard Shaw
Meghdoot	Kalidas
Merchant of Venice	William Shakespeare
Midnight's Children	Salman Rushdie
Mother	Maxim Gorky
Much Ado About Nothing	William Shakespeare
Mudra Rakshas	Vishakadutta
My Experiments with Truth	Mahatma Gandhi
My Music, My Life	Ravi Shankar
My Truth	Indira Gandhi

Name of the book	Author
Natya Shastra	Bharat Muni
Nine Days Wonder	John Masefield

Name of the book	Author
Odyssey	Homer
Oliver Twist	Charles Dickens
Origin of Species	Charles Darwin
Othello	William Shakespeare

Name of the book	Author
Panchatantra	Vishnu Sharma
Passage to England, A	Nirad C. Choudhury
Paradise Lost	John Milton
Passage to India, A	E. M. Forster
Patriot, The	Pearl S. Buck
Post Office	Rabindranath Tagore
Pride and Prejudice	Jane Austen

Name of the book	Author

Raghuvamsa	Kalidas
Ram Charita Manas	Tulsidas
Ramayana	Valmiki
Ratnavali	Harsha Vardhan
Ritu Samhara	Kalidas
Romeo and Juliet	William Shakespeare
Rubaiyat	Omar Khayyam

Sadar-i-Riyasat	Karan Singh
Satyartha Prakash	Swami Dayanand Saraswati
Savitri	Sri Aurobindo Ghosh
Sense and Sensibility	Jane Austen
Satanic Verses, The	Salman Rushdie
Shahnama	Firdausi
Shakuntala	Kalidas
Shape of Things to Come	H.G. Wells
Shame	Salman Rushdie
Sohrab and Rustum	Mathew Arnold
Sunny Days	Sunil Gavaskar

Tale of Two Cities, A	Charles Dickens
Tempest, The	William Shakespeare
Three Musketeers	Alexander Dumas
Time Machine	H.G. Wells
To Live or Not to Live	Nirad C. Choudhury
Triumph	John Kenneth Galbraith
Twelfth Night	William Shakespeare
Twenty Years After	Alexander Dumas
Two Leaves and a Bud	Mulk Raj Anand

Name of the book	**Author**

Name of the book	Author
Ulysses	James Joyce
Unto This Last	John Ruskin
Utopia	Thomas Moore
Uttar Ramcharita	Bhavbhuti

Name of the book	Author
Valley of Dolls	Jacqueline Susann
Vanity Fair	William Thackeray
Vinay Patrika	Tulsidas
Virginians, The	William Thackeray
Vish Vriksha	Bankim Chandra Chatterjee
Voice of Conscience	V.V. Giri

Name of the book	Author
Wake up India	Annie Beseant
War and Peace	Leo Tolstoy
Wealth of Nations	Adam Smith
Wonder that Was India, The	A.L. Basham

Name of the book	Author
Yama	Mahadevi Verma

AAFI	The Amateur Athletics Federation of India
ABC	Audit Bureau of Circulation
ACPC	Agricultural Costs and Prices Commission
AEZ	Agri Export Zone
AD	Anno Domini
AGM	Annual General Meeting
ADB	Asian Development Bank
AFP	Agence France Presse
AC	Ante Christum; Alternating Current
AI	Artificial Intelligence; Air India
AG	Accountant General
ARM	Additional Resource Mobilisation
AM	Ante Meridiem
APM	Administered Price Mechanism
ASLV	Augmented Satellite Launch Vehicle
AICTE	All India Council for Technical Education
ASEAN	Association of South East Asian Nations
ASP	Application Service Provider; Association of Shareware Professionals
AIIMS	All India Institute of Medical Sciences
AITUC	All India Trade Union Congress
ASCII	American Standard Code for Information Interchange
AIDS	Acquired Immuno Deficiency Syndrome
ANC	African National Congress
APEC	Asia Pacific Economic Cooperation
AGMARK	Agricultural Marketing Development
ALGOL	Algebraic Oriented Language (Algorithmic Language)
ASSOCHAM	Associated Chamber of Commerce and Industry
AT&T	American Telegraphic and Telephone Co. Ltd.
ATM	Automated Teller Machine
AWACS	Airborne Early Warning and Control System

B2B	Business to Business
BBC	British Broadcasting Corporation
BAT	British American Tobacco
BC	Before Christ
BHEL	Bharat Heavy Electricals Ltd.
BIFR	Board for Industrial and Financial Reconstruction
BICP	Bureau of Industrial Cost and Prices
B2C	Business to Consumer
BIOS	Basic Input Output System
BIS	Bureau of Indian Standards
BOLT	Bombay Stock Exchange On-Line Trading; Build-Operate-Lease-Transfer
BoP	Balance of Payment
BSE	Bombay Stock Exchange
BIMARU	Bihar, Madhya Pradesh, Rajasthan, Uttar Pradesh
BSF	Border Security Force

CABE	Central Advisory Board on Education
C2C	Consumer to Consumer
CACP	Commission for Agricultural Costs and Prices
C&W	Cable and Wireless
CAG	Comptroller and Auditor General of India
CAT	Computed Axial Tomography
CBC	Commonwealth Business Council
CBDT	Central Board of Direct Taxes
CCEA	Cabinet Committee on Economic Affairs
CBM	Confidence Building Measures
CDAC	Centre for the Development of Automatic Computing
CEA	Central Electricity Authority
CEO	Chief Executive Officer
CERC	Central Electricity Regulatory Commission
CFC	Chlorofluorocarbon

CHOGM	Commonwealth Heads of Government Meeting
CIA	Central Intelligence Agency
CBI	Central Bureau of Investigation
CMA	Credit Monitoring Arrangement
CII	Confederation of Indian Industry
CISC	Complex Instruction-set Computing
CRISIL	Credit Rating Information Services of India Ltd.
CNC	Computer Numerical Control
CSO	Central Statistical Organisation
CRM	Customer Relations Management
COPRA	Consumer Protection Act
CMIE	Centre for Monitoring the Indian Economy
CIS	Commonwealth of Independent States
COPU	Committee on Public Undertakings
CID	Criminal Investigation Department
CSIR	Council of Scientific and Industrial Research
CNN	Cable News Network
CRR	Cash Reserve Ratio
CITU	Centre of Indian Trade Unions
CTBT	Comprehensive Test Ban Treaty

DNA	Deoxyribonucleic Acid
DFIs	Development Financial Institutions
DMRC	Delhi Metro Rail Corporation
DMZ	Demilitarised Zone
DTP	Desktop Publishing
DMAT	Dematerialized Account

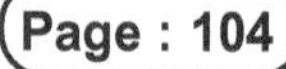
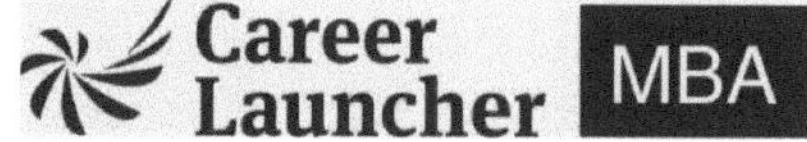

E-MAIL	Electronic Mailing
ECG	Electrocardiography
ECOSOC	Economic and Social Council (UN)
EDI	Electronic Data Interchange
EEG	Electroencephalography
EIS	Executive Information System
ELISA	Enzyme Linked Immuno-Sorbent Assay
EOU	Export Oriented Unit
EFTA	European Free Trade Association
EPZ	Export Processing Zone
ESMA	Essential Services Maintenance Act
ECGC	Export Credit Guarantee Corporation of India
EEZ	Exclusive Economic Zone
EPABX	Electronic Private Automatic Branch Exchange
ESP	Extra Sensory Perception

FRS	Fellow of the Royal Society
FAO	Food and Agriculture Organisation
FBI	Federal Bureau of Investigation
FCI	Food Corporation of India; Fertilizer Corporation of India
FCRA	Foreign Contribution Regulation Act
FDA	Food and Drug Administration
FDI	Foriegn Direct Investment
FII	Foreign Institutional Investors
FRCP	Fellow of the Royal College of Physicians
FM	Frequency Modulation
FMCG	Fast Moving Consumer Goods
FERA	Foreign Exchange Regulation Act
FEMA	Foreign Exhchange Management Act
FRCS	Fellow of the Royal College of Surgeons
FMCT	Fissile Material Cut-off Treaty
FIR	First Information Report
FOREX	Foreign Exchange
FICCI	Federation of Indian Chambers of Commerce and Industry
FTII	Films and Television Institute of India

GATT	General Agreement on Tariffs and Trade
GDP	Gross Domestic Product
GAIL	Gas Authority of India Ltd.
GDR	Global Depository Receipt
GIS	Geographical Information System
GMAT	Graduate Management Aptitude Test
GMO	Genetically Modified Organisms
GE	General Electric (USA)
GMT	Greenwich Mean Time
GNP	Gross National Product
GIC	General Insurance Corporation
GPS	Global Positioning System
GRE	Graduate Record Examination
GM	General Motors (USA)
GSI	Geological Survey of India
GSM	Global System for Mobile Communications
GUI	Graphical User Interface
GATE	Graduate Aptitude Test in Engineering
GSTP	Global System of Trade Practices
GSLV	Geo-Synchronous Satellite Launch Vehicle
GTO	Geo-Synchronous Transfer Orbit

HYV	High Yielding Varieties
HUL	Hindustan Unilever Limited
HIV	Human Immunodeficiency Virus
HANGSENG	Hong Kong Stock Exchange Index
HMV	His Master's Voice; Heavy Motor Vehicle
HDFC	Housing Development Finance Corporation
HTML	Hypertext Markup Language
http	hypertext transfer protocol
HUDCO	Housing and Urban Development Corporation
HDI	Human Development Index
HINDALCO	Hindustan Aluminium Company Limited

IAEA	International Atomic Energy Agency
IARI	Indian Agricultural Research Institute
IBM	International Business Machines
ICAR	Indian Council of Agricultural Research
ICC	International Cricket Council / International Criminal Court
INA	Indian National Army
ICCR	Indian Council for Cultural Relations
ICJ	International Court of Justice
IDBI	Industrial Development Bank of India
IPC	Indian Penal Code
IIT	Indian Institute of Technology
IJRY	Integrated Jawahar Rozgar Yojana
IDRA	Industrial Development and Regulation Act
IBRD	International Bank for Reconstruction and Development
ICBM	Inter-Continental Ballistic Missile
ILO	International Labour Organisation
IGNOU	Indira Gandhi National Open University
ICICI	Industrial Credit Investment Corporation of India
INDU	Indian National Defence University
INSAT	Indian National Satellite
IOC	Indian Oil Corporation
IP	Internet Protocol
IQ	Intelligence Quotient
IRA	Irish Republican Army
IRBM	Intermediate Range Ballistic Missile
IRDP	Integrated Rural Development Programme
ISBN	International Standard Book Number
ISI	Indian Standards Institution; Inter Service Intelligence
IFCI	Industrial Finance Corporation of India
ISO	International Standards Organisation
IST	Indian Standard Time
ITU	International Telecommunication Union
IVF	Invitro Fertilisation
ISRO	Indian Space Research Organisation

IMF	International Monetary Fund
IIP	Index of Industrial Production
IDA	International Development Agency
ICRA	Investment Information and Credit Rating Agency of India
ITC	Indian Tobacco Company
ICMR	Indian Council of Medical Research
INTUC	Indian National Trade Union Congress
IOU	I Owe You
IPR	Intellectual Property Rights
ISDN	Integrated Services Digital Network
IRDA	Insurance Development and Development Authority

LAC	Line of Actual Control
LIBOR	London Inter Bank Offer Rate
LCA	Light Combat Aircraft
L&T	Larsen and Toubro
LSD	Lysergic acid diethylamide
LDC	Least Developed Countries
LIC	Life Insurance Corporation (of India)
LPG	Liquefied Petroleum Gas
LPSC	Liquid Propulsion System Centre

MDC	Movement for Democratic Change
MCF	Master Control Facility
M&A	Mergers and Acquisitions
MFN	Most Favoured Nation
MF	Mutual Fund
MNC	Multinational Corporation
MODVAT	Modified Value Added Tax
MRI	Magnetic Resonance Imaging
MOU	Memorandum of Understanding
MRTPC	Monopolies and Restrictive Trade Practices Commission
MSP	Minimum Support Price
MTCR	Missile Technology Control Regime
MUL	Maruti Udyog Limited
MODEM	Modulator / Demodulator

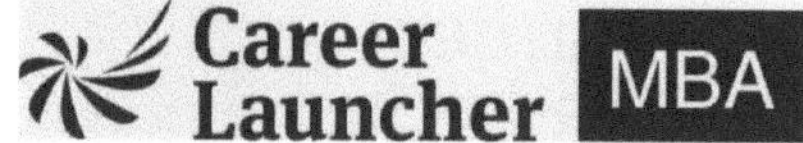

NABARD	National Bank for Agriculture and Rural Development
NCAER	National Council of Applied Economic Research
NCCF	National Consumers Cooperative Federation
NCFSE	National Curriculum Framework for Secondary Education
NAFTA	North American Free Trade Agreement
NASDAQ	National Association of Securities Dealers Automated Quotation
NATO	North Atlantic Treaty Organisation
NCL	National Commission on Labour / National Chemical Laboratory
NCRWC	National Commission to Review the Working of the Constitution
NDC	National Development Council
NGO	Non-Government Organisation; Non-Gazetted Officer
NMR	Nuclear Magnetic Resonance
NPT	Nuclear Non-Proliferation Treaty
NPC	National Productivity Council
NPA	Non Performing Assets
NASSCOM	National Association of Software and Service Companies
NAFED	National Agricultural Cooperative Marketing Federation
NREP	National Rural Employment Programme
NTPC	National Thermal Power Corporation
NCC	National Cadet Corps
NMS	Network Management System
NASA	National Aeronautics and Space Administration
NAV	Net Asset Value
NSIC	National Small-scale Industries Corporation
NCERT	National Council of Educational Research and Training
NWP	National Water Policy

OAPEC	Organisation of Arab Petroleum Exporting Countries
OAU	Organisation of African Unity
OBU	Overseas Banking Unit
OECD	Organisation for Economic Cooperation and Development
OIC	Organisation of Islamic Conference
ONGC	Oil and Natural Gas Corporation
OPEC	Organisation of Petroleum Exporting Countries
OOP	Object Oriented Programme

PAC	Public Accounts Committee
P&G	Proctor and Gamble Limited
PAN	Permanent Account Number
PAL	Premier Automobiles Limited
PFI	Petroleum Federation of India
Ph.D.	Doctor of Philosophy
PIL	Public Interest Litigation
PGA	Professional Golf Association
PIN	Postal Index Number
PM	Post Meridiem; Prime Minister
PPA	Power Purchase Agreement
PDS	Public Distribution System
PMRY	Prime Minister's Rozgar Yojana
PPP	Purchasing Power Parity; Point-to-Point Protocol
PROLOG	Programming Logic
PRI	Panchayati Raj Institution
PSE	Public Sector Enterprises
PSLV	Polar Satellite Launch Vehicle
PTA	Pilotless Target Aircraft
PTO	Please Turn Over
PAYE	Pay as You Earn
PHDCCI	Punjab, Haryana, Delhi Chamber of Commerce and Industries
PCA	Professional Chess Association
Pixel	Picture element
POTA	Prevention of Terrorism Act
POTO	Prevention of Terrorism Ordinance
PS	Post Scriptum
PTI	Press Trust of India
PSU	Public Sector Undertaking

QR	Quantitative Restriction

General Knowledge

R&D	Research and Develoment
RAM	Random Access Memory
RAW	Research and Analysis Wing
RBO	River Basin Organisation
RIDF	Rural Infrastructure Development Fund
RPM	Revolutions Per Minute
RSS	Rashtriya Swayam Sewak Sangh
RBI	Reserve Bank of India
RAF	Rapid Action Force
REC	Rural Electrification Corporation
RISC	Reduced Instruction–Set Computing
RRBs	Regional Rural Banks

SAIL	Steel Authority of India Limited
SEBs	State Electricity Boards
SAPTA	South Asian Preferential Trade Agreement
SCI	Shipping Corporation of India
SCM	Supply Chain Management
SEA	Satellite Education Authority
SFCs	State Financial Corporations
SDR	Special Drawing Rights
SEBI	Securities and Exchange Board of India
SENSEX	Sensitivity Index (of Share Price)
SEZ	Special Export Zone
SRTCs	State Road Transport Corporations
SSI	Small Scale Industries
SCOPE	Standing Committee of Public Enterprise
SLR	Statutory Liquidity Ratio
SPCA	Society for Prevention of Cruelty to Animals
STC	State Trading Corporation
SUV	Sports Utility Vehicle
STP	Software Technology Park
SLV	Satellite Launch Vehicle
SPIC	Southern Petrochemical Industries Corporation
SAI	Sports Authority of India
STD	Subscriber Trunk Dialing; Sexually Transmitted Diseases

TCP	Transfer Call Protocol; Transmission Control Protocol
TELCO	Tata Engineering and Locomotive Company
TIFR	Tata Institute of Fundamental Research
TISCO	Tata Iron and Steel Company
TNT	Trinitrotoluene
TQM	Total Quality Management
TCS	Tata Consultancy Services
TRIMS	Trade Related Investment Measures
TRIFED	Tribal Cooperative Marketing Development Federation of India Ltd.
TRIPS	Trade Related Intellectual Property Rights
TADA	Terrorist and Disruptive Activities (Prevention) Act
TRYSEM	Training of Rural Youth for Self-employment
TWAS	Third World Academy of Science

UGC	University Grants Commission
UNCTAD	United Nations Conference on Trade and Development
UNESCO	United Nations Educational, Scientific and Cultural Organisation
UNFCCC	United Nations Framework Convention on Climate Change
UNIDO	United Nations Industrial Development Organisation
UNFPA	United Nations Population Fund
UPSC	Union Public Service Commission
UNEP	United Nations Environment Programme
UFO	Unidentified Flying Objects
UHF	Ultra-high Frequency
UNI	United News of India
USP	Unique Selling Proposition
UPS	Uninterrupted Power Supply
UNICEF	United Nations International Children's Emergency Fund (At present known as 'United Nations Children's Fund')

VAN	Virtual Area Network
VDIS	Voluntary Disclosure of Income Scheme
VSAT	Very Small Aperture Terminal
VAT	Value Added Tax

WEF	World Economic Forum
WHO	World Health Organisation
WMO	World Meteorological Organisation
WWW	World Wide Web
WPI	Wholesale Price Index
WWF	World Wildlife Fund (At present known as Worldwide Fund for Nature)
WWF	World Wrestling Federation
WTDC	World Telecommunication Development Conference
WTO	World Trade Organisation

XML	Extensible Mark-up Language
XMS	Extended Memory System

///////////Important Facts about World and India///////////

(A) World's Largest, Longest and Highest Man-made Structures

Structure	Name	Location
Longest Rail Line	Trans-Siberian line from Moscow to Nakhodka, 9,438 kilometres long	Russia
Largest Temple (Hindu)	Angkor Vat	Cambodia
Longest Wall	The Great Wall of China	China
Longest Railway Platform	Gorakhpur (1,366.33 m)	Gorakhpur, Uttar Pradesh
Largest Cathedral	Diocese of New York	New York
Longest Railway Bridge	Huey P. Long Bridge	Metairie, Louisiana, US
Busiest Airport	Hartsfield-Jackson Atlanta International Airport	Georgia, USA
Highest Road Bridge over Water	Royal Gorge	River Arkanas, Colorado
Largest Library	The Library of Congress	Capital Hill, Washington, DC

(B) Important Natural Entities of the World

Natural Entity	Names
Largest Ocean	Pacific
Largest Gulf	Gulf of Mexico
Largest Island	Greenland (renamed Kalaatlit Nunaat)
Largest Bay	Hudson Bay, Northern Canada
Tallest Animal	Giraffe
Largest Bird	North American Ostrich
Largest Animal	Blue Whale
Largest Egg	Ostrich Egg
Smallest Bird	Bee Hummingbird
Smallest River (shortest)	Roe River in Montana
Largest Sea	South China Sea
Largest Delta	Sunderbans
Driest Place	Atacama Desert, Chile
Highest Waterfall	Salto Angel, Venezuela
Largest Desert	The Sahara, North Africa
Hottest Place	Aziza, Libya
Largest Glacier	Siachen, Indo-Pak border
Coldest Place	Vostok Staion (Antarctica)

(C) Important Facts of India.

National Insignia and Other Important Facts

1. **National Flag:** It was **adopted** by Constituent Assembly on July **22 1947**. Ratio of width to length is 2 : 3 having three bands of equal width; lowest is green, middle one is white and saffron is the colour at the top. A wheel is at the centre of the flag of navy blue colour **having 24 spokes. Madam Bhikaji Cama was the first to unfurl the tri-colour at an international body.**

2. **National Anthem:** Composed by **Rabindranath Tagore,** have wordings: Jana Gana Mana..., in 1911. Adopted on January 24, 1950, by the Constituent Assembly of India and takes about **52 seconds** to sing it completely. It was first sung on 27th Dec. 1911 at Calcutta session of Congress.

3. **National Song: Composed by Bankim Chandra Chatterjee,** wordings: Vande Mataram ..., **taken** from **'Anand Math'**, a novel by him and was adopted on **January 24, 1950.**

4. **National Flower** is **Lotus.**

5. **National Animal** is **Tiger.**

6. **National Bird** is **Peacock.**

7. **State Emblem of India**
   The state emblem is an adaptation from the Sarnath Lion Capital of Ashoka. In the original, there are four lions, standing back to back, mounted on an abacus with a frieze carrying sculptures in high relief of an elephant, a galloping horse, a bull and a lion separated by intervening wheels over a bell-shaped lotus. Carved out of a single block of polished sandstone, the Capital is crowned by the Wheel of the Law (Dharma Chakra). In the state emblem, adopted by the Government of India on 26 January 1950, only three lions are visible, the fourth being hidden from view. The wheel appears in relief in the centre of the abacus with a bull on right and a horse on left and the outlines of other wheels on extreme right and left. The bell-shaped lotus has been omitted. **The words Satyameva Jayate from Mundaka Upanishad,** meaning 'Truth Alone Triumphs', are inscribed below the abacus in Devanagari script.

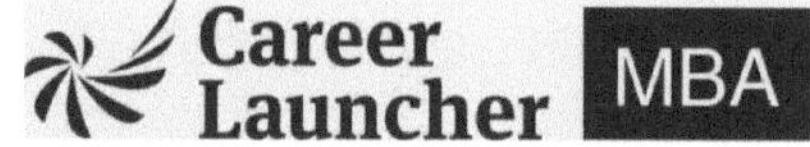

(D) Important Boundaries and Lines of the World

1. **Durand Line:**   It is the line which separates India and Afghanistan.
2. **MacMahon Line:**   It demarcates the boundries of China and India.
3. **Radcliffe Line:**   It demarcates the boundary between India and Pakistan.
4. **38th Parallel:**   It is the parallel separating North Korea and South Korea.
5. **49th Parallel:**   It is the boundary between USA and Canada.
6. **Siegfried Line:**   It is the line between Germany and France, from German side.
7. **Maginot Line:**   It is the line between Germany and France from French side.
8. **17th parallel:**   It is the parallel (latitude) which separated north Vietnam from south Vietnam.

(E) States of India and Their Capitals

States	Capitals	States	Capitals
1. Andhra Pradesh	Hyderabad /Amaravati	16. Manipur	Imphal
2. Arunachal Pradesh	Itanagar	17. Meghalaya	Shillong
3. Assam	Dispur	18. Mizoram	Aizawl
4. Bihar	Patna	19. Nagaland	Kohima
5. Chhatisgarh	Raipur	20. Orissa	Bhubaneswar
6. Goa	Panaji	21. Punjab	Chandigarh
7. Gujarat	Gandhinagar	22. Rajasthan	Jaipur
8. Haryana	Chandigarh	23. Sikkim	Gangtok
9. Himachal Pradesh	Shimla	24. Tamil Nadu	Chennai
10. Jammu & Kashmir	Srinagar/Jammu	25. Telangana	Hyderabad
11. Jharkhand	Ranchi	26. Tripura	Agartala
12. Karnataka	Bangalore	27. Uttarakhand	Dehra Dun
13. Kerala	Thiruvananthapuram	28. Uttar Pradesh	Lucknow
14. Madhya Pradesh	Bhopal	29. West Bengal	Kolkata
15. Maharashtra	Mumbai		

National Capital Territory	Capital
Delhi	Delhi

Union Territories	Capitals
1. Andaman & Nicobar Islands	Port Blair
2. Chandigarh	Chandigarh
3. Dadra & Nagar Haveli	Silvassa
4. Daman & Diu	Daman
5. Lakshadweep	Kavaratti
6. Puducherry	Puducherry

***Please know that there are 29 States and 7 Union Territories in India. Delhi is counted as a Union territory.**

Islands: India possesses two groups of Islands, i.e. (i) Lakshadweep, (ii) Andaman & Nicobar group.

(i)   **Lakshadweep:** It is a collection of 27 islands present in the Arabian Sea lying about 300 kilometres west of Kerala.

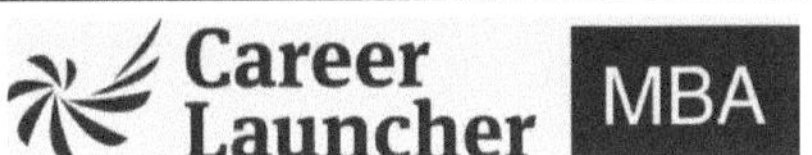

(ii)   **Andaman & Nicobar group:** Nicobar consists of 19 small islands and Andaman has a collection of 204 small islands.

(iii) **Indira point** is the Southmost extremity of India.

(F) Important Indian Towns and Associated Industries

Town	Industry	Town	Industry
Aligarh	Locks	Mysore	Silk
Ankleshwar	Oil	Nangal	Fertilizers
Bhilai	Steel plant	Nepanagar	Newsprint
Chittaranjan	Locomotive	Perambur	Railway coach factory
Digboi	Oil	Pimpri	Penicillin factory
Durgapur	Steel plant	Raniganj	Coal mining
Jhamshedpur	Steel	Rourkela	Steel plant
Jharia	Coal	Sindri	Fertilizers
Katni	Cement	Surat	Textiles
Khetri	Copper	Titagarh	Paper
Ludhiana	Hosiery, cycles, sewing machines	Vishakhapatnam	Ship-building

(G) Important Indian Cities on River Banks

City	River	City	River
Ahmedabad	Sabarmati	Ludhiana	Sutlej
Ayodhya	Sarayu	Nashik	Godavari
Delhi	Yamuna	Srinagar	Jhelum
Guwahati	Brahmaputra	Tiruchirapalli	Cauvery
Howrah	Hugli	Ujjain	Shipra
Hyderabad	Musa	Varanasi	Ganges
Kota	Chambal	Vijayawada	Krishna
Lucknow	Gomti		

(H) Important Indian Sites and Monuments and Their Locations

Site/Monument	Location	Site/Monument	Location
Ajanta Caves	Aurangabad	Jantar Mantar	Delhi
Anand Bhawan	Allahabad	Kanyakumari	Tamil Nadu
Buland Darwaza	Fatehpur Sikri near Agra	Khajuraho	Bhopal
Char Minar	Hyderabad	Kranti Maidan	Mumbai
Dilwara Temples	Mount Abu	Minakshi Temple	Madurai
Elephanta Caves	Mumbai	Red Fort	Delhi
Ellora Temples	Aurangabad	Sabarmati	Ahmedabad
Gol Gumbaz	Bijapur	Sanchi	Madhya Pradesh
Golden Temple	Amritsar	Sarnath	Varanasi
Gomateshwara Statue	Mysore	Shantiniketan	Birbhumi
Jallianwala Bagh	Amritsar	Victoria Memorial	Kolkata
Jama Masjid	Delhi		

(I)   Major Indian Crops and Their Leading Producers

Name of the Crop	Main Proucer
Cashew nuts	Tamil Nadu, Kerala
Cloves	Kerala
Coconut	Tamil Nadu, Kerala
Coffee	Karnataka, Kerala
Cotton	Gujarat, Maharashtra
Groundnut	Gujarat, Andhra Pradesh, Tamil Nadu
Jute	Bihar, W. Bengal, Odisha
Mustard	Uttar Pradesh, Rajasthan
Rice	West Bengal, Tamil Nadu
Rubber	Kerala, Karnataka
Saffron	Karnataka, Tamil Nadu
Silk	Karnataka, Kerala
Sugar cane	Uttar Pradesh, Maharashtra
Tea	Assam, West Bengal, Kerala
Tobacco	Maharashtra, Gujarat, Madhya Pradesh
Wheat	U.P., Punjab, Haryana

(J)   Minerals and Their States of Abundance

Minerals	States
Bauxite	Odisha is the largest producer of bauxite in the country and contributes about one-third of the total production. Jharkhand is the second largest producer of bauxite and produces about 22% of India's total.
Coal	Bihar, West Bengal (Raniganj and Jharia)
Copper	Major copper ore deposits are located in Singhbhum district (Jharkhand), Balghat district (Madhya Pradesh) and Jhunjhunu and Alwar districts (Rajasthan).
Diamond	Madhya Pradesh (Panna)
Iron	Odisha (Mayurbhanj, Bonai, Keonjhar)
Lignite	Tamil Nadu (Neyveli fields)
Limestone	Madhya Pradesh
Manganese	Odisha
Mica	India has monopoly in the production of mica, producing about 60% of the world's total production. About 95% of India's mica is distributed in just three states of Jharkhand, Andhra Pradesh and Rajasthan.

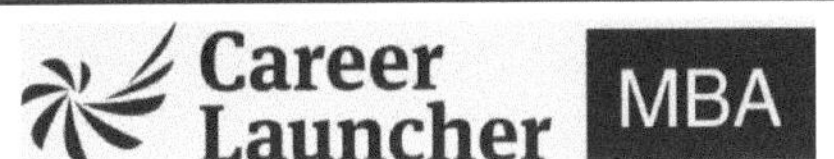

(K)   Important River-based Projects

Name of the project	River
Bhakra Nangal Project	Sutlej
Chambal Project	Chambal
Damodar Valley Project	Damodar
Farakka Project	Bhagirathi, Ganga
Gandak River Project	Gandak
Hirakud Dam Project	Mahanadi
Idukki Project	Periyar
Kosi Project	Kosi
Koyna Project	Koyna
Mayurakshi Project	Murali
Nagarjunasagar Project	Krishna
Rihand Scheme	Rihand
Tawa Project	Tawa
Tehri Dam Project	Bhilangana, Bhagirathi
Tungabhadra Project	Tungabhadra
Ukai Project	Tapti

(L)   Important Dances of India

Name of the dance	State which it belongs to
Bihu	Assam
Bidesia	Bihar
Bharatanatyam	South India (Tamil Nadu)
Bhangra, Gidda	Punjab
Chiraw	Mizoram
Jatra, Chau	West Bengal
Jhulan leela, Jhumar or Ghumar	Rajasthan
Kathak	North India (Uttar Pradesh)
Kuchipudi, Kottam	Andhra Pradesh
Lota, Pandavani	Madhya Pradesh
Mohiniattam, Kathakali, Theyyam	Kerala
Manipuri, Maharasa	Manipur
Nautanki	Uttar Pradesh
Odissi	Odisha
Bhavai	Gujarat
Tamasha, Lavani	Maharashtra
Yakshagana	Karnataka
Kathakali	Kerala

Career Launcher MBA

General Knowledge

(M) Important Indian Tribes and Their Habitats

Name of the tribe	Habitat
Abors	Assam, Arunachal Pradesh
Baiga	Madhya Pradesh
Bhils	Madhya Pradesh, Rajasthan
Bhotias	Uttar Pradesh
Garos	Meghalaya
Gonds	Madhya Pradesh, Bihar, Odisha, Andhra Pradesh
Khonds	Odisha
Khasis	Assam, Meghalaya
Kuki	Manipur
Mina	Rajasthan
Mundas	Jharkhand
Murias	Chhattishgarh
Santhals	West Bengal, Bihar, Chhattisgarh.
Todas (it is a **polyandrous** tribe)	Tamil Nadu
Warlis	Maharashtra

(N) Heads of Important International Organisations

	Organisations	Head
1	United Nations (UN)	Antonia Guterres
2	World Trade Organisation (WTO)	Robert Azevedo
3	World Bank (WB)	David Malapass
4	World Economic Forum (WEF)	Klaus Schwab
5	International Monetary Fund (IMF)	David Lipton
6	International Olympic Committee	Thomas Bach
7	FIFA	Gianni infantino
8	International Cricket Council (ICC)	Shashank Manohar

Important Demographic Facts of India

Census 2011

Following are few selected, important demographic facts, that you should always keep on your finger tips. You can expect atleast one question from them.

The 15th Indian National census was conducted in two phases, house listing and population enumeration. House listing phase began on April 1, 2010 to collect of information on all buildings. Information for National Population Register was also collected in the first phase, which will be used to issue a 12-digit unique identification number

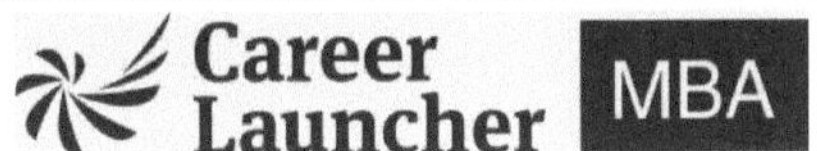

(Aadhar) to all registered Indians by Unique Identification Authority of India (UIAI). The second phase of population enumeration was conducted between 9 to 28 February 2011. Census has been conducted in India since 1872. In Census - 2011 biometric information was collected for the first time. Shri C. Chandramouli is the Registrar General and commissioner of 2011 indian census.

1.   Absolute population of India - 121.02 crores. It comprises 62.37 crores males and 58.65 crores females.
2.   Population growth during the decade remained 17.64 percent.
     ⇒ Total absolute increase in population during the decade is 18.15 crores.
     ⇒ Sex ratio - 940 females per 1000 males. Child sex ratio for females is 914 per 1000 males.
3.   Highest sex ratio - Kerala
4.   Lowest sex ratio - Haryana
5.   Most populous state - Uttar Pradesh
6.   Least populous state - Sikkim
7.   Most populous union territory - Delhi
8.   Least populous union territory - Lakshadweep
9.   Population density (people living in one square km) of India - 382.
10. Highest population density - Bihar
11. Lowest population density - Arunachal Pradesh
12. Literacy rate of India - 74.04% (males: 82.14%, female: 65.46%). Literacy rate of India has gone up to 74.04 percent from previous figure of 64.83 percent.
13. States with highest literacy - Kerala (93.9%)
14. State with lowest literacy - Bihar (63.82%)
15. Urbanization (% of population living in urban areas) - 27.8% (India)
16. Most urbanised state (1991 census) - Mizoram
17. Speakers of language (in descending order) - Hindi > Bengali > Telugu > Marathi > Tamil > Urdu
18. Census commissioner of India for the census 2011 is Dr. C. Chandramouli

Different UN Agencies

	Name of Agency	Abbrev-iation	Date of Establishment	Headquarter	Purpose	Heads
1.	International Labour Organization	ILO	1919	Geneva	To promote social justice, improve conditions and living standard of workers and promote economic stability	Guy Ryder
2.	International Atomic Energy Agency	IAEA	1957	Vienna	To promote peaceful uses of atomic energy	Yukiya Amano (Director General)
3.	Food and Agriculture Organization	FAO	1945	Rome	To raise nutritional levels, living standards, production and distribution of food and agricultural products, improving living conditions of rural population	Jose Grazianoda Silva
4.	United Nations Education, Scientific and Cultural Organization	UNESCO	1946	Paris	To promote collaboration among nations through education, science and culture in order to further justice, human rights and freedom	Audrey Azoulay (Director general)
5.	World Health Organization	WHO	1948	Geneva	Attainment of the highest possible level of health by all people	Tedros Adhanom (Director general)
6.	International Bank for Reconstruction and Development	IBRD	1945	Washington	Development of economies of members by facilitating investment of capital and foreign investment, through provision of loans	Jim Yong Kim (President of WB)

7.	World Meteorological Organization	WMO	1950	Geneva	To promote international exchange of weather reports and other weather related services	Petteri Taalas (Head)
8.	International Maritime Organization	IMO	1958	London	Promotes cooperation on technical matters of maritime safety, navigation and encourages anti-pollution measures	Kitack Lim (Head)
9.	United Nations International Children's Emergency Fund	UNICEF	1946	New York	Children's welfare all over the world	Henrietta H. Fore (Ex.Directors)
10.	General Agreement on Tariffs and Trade (from 1994 it is known as WTO)	WTO	1948 - 1994	Geneva	Treaty setting rules for world trade, to reduce tariffs and other barriers to international trade	Rober Azevedo
11.	United Nations Development Programme	UNDP	1965	New York	Help developing countries increase the wealth producing capabilities and resources	Achim Steiner (Chairperson)
12.	United Nations Environment Programme	UNEP	1972	Nairobi	Promotes international cooperation in matters relating to human environment	Erik Solheim (Dir Gen)
13.	United Nations Fund for Population Activities	UNFPA	1967	New York	Promotes Population related programmes	Natalia Kanem
14.	United Nations High Commissioner for Refugees	UNHCR	1950	Geneva	Provides international protection to refugees	Filippo Grandi
15.	United Nationas Industrial Development Organization	UNIDO	1967	Vienna	Extends assistance to developing countries for development and modernisation of industries	Li Yong
16.	International Finance corporation	IFC	1955	Washington	Promote economic development by encouraging private enterprise in its member countries	Philippe Le Houerou (CEO)
17	International Monetary Fund	IMF	1945	Washington	Promotes international monetary co-operation and expansion of international trade	David Lipton (Acting M.D of IMF)
18	International Civil Aviation	ICAO	1947	Montreal	Promotes safety of international aviation and establishes international standards and regulations	Dr. Fang Liu
19	Universal Postal Union	UPU	1947	Berne	Improves various postal services and promotes international collaboration	Bishar Abdirahenan Hussein
20	International Telecommunication Union	ITU	1947	Geneva	Sets international regulations for radio, telegraph, telephone and space radio communications	Houlin Zhao
21	United Nations Conference on Trade and Development	UNCTAD	1964	Geneva	Promotes international trade with a view to accelerate economic growth of developing countries	Mukhisa Kituyi (Secretary- General)
22	United Nations Institute for Training and Research	UNITAR	1965	New York	Provides high priority training and of projects to help facilitate the UN research objectives of world peace and security, and of economic and social progress	Nikhil Seth (Executive Director)
23	United Nations Relief and Work for Palestine Refugees in the North East	UNRWA	1949	New York	Provides food, health services, education vocational training for those displaced in the Arab-Israel war	Pierre Krahenbuhl (Commissioner Gen)
24	International Olympic Committee	IOC	1894	Lousanne Switzerland	Responsible for Organizing Modern Summer & Winter Olympic Games	Thomas Bach

A list of programmes by Narendra Modi Government:

Pradhan Mantri Jan Dhan Yojana (PMJDY)

It is a national mission for financial inclusion to ensure access to financial services, namely Banking Savings & Deposit Accounts, Remittance, Credit, Insurance, and Pension in an affordable manner. This financial inclusion campaign was launched by the Prime Minister Narendra Modi on 28 August 2014.He had announced this scheme on his first Independence Day speech on 15 August 2014.Run by Department of Financial Services, Ministry of Finance, on the inauguration day, 1.5 Crore (15 million) bank accounts were opened under this scheme. Guinness World Records recognises the achievements made under PMJDY, Guinness World Records Certificate says "The most bank accounts opened in 1 week as a part of financial inclusion campaign is 18,096,130 and was achieved by Banks in India from 23 to 29 August 2014". By 7 October 2015, 18.70 crore accounts were opened, with around Rs. 25146.97 crore (US$3.8 billion) were deposited under the scheme.

Digital India

Digital India is an initiative by the Government of India to ensure that Government services are made available to citizens electronically by improving online infrastructure and by increasing Internet connectivity. It was launched on July 1, 2015 by Prime Minister Narendra Modi. The initiative includes plans to connect rural areas with high-speed internet networks. Digital India has three core components. These include: The creation of digital infrastructure, delivering services digitally and digital literacy. The Government plans to complete this project in five years. That is, by 2019, the Digital India project is expected to be fully functional.

Swachh Bharat Abhiyan

The Swachh Bharat Abhiyan was launched formally on October 2, 2014, the birth anniversary of Mahatma Gandhi. The objective is to make India a clean India by 2019, the 150th birth anniversary of Mahatma Gandhi. The plan is to provide toilet and sanitation facilities in all rural and remote areas, to create public awareness of cleanliness, to clean roads, streets, encroachments and make India one of the cleanest countries of the world.

Make in India

Make in India is an initiative of the Government of India to encourage multinational, as well as domestic companies to manufacture their products in India. It was launched by Prime Minister Narendra Modi on 25 September 2014. India would emerge, after initiation of the programme in 2015, as the top destination globally for foreign direct investment, surpassing the People's Republic of China as well as the United States. The Make in India campaign is completely under the Central Government, in which the Government has identified 25 major sectors which have the potential of becoming a global leader.

Saansad Adarsh Gram Yojana

Sansad Adarsh Gram Yojana is a rural development programme broadly focusing upon the development in the villages which includes social development, cultural development and spread motivation among the people on social mobilization of the village community. The programme was launched by the Prime Minister of India, Narendra Modi on the birth anniversary of Jayaprakash Narayan, on 11 October 2014. According to this yojana, each MP will take the responsibility of developing three villages by 2019. The idea is to make India's villages to be fully developed with physical and institutional infrastructure. There are certain guidelines for this scheme, which has been formulated by the Department of Rural Development. The Prime Minister released the guidelines on October 11, 2014 and requested all MPs to develop one model village by year 2016 in their constituency and two more by 2019.

Atal Pension Yojana (APY)

Atal Pension Yojana is a government-backed pension scheme in India targeted at the unorganized sector. It was originally mentioned in the 2015 Budget speech by Finance Minister Arun Jaitley in February 2015.It was formally

launched by Prime Minister Narendra Modi on 9 May in Kolkata. As of May 2015, only 11% of India's population has any kind of pension scheme, this scheme aims to increase the number. In Atal Pension Yojana, for every contribution made to the pension fund, the government will contribute an equal amount to his/her fund. Depending on the contribution made between 18 and 40, at the age of 60 a sum of Rs. 1000 (US$15), Rs. 2000 (US$30), Rs. 3000 (US$45), Rs. 4000 (US$60), or Rs. 5000 (US$75) will be paid monthly.

Pradhan Mantri Jeevan Jyoti Bima Yojana (PMJJBY)

Pradhan Mantri Jeevan Jyoti Bima Yojana is a government-backed Life insurance scheme in India. It was originally mentioned in the 2015 Budget speech by Finance Minister Arun Jaitley in February 2015. It was formally launched by Prime Minister Narendra Modi on 9 May in Kolkata.As of May 2015, only 20% of India's population has any kind of insurance, this scheme aims to increase the number. Pradhan Mantri Jeevan Jyoti Bima Yojana is available to people between 18 and 50 years of age with bank accounts. It has an annual premium of Rs. 330 (US$5.00) excluding service tax, which is above 14% of the premium. The amount will be automatically debited from the account. In case of death due to any cause, the payment to the nominee will be 2 lakh (US$3,000).This scheme will be linked to the bank accounts opened under the Pradhan Mantri Jan Dhan Yojana scheme. Most of these account had zero balance initially. The government aims to reduce the number of such zero balance accounts by using this and related schemes.

Pradhan Mantri Suraksha Bima Yojana (PMSBY)

Pradhan Mantri Suraksha Bima Yojana is a government-backed accident insurance scheme in India. It was originally mentioned in the 2015 Budget speech by Finance Minister Arun Jaitley in February 2015.It was formally launched by Prime Minister Narendra Modi on 9 May in Kolkata.As of May 2015, only 20% of India's population has any kind of insurance, this scheme aims to increase the number. Pradhan Mantri Suraksha Bima Yojana is available to people between 18 and 70 years of age with bank accounts. It has an annual premium of 12 (18¢ US) excluding service tax, which is about 14% of the premium. The amount will be automatically debited from the account. In case of accidental death or full disability, the payment to the nominee will be 2 lakh (US$3,000) and in case of partial disability 1 lakh (US$1,500). Full disability has been defined as loss of use in eyes, hands or feet. Partial disability has been defined as loss of use in one eye, hand or foot.

Beti Bachao, Beti Padhao Scheme

It is a Government of India scheme that aims to generate awareness and improving the efficiency of welfare services meant for women. The scheme was initiated with an initial corpus of Rs 100 crore. Prime Minister Modi launched the programme on January 22, 2015 from Panipat, Haryana. This is being implemented through a national campaign and focussed multi sectoral action in 100 selected districts low in CSR, covering all States and UTs. This is a joint initiative of Ministry of Women and Child Development, Ministry of Health and Family Welfare and Ministry of Human Resource Development. The objectives of this initiative are: Prevention of gender biased sex selective elimination, ensuring survival & protection of the girl child and ensuring education and participation of the girl child.

Sukanya Samriddhi Yojana

Sukanya Samriddhi Account (literally Girl Child Prosperity Account) in a Government of India backed saving scheme targeted at the parents of girl children. The scheme encourages parents to build a fund for the future education and marriage expenses for their female child. The scheme was launched by Prime Minister Narendra Modi on 22 January 2015 as a part of the Beti Bachao, Beti Padhao campaign. The scheme currently provides an interest rate of 9.2% and tax benefits. The account can be opened at any India Post office or a branch of some authorised commercial banks.

Pradhan Mantri Krishi Sinchai Yojana

PMKSY is central scheme that aims at providing irrigation facilities to every village in the country by converging ongoing irrigation schemes implemented by various ministries. It will have an outlay of Rs. 50,000 crore over a period of five years (2015-16 to 2019-20). The allocation for the current financial year is Rs. 5300 crore. The major objective of the PMKSY is to achieve convergence of investments in irrigation at the field level, expand cultivable area under assured irrigation (Har Khet ko pani), improve on-farm water use efficiency to reduce wastage of water, enhance the

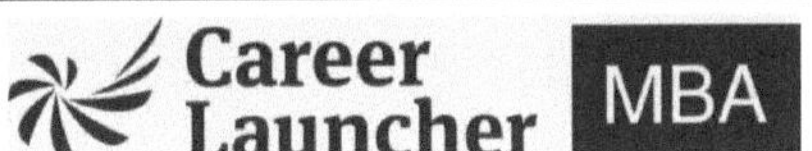

adoption of precision-irrigation and other water saving technologies (More crop per drop), enhance recharge of aquifers and introduce sustainable water conservation practices by exploring the feasibility of reusing treated municipal based water for peri-urban agriculture and attract greater private investment in precision irrigation system.

Pradhan Mantri Kaushal Vikas Yojana (PMKVY)

This will be the flagship scheme for skill training of youth to be implemented by the new Ministry of Skill Development and Entrepreneurship through the National Skill Development Corporation (NSDC). The scheme will cover 24 lakh persons. Skill training would be done based on the National Skill Qualification Framework (NSQF) and industry led standards. Under the scheme, a monetary reward is given to trainees on assessment and certification by third party assessment bodies. The average monetary reward would be around Rs. 8000 per trainee.

Atal Mission for Rejuvenation and Urban Transformation

The initiative was announced by PM Narendra Modi on 25 June 2015, and is said to be aiming to transform 500 cities and towns into efficient urban living spaces, with special focus on a healthy and green environment for children. it was also reported that Cabinet has approved Rs 50,000 crore for this mission which is to be spent over the next five years. The purpose of Atal Mission for Rejuvenation and Urban Transformation (AMRUT) is to (i) ensure that every household has access to a tap with assured supply of water and a sewerage connection; (ii) increase the amenity value of cities by developing greenery and well maintained open spaces (parks); and (iii) reduce pollution by switching to public transport or constructing facilities for non-motorized transport (e.g. walking and cycling).

Smart Cities Project

The government of India under Prime Minister, Shri Narendra Modi has a vision of developing 100 smart cities as satellite towns of larger cities and by modernizing the existing mid-sized cities. The government plans to identify 20 smart cities in 2015, 40 in 2016 and another 40 in 2017. The 100 potential smart cities nominated by all the States and UTs based on Stage1 criteria will prepare Smart City Plans which will be rigorously evaluated in the Stage2 of the competition for prioritizing cities for financing. In the first round of this stage, 20 top scorers will be chosen for financing during this financial year. The remaining would be asked to make up the deficiencies identified by the Apex Committee in the Ministry of Urban Development for participation in the next two rounds of competition. 40 cities each will be selected for financing during the next rounds of competition.

Swarnajayanti Gram Swarozgar Yojana (SGRY)

- Started on April 1, 1999. It has replaced the following programs.
    - **Integrated Rural Development Programme (IRDP):** Started in 1978-79.
    - **Development of Women and Children in Rural Areas (DWCRA) :** Started in 1978-79.
    - **Ganga Kalyan Yojana (GKY) :** Started in 1997.
    - **Million Wells Scheme (MWS):** Started in 1989.
    - **Supply of Improved Tool-kits to Rural Artisans (SITRA) :** Started in 1992.
- The Yojana takes into account all the strengths and weaknesses of the earlier self-employment programs.
- It aims at establishing a large number of micro-enterprises in the rural areas.
- Every assisted family will be brought above the poverty line. It is proposed to cover 30% of the rural poor in each block.
- To target at least 50% Scheduled Castes and Scheduled Tribes, 40% Women and 3% disabled.
- Shared 75 : 25 by Centre and States.

Pradhan Mantri Gramodaya Yojana (PMGY)

- It was introduced in 2000-01 with the objective of focusing on village level development in five critical areas, i.e., primary health, primary education, housing, rural roads and drinking water and nutrition with the overall objective of improving the quality of life of people in rural areas. Rural electrification was added as an additional component from 2001-02.

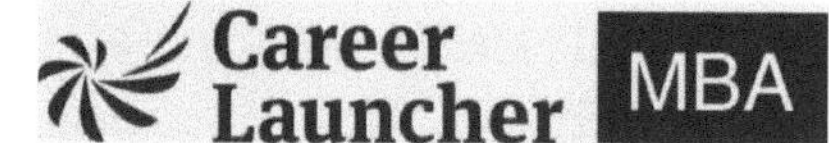

- It has the following components.

    1. **Pradhan Mantri Gram Sadak Yojana (PMGSY)**
        - It was launched on Dec 25, 2000 with the objective of providing road connectivity through good all weather roads to all rural habitations with a population of more than 1000 persons by the year 2003 and those with a population of more than 500 persons by the year 2007.
    2. **Pradhan Mantri Gramodaya Yojana (Gramin Awas)**
        - Launched on Apr 1, 2000. Based on the pattern of Indira Awas Yojana, the scheme is being implemented in the rural areas throughout the country with the objective of sustainable habitat development.
    3. **Pradhan Mantri Gramodaya Yojana (Rural Drinking Water Project)**

National Rural Employment Guarantee Scheme (NREGS)

- It was launched on Feb 2, 2006. The on-going programs of Sampoorna Grameen Rozgar Yojana (SGRY) and National Food for Work Programme (NFFWP) were subsumed within the NREGS in the 200 districts identified in the initial stage. All the districts in the country are covered under the scheme now. The features of the scheme are:

(a) State Government to provide at least 100 days of guaranteed wage employment in every financial year to every household whose adult members volunteer to do unskilled manual work.

(b) Until such time as a wage rate is fixed by the Central Government, the minimum wage for agricultural laborers shall be applicable for the scheme.

(c) An applicant not provided employment within fifteen days, to be entitled to a daily unemployment allowance as specified by the State Government subject to its economic capacity, provided such rate is not less than quarter of the wage rate for the first thirty days during the financial year and not less than a half of the wage rate for the remaining period of the financial year.

Sampoorna Gramin Rozgar Yojana (SGRY)

- It was started on September. 25, 2001, with the mergence of the **Employment Assurance Scheme (EAS)** and the **Jawahar Gram Samriddhi Yojana (JGSY).** Earlier **Jawahar Rozgar Yojana**, which started in 1989, was merged with Jawahar Gram Samriddhi Yojana.
- This scheme has been subsumed in National Rural Employment Guarantee Scheme.

Bharat Nirman Yojana

- Accepting the policy 'a step towards village', Union Government launched a new scheme, named **'Bharat Nirman Yojana'** on Dec 16, 2005. This scheme aims at developing rural infrastructure. The duration of implementing this scheme has been determined for four years with the expected expenditure of Rs. 1,74,000 crore.
  The major six sectors and their targets for next four years are
- **Irrigation :** To ensure irrigation for additional one crore hectare of land by 2009.
- **Roads :** To link all villages of 1,000 population with roads and also to link all ST and hilly villages upto 500 population with roads.
- **Housing :** Construction of 60 lakh additional houses for the poor.
- **Water Supply :** To ensure drinking water to all remaining 74,000 villages.
- **Electrification :** To supply electricity to all remaining 1,25,000 villages and to provide electricity connection to 2.3 crore houses.
- **Rural Communication :** To provide telephone facility to all remaining 66,822 villages.

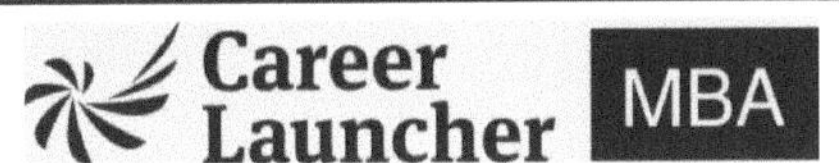

Swarnajayanti Shahari Rozgar Yojana (SJSRY)

- The SJSRY came into operation in Dec 1997, through a restructuring and streamlining of the earlier urban poverty alleviation programs, the **Nehru Rozgar Yojana (NRY)**, the **Urban Basic Services for the Poor (UBSP)** and the Prime Minister's **Integrated Urban Poverty Alleviation Programme (PMIUPEP)**.
- It seeks to provide employment to the urban employed or underemployed living below poverty line and educate up to IX standard through encouraging the setting up of self-employment ventures or provision of wage employment.
- It is funded by the Centre and States on 75 : 25 bases.

Antyodaya Anna Yojana

- Launched on Dec 25, 2000, the scheme aims at providing food security to poor families.
- The Scheme contemplates identification of 10 million poorest of the poor families and providing them with 35 kg of food grains per family per month at a low price of Rs. 2 per kg of wheat and Rs. 3 per kg for rice.

Annapurna Yojana

- Inaugurated on Mar 19, 1999.
- Initially the scheme provided 10 kg food grains to senior citizens who were eligible for old age pension but could not get it due to one reason or the other. Later on, it was extended to cover those people also who get old age pensions.
- Food grains are provided to the beneficiaries at subsidized rates of Rs. 2 per kg of wheat and Rs. 3 per kg of rice.

Sarva Shiksha Abhiyan

- The Scheme of Sarva Shiksha Abhiyan (SSA) was launched in 2001. The goals of SSA are as follows: (i) All 6-14 age children in school/Education Guarantee Scheme Centre/bridge course by 2003, (ii) All 6-14 age children complete five year primary education by 2007; (iii) All 6-14 age children complete eight years of schooling by 2010; (iv) Focus on elementary education of satisfactory quality with emphasis on education for life; (v) Bridge all gender and social category gaps at primary stage by 2007 and at elementary education level by 2010; and (vi) Universal retention by 2010.
- The assistance under the program of SSA was on a 85:15 sharing arrangement during the Ninth Plan, 75:25 sharing arrangement during the Tenth Plan, and 50:50 sharing thereafter between the Central Government and State Government.
- SSA addresses the needs of 194 million children in the age group of 6-14 years. Under the scheme, 9.72 lakh existing primary and upper primary schools and 36.95 lakh existing teachers have been covered.

Mid-Day Meal Scheme for School Children

- The National Program of Nutritional Support to Primary Education (NPNSPE), popularly known as the Mid-Day Meal (MDM) Scheme, was formally launched on Aug 15, 1995. The objective of the program is to give a boost to universalization of primary education by increasing enrolment, attendance and retention, and also improving nutritional status of children in primary classes.
- Under the MDM scheme, cooked mid-day meal with a nutritional content of 450 calories and 12 grams protein is served to children studying at primary level.
- About 12 crore children studying in over 9.50 lakh schools are presently covered under the scheme. In order to improve the quality of meal, the scheme was last revised in June, 2006. The cooking cost norm has been fixed at Rs. 2 per child per school day with Rs. 1.80 as Central assistance for North East States and Rs. 1.50 for other States and UTs. Assistance to States has been provided at the rate of Rs 5,000 per school to procure/repair kitchen devices.

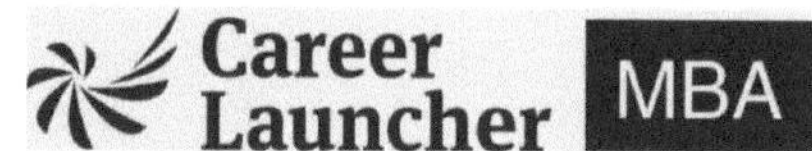

Part – II
Basics of Economics
and Indian Economy
since Independence

Career Launcher MBA

Important Basic Concepts of Economics

Economic and non-economic activities

Economic activities: The activities which give income in return are called economic activities.

Non-economic activities: The activities which do not give any income in return are called non-economic activities.

All the economic activities are broadly divided into three categories:

Primary activities: All the economic activities, which result in the production of goods with the help of land and water are known as primary activities, e.g., agriculture, rearing of animals, hunting, fishing, mining, etc. Some examples of goods produced through primary activities are wheat, vegetables, milk, marble, coal, etc.

Secondary activities: When primary goods are used to produce some other commodity manually or by machines then the activities involved in the conversion are known as secondary activities, e.g., paper from wood, bread from wheat, etc. In other words, we can say that there is interdependence between the primary and secondary activities.

Tertiary activities: For all the primary and secondary activities we need a support system like transportation, postal services, telephones, etc. These support systems are in the form of tangible goods that cannot be measured. In other words, the services are the link between the producer and the customer.

Based on the national income and per capita income, various countries are divided into three categories:
Underdeveloped countries (Ethiopia, Sudan, etc.)
Developing countries (India, China, Pakistan, etc.)
Developed countries (USA, UK, Japan, Singapore, etc.)
In an economically developed country, majority of the people earn an income higher than their requirements. If they lack in a particular segment of goods or food production, they have the ability to buy and import that from other countries.

Profit

It is the reward for the organization in the production of goods and services. According to Taussing, profit is a mixed and vexed income. Hawley referred to profit as a reward for taking risk while Samuelson considered it as the return coming from implicit factors. Professor Knight regarded profits as a reward for bearing uncertainties while Schumpeter interpreted profits as reward for innovative functions of the entrepreneur. Karl Marx criticized profits as a legalised robbery. In other words, profit is equal to the difference between total revenue and total cost of production.

Profits are classified into two types: (i) Gross profits and (ii) Net profits

(i) **Gross profit:** Any profit usually means gross profit as it includes following items.
   (a) Input costs (e.g., maintenance cost, depreciation charges, etc.)
   (b) Implicit returns (e.g., implicit interests, implicit wages, implicit interests, etc.)
   (c) Non-entrepreneurial profit (e.g., windfall gain, monopoly gains, etc.)
   (d) Net profit (pure economic profit)

So, mathematically gross profit can be calculated by the following formula.

Gross profit = Net profit + Implicit rent + Implicit wages + Implicit interest + Depreciation charges + Maintenance costs + Non-entrepreneurial profit

(ii) **Net profit:** It is the total revenue of a firm less explicit and implicit cost. Mathematically net profit can be calculated by the following formula.
   Net profit = Gross profit − (Implicit costs + Depreciation charges + Insurance charges)

   Entrepreneurs get net profits for:
   (a) successful coordination between different factors of production;
   (b) taking risks;
   (c) bearing uncertainties in production, and
   (d) making innovations.

Rewards of other factors of production always remain positive but the profit received by the entrepreneur may be either positive or negative. Net profit could be normal (minimum profit that an entrepreneur should get) or super normal (more than the normal profit).

National income

It is the money value of all the goods and services produced in a country in a year. National income can be calculated in following three ways:
- The total value of output in a country in a year
- The total value of all incomes received by the owners of factors of production in a year
- The total expenditure incurred on all goods and services in a year

According to Alfred Marshall, the labour and capital of a country, acting upon its natural resources produce annually a certain net aggregate of commodities, material and immaterial including services of all kinds. This is the true net annual income or revenue of the country or national dividend. This definition was criticized on the ground of difficulty in the accurate measurement of the value of output of innumerable varieties of goods and services, danger of counting the same good more than once, and goods and services produced, consumed by the producers themselves makes evaluation difficult.

Pigou defined national income as the national dividend, or that part of the objective income of the community including, of course, income derived from abroad, which can be measured in money. This definition was better than Marshall's definition but was criticized on the ground of not being applicable to underdeveloped countries where bartering still prevails and complexities in the calculation of national income because of discontinuation (because of any improbable reasons).

Irving Fisher described it as the national dividend or income consisting solely of services as received by ultimate consumers; whether from their material or from their human environments. Fischer states that national income is determined not by production but by consumption in a year. Fischer's definition seems to be more scientific but is less practical as it is very difficult to measure the money value of consumed goods and services in a year because for that, one must know the life span of the goods which varies from goods to goods and at the same time it is difficult to estimate the value of durable goods when they change hands.

Concepts related to national income

Concept of value added: Value added is defined as the difference between total value of output of a firm and value of inputs bought from other firms. Thus, it is value added in the process of production.

Value of output by a firm = Sales + Change in stock
Value added = Value of output – Intermediate goods cost
Net value added at market price = Gross value added at market price – Consumption of fixed capital (depreciation)
Net value added at factor cost = Net value added at market price – Net indirect taxes (= Indirect taxes – Subsidies) = Total factor income

Gross national product (GNP): It is the money value of all the final goods and services produced by an economy in a year. Since prices vary throughout the year, economists calculate gross national product at constant prices, i.e. the output is multiplied with prices of goods during a stable year. Following are the items that are excluded from the gross national product measurement as they are not production activities but only the exchange of funds:

(i) Purely financial transactions like buying and selling of securities, Government transfer payments and Private transfer payments,
(ii) Transfer of used goods,
(iii) Non-market goods and services,
(iv) Illegal activities like smuggling, gambling, etc., and
(v) The value of leisure.

Real gross national product and nominal gross national product are figured out by taking the value of national product at constant price and current price respectively.

Gross Domestic Product (GDP): It is actual gross product within a country. The only difference between GNP and GDP is that GDP does not include income from abroad.

Net National Product (NNP): It is the money value of net production of goods and services. It facilitates the observation of the change in output from year to year. (sometimes it becomes difficult to estimate it when depreciation of plants and machineries are included).

Net national product =
Gross national product – Depreciation

National income or national income at factor prices: This facilitates in estimating the value of what is produced in a year exactly.

National income = Net national product – Indirect taxes + Depreciation

National disposable income: It is the income from all sources of the residents of a nation for spending on consumption as well as saving during a financial year. It is the maximum available income of a country.
National disposable income = Net national product at market price + Other current transfers from the rest of the world

Personal income: It is the income received by all the people in the country.

Personal income = National income – (Corporate taxes + Undistributed corporate profits + Contribution to social security schemes by employers and employees) + Transfer payments

Transfer payments: These are certain incomes, which are not correctly earned but paid to the individuals like old age pension, widow pension, payment for unemployment and other such welfare expenditures. These payments are made out of the funds of exchequer by the government. These incomes are added to the personal income.

Disposable personal income: It is the income that people can spend as they like. It includes personal consumption and personal saving.

$$\text{Disposable personal income} =$$
$$\text{Personal income} - \text{Personal taxes (i.e. direct taxes)}$$

Per capita income: It is the average income received by a citizen of a country in a year. It is an indicator of the improvement in the economic position of a person.

$$\text{Per capita income} = \frac{\text{National income}}{\text{Population}}$$

Direct and indirect tax

According to JS Mill, a direct tax is one which is demanded from the very person who it is intended or desired should pay it. Indirect taxes are those which are demanded from one person in the expectation and intention that he shall indemnify himself at the expense of another. Dalton defines the direct tax as a tax that is really paid by a person on whom it is legally imposed. While an indirect tax is imposed on a person but paid partly or wholly by another owing to consequential changes in terms of some contract or bargain between them.

In the Indian tax system, following come under direct taxes:
(i)   Income tax,
(ii)   Corporation tax,
(iii)   Wealth tax,
(iv)   Gift tax,
(v)   Capital gains and
(vi)   Estate duty

Goods and Services Tax (GST)

GST is an Indirect Tax which has replaced many Indirect Taxes in India. In order to implement GST, Constitutional (122nd Amendment) Bill (CAB)was introduced in the Parliament and passed by Rajya Sabha on 03rd August, 2016 and Lok Sabha on 08th August, 2016. The CAB was passed by more than 15 states and thereafter Hon'ble President gave assent to "The Constitution (One Hundred And First Amendment) Act, 2016" on 8th of September, 2016. Since then the GST council and been notified bringing into existence the Constitutional body to decide issues relating to GST. The Goods and Service Tax Act was passed in the Parliament on 29th March 2017. The Act came into effect on 1st July 2017. The GST would apply to all goods other than alcoholic liquor for human consumption and five petroleum products, viz. petroleum crude, motor spirit (petrol), high speed diesel, natural gas and aviation turbine fuel. It would apply to all services barring a few to be specified.

At the **Central** level, the following taxes are being subsumed:

1.   Central Excise Duty,
2.   Additional Excise Duty,
3.   Service Tax,
4.   Additional Customs Duty commonly known as Countervailing Duty, and
5.   Special Additional Duty of Customs.

At the **State** level, the following taxes are being subsumed:

1.   Subsuming of State Value Added Tax/Sales Tax,
2.   Entertainment Tax (other than the tax levied by the local bodies), Central Sales Tax (levied by the Centre and collected by the States),
3.   Octroi and Entry tax,
4.   Purchase Tax,
5.   Luxury tax, and
6.   Taxes on lottery, betting and gambling.

GST Council

As per Article 279A (1) of the amended Constitution, the GST Council has to be constituted by the President within 60 days of the commencement of Article 279A. The notification for bringing into force Article 279A with effect from 12th September, 2016 was issued on 10th September, 2016. The Union Cabinet under the Chairmanship of Prime Minister Shri Narendra Modi approved setting up of GST Council on 12th September, 2016.

As per Article 279A of the amended Constitution, the GST Council which will be a joint forum of the Centre and the States shall consist of the following members: -

1.   Union Finance Minister - Chairperson
2.   The Union Minister of State, in-charge of Revenue of finance - Member
3.   The Minister In-charge of finance or taxation or any other Minister nominated by each State Government - Members

As per Article 279A (4), the Council will make recommendations to the Union and the States on important issues related to GST, like the goods and services that may be subjected or exempted from GST, model GST Laws, principles that govern Place of Supply, threshold limits, GST rates including the floor rates with bands, special rates for raising additional resources during natural calamities/disasters, special provisions for certain States, etc.

Classification of taxation system

Taxes are categorized in the following four types:

Proportional taxes: In this type of taxation system, each income is taxed at a uniform or flat rate. This type of taxation is not suitable to bring about the desired changes in the distribution of wealth in the society and affects poor more. So, this type of taxation system is not preferred much nowadays.

Progressive taxes: In this type of taxation system, higher income groups pay higher percentage of their income as tax. Here, marginal utility of money falls with addition to money income. This helps in better distribution of wealth among different sections of society. This system is preferred by most of the governments.

Regressive taxes: This is opposite form of the progressive taxation system where rich are imposed with less taxes and poor are charged higher taxes because of their vast number. This is just a hypothetical system and does not exist nowadays.

Degressive taxes: It is milder form of progressive taxation system where rate of taxes does not increase in the same proportion as the income rises. Higher income groups make higher sacrifice than smaller income groups.

Budget

Budget is an itemized summary of expected income and expenditure of a country, company, etc., over a specified period, usually a financial year. In economics, the budget is an annual statement of the estimated receipts and expenditures by the government over the fiscal year. (In India, April 1 to March 31)

Objectives of budget: (i) To secure the reallocation of resources, if market fails or performs poorly, (ii) redistribution of income and wealth to reduce inequality, (iii) to maintain economic stability and prevent business fluctuation, i.e. high level of employment and price stability, (iv) management of public sector efficiently in order to achieve maximum social welfare.

Constituents of budget: Budget is primarily divided into two parts, i.e. the revenue budget and capital budget. The revenue budget constitutes revenue receipts of the government and the expenditure of this collected revenue. The capital budget constitutes capital receipts and expenditures.

Receipts

Revenue receipts: It is divided into two classes, i.e. tax revenue and non-tax revenue. Tax revenue consists of all the receipts of taxes (both direct and indirect) and other duties levied by the Union Government (budget also states the proposed changes in the existing taxation policy). Non-tax revenue includes all other receipts like revenue received by the government in the form of prices paid for government supplied goods and services, e.g., postage, tolls, railways, electricity, etc., and also includes interest and dividend earned by the governmental investment and revenue earned on account of the administrative function of the government like licence fee, registration fee (for automobiles, fire arms, etc.), fines and penalties, escheats, etc.

Capital receipts: This includes market loans (loans raised from the public), borrowings from the Reserve Bank of India and other parties through the sale of treasury bills, loans received by the foreign governments and international institutions (World Bank, Asian Development Bank, etc.), recoveries of loans granted to the state governments, Union Territory governments and other parties, small savings and deposits in Public provident fund (PPF), etc.

Expenditures

Revenue and capital expenditures

Revenue expenditure: It includes expenditure incurred for the normal running of the government, payment of interests on the loans taken, subsidies, etc. In other words, all those expenditures, which do not result in the creation of assets, are considered as revenue expenditures.

Capital expenditure: It includes expenditure on acquisition of assets like land, buildings, machinery, equipments, investments, loans and advances given to the state governments, Union Territories, government companies and corporations, and other parties.

Planned and unplanned expenditures

Planned expenditures are all those public expenditures incurred for the current development and investment as in the planned proposals. All other expenditures are known as unplanned expenditure.

Developmental and non-developmental expenditures

Developmental expenditure: It includes plan expenditure of railways, post offices and telecommunications and non-departmental commercial undertakings (financed out of their internal and extra budgetary resources, including market loans and term loans from financial institutions to the state government public enterprises and also the developmental loans to non-departmental undertakings and other parties by the central or state governments).

Non-developmental expenditure: It includes expenditure on defence, interest payment, tax collection, police, judiciary and other expenditures like expenditures on general administration, natural and accidental calamities relief, grant and loans for non-development works to the foreign countries, subsidies, etc.

Balanced, surplus and deficit budget

Size of estimates	Types of budget	Remarks
Revenue less than expenditure	Deficit	Increases the aggregate demand. So, it is a good policy to combat recession but the economy comes in under employment equilibrium because of deficient demand
Revenue is equal to expenditure	Balanced	Slightly increases the aggregate demand and is a good policy to bring the economy near full employment to a full employment equilibrium
Revenue is greater than expenditure	Surplus	Surplus budget lowers the aggregate demand (good for combating inflation but a poor strategy against deflation and recession)

Types of deficit

Following are the four types of deficit.

(i) **Budget deficit:** It is the difference between the total expenditure and current revenue and net internal and external capital receipts of the government put together. This deficit is essentially financed by internal and external capital.

(ii) **Fiscal deficit:** It is the difference between the total expenditure of the government (revenue expenditure, capital expenditure and loans net of repayment) and the revenue receipts and all those capital receipts (not borrowing) which finally accrue to the government. Fiscal deficit indicates more inflation, as more the deficit more will be the government borrowings that will result in more the burden of interest payments.

(iii) **Primary deficit:** It is the difference between fiscal deficit and interest payments. It is an indicator of the situation when to tighten the belt. A zero primary deficit refers to the interest commitments on earlier loan forcing government to borrow. In other words, it is a measure of fiscal irresponsibility.

(iv) **Revenue deficit:** It is the difference between the government's revenue expenditures and revenue receipts. In the same level of fiscal deficit, higher revenue deficit is worse than a lower revenue deficit.

Important Economics Terms

Administered price: The administrative body, e.g., the government, a marketing board or a trading group determines the price. The competitive market force are not entitled to determine this price. The government fixes a price in accordance with demand-supply position in the market.

Ad valorem tax: A type of indirect tax in which goods are taxed by their values. In the case of ad valorem tax, the tax amount is calculated as the proportion of the price of the goods. Value Added Tax (VAT) is an ad valorem tax.

Appreciation: An increase in the value of something, e.g., stock of raw materials or manufactured goods, inclusive of increase in the traded value of a currency. It is the opposite of depreciation. Appreciation may occur when the prices rise due to inflation. It also causes scarcity or increase in earning power. It is opposite of depreciation.

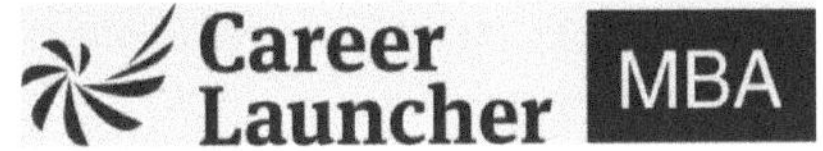

Arbitrage: When the middle man buys and sells goods at a particular time to cash the price differences of two markets, then this action is termed as arbitrage. Purchases are done when prices are low in one market and then sold in another market where the prices are high in order to earn the profit due to price difference in the two markets.

Average cost: Total cost divided by the output.

Balance of payment: A systematic record of all economic transactions completed between the residents of a country and the residents of the remaining world during a year. The balance of payment shows the relationship between total payment of one country to all other countries and its total receipts from them. Balance of payment includes both visible and invisible items. Balance of payment includes visible export and imports along with invisible trade like shipping, banking, insurance, tourism, royalty and payments of interest on foreign debts.

Balance of Trade: The total value of a country's export commodities and total value of import commodities. Thus, balance of trade includes only visible trade, i.e. movement of goods (exports and imports of goods). Balance of trade is a part of balance of payment statement.

Bank Rate: The rate of discount at which the central bank of the country discounts first class bills. It is the rate of interest at which the central bank lends money to the lower banking institutions. Bank rate is a direct quantitative method of credit control in the economy.

Bills of Exchange: Document acknowledging an amount of money owned in consideration for goods received.

Blue Chip: Equity shares whose purchase is extremely safe. It is a safe investment as it does not involve any risk.

Blue Collar Jobs: Jobs concerned with a factory. Persons who are unskilled and depend upon manual jobs that require physical strain on human muscle are said to be engaged in Blue Collar Jobs. Such jobs are on the decline these days with the advancement of technology.

Break-even price: Price at which firms make zero abnormal profits. It is equal to the average cost.

Bridge loan: Loan made by a bank for a short period to make up for a temporary shortage of cash. On the part of borrower, mostly the companies, for example, a business organisation wants to install a new company with new equipments etc. while its present installed company/ equipments etc. are not yet disposed off. Bridge loan covers this period between the buying of the new and disposing of the old one.

Budget deficit: It is the difference between the total expenditure on one hand, and current revenue and net internal and external capital receipts of the government. It has to be financed by net internal and external capital receipts.

Bull: Bull is that type of speculator who gains with the rise in prices of shares and stocks. He buys share or commodities in anticipation of rising prices and sells them later at a profit.

Bull market: A market where the speculators buy shares or commodities in anitcipation of rising prices. This market enables the speculators to resell such shares and make a profit.

Business cycle: Type of fluctuations in the economic activity of organised communities. It is composed of period of good trade characterised by rising prices and low unemployment, alternating with period of bad trade characterised by falling prices and high unemployment. Every trade cycle has five different sub-phases: depression (dip), recovery, full employment, prosperity (boom) and recession.

Call Money: It is a form of loans and advances which is payable on demand or within the number of days specified for the purpose.

Capital expenditure: Consists mainly of expenditure on acquisition of assets like land, buildings, machinery, equipment; investments in shares, etc. and loans and advances granted by the central government to state and union territory governments, government companies, corporations and other parties.

Capital market: Capital market is the market that gives medium term and long term loans. It is different from money market that deals only in short term loans.

Capitalism: It is an economic system in which all means of production are owned by private individuals. Self profit motive is the guiding feature for all economic activates under capitalism. Under pure capitalism system,

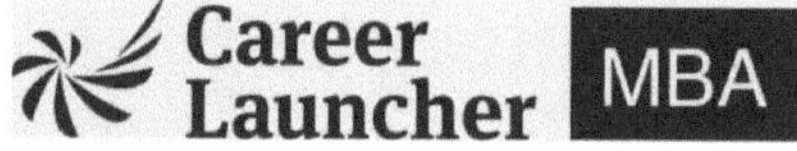

economic conditions are regulated solely by free market forces. This system is based on 'Laissez-faire system', i.e. no state intervention. Sovereignty of consumer prevails in this system. Consumer behaves like a king under capitalism.

Capital receipts: Items included in capital receipts are loans raised by the government from the public (also called market loans), borrowings by the government from the Reserve Bank of India and other parties through the sale of treasury bills, loans received from foreign governments and other international bodies (For example, World Bank, Asian Development Bank etc.), recoveries of loans granted to state and union territory governments and other parties, small savings and deposits in the public provident fund (PPF), etc.

Cash credit: Credit which is advanced against the value of the borrower's current assets, which comprise mainly stocks of goods — raw materials, semi-manufactured or finished goods, and bills receivable (dues) from others.

Cash Reserve Ratio (CRR): The portion of net demand and time liabilities every bank is required to deposit with the RBI.

Closed Economy: Closed economy refers to an economy having no foreign trade (i.e. export and import). Such economies depend exclusively on their own internal domestic resources and have no dependence on outside world.

Control price: A product price fixed by the government, which is below the equilibrium price.

Core sector: Economy needs basic infrastructure for accelerating development. Development of infrastructure industries like cement, iron and steel, petroleum, heavy machinery etc. can only ensure the development of the economy as a whole. Such industries are core sector industries.

Corporation tax: It is a tax on company's profit. It is a direct tax which is calculated on profits after interest payments and allowance (i.e. Capital allowance) have been deducted but before dividends are allowed for.

Credit money: This refers to money, whose value is greater than the commodity value of the material from which the money is made.

Custom duty: A duty that is imposed on the products received from exporting nations of the world. It is also called protective duty as it protects the home industries.

Dear money: This is a condition in which loans or money are very difficult to obtain.

Death rate: Death rate signifies the number of deaths in a year per thousand of the population. It is mostly known as crude death rate. Life expectancy is an important determinant of death rate.

Deficit financing: It is a practice resorted to by modern governments of spending more money than they it receives in revenue. It is a policy of bridging a deficit between government expenditure and revenue. Deliberately budgeting for a deficit is called deficit financing. This practice was popularised by Prof. JM Keynes to deal with depression and unemployment situations and to stimulate economic activity. Deficit financing, though having inflationary effects, has now become a common practice in all countries.

Deflation: Deflation is the opposite case of inflation. Deflation is that state of falling prices which occurs at that time when the output of goods and services increases more rapidly than the volume of money in the economy. During deflation, the general price level falls and the value of money rises.

Depreciation: The value of the existing capital stock that has been consumed or used up in the process of producing output.

Devaluation: The loss of value of currency of a country relative to other foreign currencies is known as devaluation. Devaluation is a process in which the government deliberately cheapens the exchange value of its own currency in terms of other currencies by giving it a lower exchange value. Devaluation is used for improving the balance of payment situation in the country.

Direct tax: Those taxes that are levied immediately on the property and income of persons, and those that are paid directly by the consumers to the state. Income tax, interest tax, wealth tax, corporation tax are all examples of direct taxes.

Disinflation: It refers to a process of bringing down prices moderately from their high level without any adverse impact on production and employment. Thus, disinflation is an anti-inflationary measure.

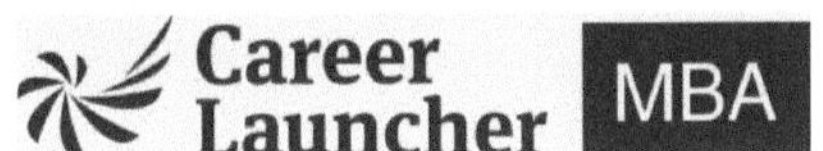

Dividend: Dividend is the amount which the company distributes to share holders when the profits of the company are calculated by the board of directors.

Excise duty/Excise tax: It is a tax imposed on total cost incurred by a firm. It is a tax which is imposed on certain indigenous production (e.g., petroleum products, cigarettes, etc.) of the country. Excise duty may be imposed either to raise revenue or to check the consumption of the commodities on which they are imposed. Excise duty is progressive in nature.

Fiscal policy: It is that part of government economic policy which deals with taxation, expenditure, borrowing, and the management of public debt in the economy. Fiscal policy primarily concerns itself with the flow of funds in the economy. It exerts a very powerful influence on the working of economy as a whole.

Fiscal deficit: The difference between the total expenditure of the government and the revenue receipts plus those capital receipts which are not in the nature of borrowing, but which finally accrue to the government.

Fiscal policy: Government's expenditure and tax policy together is known as its fiscal policy.

Fiscal Year: The fiscal year runs from April 1 to March 31.

Import duty: Import duty is a tax on imports imposed on an ad valorem basis, i.e. fixed in the form of a percentage on the value of the commodity imported.

Imports: These are equal to consumption of a good minus its production.

Inflation: A situation of a steady and sustained rise in general prices is usually known as inflation. Inflation is a state in which the value of money is falling, i.e. prices are rising.

Joint sector: When a sector is jointly owned, managed and run by both public and private sectors, it is called joint sector. This sector indicates the partnership between the two, i.e. public and private sector.

Laissez Faire: It is a French word meaning 'non-interference'. This doctrine was popularised by classical economists who gave the view that government should interfere as little as possible in the economic activities of the individuals.

Liquidation: It refers to the termination (or winding up) of a registered company. Liquidation takes place because of company's insolvency. In liquidation, assets are turned into cash for settling outstanding debts and for apportioning the balance, if any, amongst the owners.

Liquidity: Assets which can easily be converted into cash money are said to have liquidity. Land does not possess liquidity at it takes longer time to get it converted into cash.

Marginal cost: It is the increase in total cost or total variable cost incurred when an extra unit of output is produced.

Monetary policy: Monetary policy comprises all measures applied by the monetary authorities with a view to produce a deliberate impact on the nature and volume of money so as to achieve the objectives of general economic policy. It aims at regulating the flow of currency, credit and other money substitutes in an economy with a view to affect the total stock of such assets as well as to influence the demand of the community for such assets.

Monopolistic competition: It is a market in which there are many sellers, they produce a differentiated product and there is free entry and exist.

Multinational company: It is a large scale company which has its production base in several countries and the bulk of the production is done in outside nations. This company produces more overseas than it does in its parent country. Increased trade and economies of scale have encouraged such type of companies in the recent years.

Oligopoly: It is that form of imperfect competition in which there are only a few firms in the industry (or group) producing either homogeneous products or may be having product differentiation in a given line of production.

Open economy: It is that economy which is left free and the government imposes no restrictions on trade with areas outside that economy.

Open market operations: Buying and selling of securities by the RBI in the open market. This is a tool of the Central Bank for monetary control.

Overhead costs: It is the total of all costs that are independent of the level of output.

Parity value: In a fixed exchange rate system, the value of a currency will be fixed in terms of another currency or in terms of gold. This value is known as the parity value of the currency.

Price index: An index number that shows how the average price of a bundle of goods has changed over a period of time.

Primary deficit: Fiscal deficit minus interest payments. It indicates how much of the government borrowing is going to meet expenses other than interest payments.

Private Sector: Private Sector is that part of the economy which is not owned by the government and is in the hands of private enterprise. In other words, private sector is not under direct government control. Private sector includes the personal as well as the corporate sector.

Privatisation: Privatisation is the antithesis of nationalisation. When the government owned public industries are denationalised and the disinvestment process is initiated, it is called privatisation.

Profit: Total revenue minus total cost.

Public sector: It signifies those undertakings which are owned, managed and run by public authorities. Public sector includes direct government enterprise, the nationalised industries and public corporations. In this sector of the economy, the government acts as an entrepreneur.

Revolving credit: It is a bank credit that is renewed automatically until notice of cancellation is received. Revolving credits may be sanctioned for an unlimited amount in total but with a limit on the amount that may be drawn at any one time or within a specified period, e.g., one month.

Seasonal unemployment: It is the unemployment which is caused by seasonal variation in demand for labour by various industries, such as agriculture, construction and tourism. Seasonal unemployment normally declines in spring as more outdoor work can be undertaken.

Security: Security refers to a share, bond or government stock that can be bought and sold, usually on the stock exchange or on a secondary market, and carries a right to some form of income, either in the form of a fixed rate of interest or dividends.

Selling costs: It is same as advertising costs.

Share capital: It is the amount of money raised by a company by issuing shares. The authorized share capital is the amount that a company is allowed to issue as laid down in its Articles of Association. The issued share capital is the amount actually issued i.e. the number of issued shares multiplied by their par value. Fully paid share capital is the amount raised by payment of the full par value of the issued shares.

Soft currency: A currency with limited convertibility into gold and other currencies, either because it is depreciating due to balance of payments difficulties or because controls have been placed on it to prevent the exchange rate from falling.

Special Drawing Rights (SDRs): It is a reserve asset (known as 'Paper Gold') created within the framework of the International Monetary Fund in an attempt to increase international liquidity, and now forming a part of countries' official reserves along with gold, reserve positions in the IMF and convertible foreign currencies.

Statutory Liquidity Ratio (SLR): The SLR requires the banks to maintain a specified percentage of their net total demand and time liabilities in the form of designated liquid assets.

Subsidies: Payments by government to firms or households that provide or consume a commodity. For example, government may subsidize food by paying for a part of the food expenditures of low-income households.

Tariff: Tax or a duty on imports, which can be levied either on physical units, e.g., per tonne (specific), or on value (advalorem). It could be imposed for a variety of reasons including; to raise government revenue, to protect domestic industry from subsidized or low-wage imports, to boost domestic employment, or to ease a deficit on the balance of payments.

Tax revenue: Revenue received from taxes and other duties levied by the Central Government.

Trade gap: Size of the deficit (or surplus) in the balance of trade (the difference in value between visible imports and exports).

Wealth tax: Tax imposed on the value of total assets but wealth up to a certain limit is exempted from such tax.

Stock Market Glossary

Bear: A person who expects prices to fall and sells securities hoping to make a profit by subsequently repurchasing at a lower price.

Bid: The price at which someone is prepared to buy shares.

Bull: A person who buys securities in the expectation that prices will rise and so give him an opportunity to resell at a profit.

Call option: An option giving the taker the right, but not the obligation, to buy the underlying shares at a specified price on or before a specified date.

Capital gains: The profit made by selling a security that has increased in value during the time you owned it. If the security has decreased in value since you purchased it, the difference between the purchase price and the selling price is called a capital loss.

Capitalisation: In stock market terms, the value of a company, that is, share price multiplied by the number of shares on issue.

Cash Balance: The cash balance is the credit or debit balance in the account. The credit cash balance usually invested in an interest paying money market account.

Equity: The general term for ownership in securities. In a margin account, equity represents the excess of securities value over debit balance.

Futures: A futures contract is an agreement between two parties to buy or sell an underlying asset at a certain time in the future at a certain price. It has standardised date and month of delivery, quantity and price.

Liabilities: Items owed by a person or company.

Mutual fund: Type of investment operated by an investment company that raises money from shareholders and invests it in a portfolio of stocks, bonds, or other securities. These funds offer investors the advantages of diversification and professional management. For these services they typically charge a management fee, which must be disclosed in the prospectus. Each mutual fund has its own investment objectives and strategies.

NASDAQ: (National Association of Securities Dealers Automated Quotations) Owned and operated by the NASD, NASDAQ is the computerized network that provides price quotations for securities traded over the counter as well as many listed securities.

Net Asset Value (NAV): The per share price of a mutual fund. NAV is calculated by subtracting a fund's liabilities from its total assets, then dividing the result by the number of fund shares currently outstanding. A mutual fund calculates its NAV at the end of every market day.

Net Tangible Asset (NTA) backing: Refers to the net assets owned by shareholders of a company at balance date. It expresses the asset value per share, i.e. shareholders' funds less intangibles, less preference capital, divided by the number of ordinary shares.

Over the Counter (OTC): The market in which securities transactions are conducted through a telephone and computer network connecting dealers in stocks and bonds, rather than on the floor of an exchange.

Premium: The amount by which a security is quoted or issued above its par value. The opposite to 'discount'.

Price/Earnings ratio: Shows the number of times the price covers the earnings per share.

Put-call ratio: Put-call ratio is the proportion of puts traded to calls traded. Puts would be bought if investors are bearish while calls would be bought if investors are bullish. Thus, this proportion is an index of investor sentiment.

Put option: An option giving the taker the right, but not the obligation, to sell the underlying shares at a specified price on or before a specified date. The taker is only required to deliver the shares if the option is exercised.

Rally: Short, spirited price rise.

Security: An instrument that represents an ownership interest in a corporation (stock), a creditor relationship with a corporation or governmental body (bond), or rights to ownership through such investment vehicles as options, rights, and warrants.

Career Launcher MBA

Secondary market: The national exchanges and over the counter markets where securities are bought and sold after their original issuance.

Share price index: Measures the level of share prices at any given time. The All Ordinaries Index is calculated using the current prices of companies listed on the Stock Exchange.

Stock split: An increase in the number of outstanding shares of a corporation's stock. In a split, the number of shares increases and the price per share decreases proportionately.

Important Economics Abbreviations

ADB: Asian Development Bank

ADR: American Depository Receipts

AGMARK: Agricultural Marketing Department

AITUC: All-India Trade Union Congress

AMCs: Asset Management Companies

APM: Administered Pricing Mechanism

ARF: Assets Reconstruction Fund

ASSOCHAM: Associated Chamber of Commerce and Industry

BIFR: Board of Industrial and Financial Reconstruction

BIMARU states: Bihar, Madhya Pradesh, Rajasthan and UP

BOP: Balance of Payment

BPL: Below Poverty Line

BSE: Bombay Stock Exchange

CAC: Capital Account Convertibility

CAD: Current Account Deficit

CAG: Comptroller and Auditor General

CBR: Crude Birth Rate

CCBs: Central Cooperative Banks

CII: Confederation of Indian Industry

CIS: Commonwealth of Independent States

CMIE: Centre for Monitoring Indian Economy

COFEPOSA: Conservation of Foreign Exchange and Prevention of Smuggling Activities

CPI: Consumer Price Index

CRISIL: Credit Rating Information Services of India Ltd.

CRR: Cash Reserve Requirements / Cash Reserve Ratio

CSIR: Council of Scientific and Industrial Research

CSO: Central Statistical Organisation

DFHI: Discount and Finance House of India Ltd.

DFIs: Development Financial Institutions

ECB: External Commercial Borrowing

EFTA: European Free Trade Area

EGS: Employment Guarantee Scheme

EOUs: Export Oriented Units

EPCG: Export Promotion Capital Goods

EPF: Employees Provident Fund

EPZs: Export Processing Zones/Export Promotion Zones

ESCAP: Economic and Social Commission for Asia and Pacific

EWS: Economically Weaker Sections

EXIM Bank: Export and Import Bank

FAO: Food and Agriculture Organisation

FCCBs: Foreign Currency Convertible Bonds

FCI: Food Corporation of India

FCNR(B): Foreign Currency Non-residents Accounts (Bank)

FDI: Foreign Direct Investment

FEMA: Foreign Exchange Management Act

FERA: Foreign Exchange Regulation Act

FBI: Federal Bureau of Investigation

FICCI: Federation of Indian Chamber of Commerce & Industry

FIIs: Foreign Institutional Investors

FIPB: Foreign Investment Promotion Board

FIPC: Foreign Investment Promotion Council

FTZ: Free Trade Zones

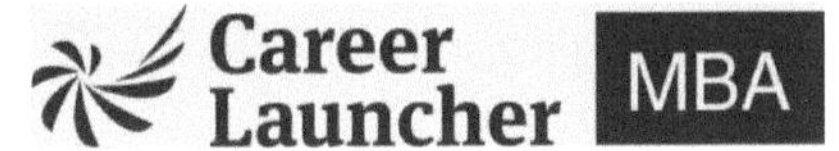

GATT: General Agreement on Tariff and Trade

GDP: Gross Domestic Product

GDRs: Global Depository Receipts

HDFC: Housing Development Finance Corporation

HDI: Human Development Index

HUDCO: Housing and Urban Development Corporation of India

HYVP: High Yielding Varieties Programme

IBM: International Business Machines

IBRD: International Bank for Reconstruction and Development

ICAR: Indian Council of Agricultural Research

ICDS: Integrated Child Development Services Scheme

ICICI: Industrial Credit and Investment Corporation of India

ICRA: Investment Information and Credit Rating Agency of India

IDA: International Development Association

IDBI: Industrial Development Bank of India

IFCI: Industrial Finance Corporation of India

IIP: Index of Industrial Production

IISCO: Indian Iron and Steel Company

IL&FS: Infrastructure Leasing and Financial Services Ltd.

ILO: International Labour Organisation

IMF: International Monetary Fund

IMR: Infant Mortality Rate

INTUC: Indian National Trade Union Congress

IPCL: Indian Petrochemicals Corporation Ltd.

IPO: Initial Public Offers

IRDA: Insurance Regulation and Development Authority

IRDP: Integrated Rural Development Programme

ISPs: Internet Service Providers

ISRO: Indian Space Research Organisation

JPC: Joint Plant Committee/Joint Parliamentary Committee

LIBOR: London Inter-bank Borrowing Rate

MAT: Minimum Alternate Tax

MIS: Management Information System

MISA: Maintenance of Internal Security Act

MNCs: Multi-national Corporations/Companies

MODVAT: Modified Value Added Tax

MOU: Memorandum of Understanding

NABARD: National Bank for Agriculture and Rural Development

NAFED: National Agricultural Cooperative Marketing Federation

NASSCOM: National Association of Software and Services Companies

NAV: Net Asset Value

NBFCs: Non-banking Finance Companies

NCAER: National Council of Applied Economic Research

NDC: National Development Council

NDDB: National Dairy Development Board

NDP: Net Domestic Product

NELP: New Exploration Licensing Policy

NGOs: Non-Government Organisations

NHAI: National Highways Authority of India Ltd.

NHB: National Housing Bank

NHPC: National Hydel Power Corporation

NLM: National Literacy Mission

NPAs: Non-performing Assets

NREP: National Rural Employment Programme

NREGS: National Rural Employment Guarantee Scheme

NRIs: Non-Resident Indians

NSIC: National Small-scale Industries Corporation

NSSO: National Sample Survey Organization

OCBs: Overseas Corporation Bodies

OECD: Organisation for Economic Cooperation and Development

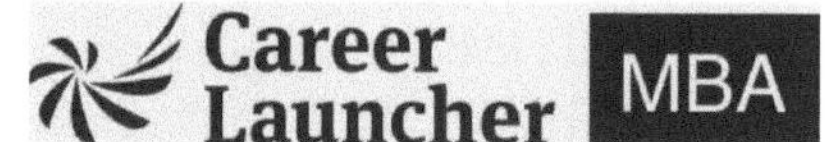

OPEC: Organisation of Petroleum Exporting Countries

OTCEI: Over the Counter Exchange of India

PBT: Profit Before Tax

PDS: Public Distribution System

PFC: Power Finance Corporation

PHDCCI: Pubjab, Haryana and Delhi Chamber of Commerce and Industry

PIO: Persons of Indian Origin

PLF: Plant Load Factor

PPPs: Purchasing Power Parities

PSE: Public Sector Enterprises

PSU: Public Sector Undertakings

RBI: Reserve Bank of India

REC: Rural Electrification Corporation

RIBs: Resurgent India Bonds

RRBs: Regional Rural Banks

SAARC: South Asian Association for Regional Cooperation

SAIL: Steel Authority of India Ltd.

SCBs: State Cooperative Banks

SCI: Shipping Corporation of India

SCOPE: Standing Conference of Public Enterprises

SEBI: Securities and Exchange Board of India

SEBs: State Electricity Boards

SEZs: Special Economic Zones

SHCIL: Stock Holding Corporation of India Ltd.

SIDBI: Small Industries Development Bank of India

SIL: Special Import Licence

SLR: Statutory Liquidity Requirements / Ratio

SSIs: Small Scale Industries

STC: State Trading Corporation

STCI: Securities Trading Corporation of India Ltd.

TISCO: Tata Iron and Steel Co.

TLM: Total Literacy Mission

UNDP: United Nations Development Programme

UNESCO: United Nations Educational, Scientific and Cultural Organisation

UTI: Unit Trust of India

VAT: Value Added Taxation / Tax

VDIS: Voluntary Disclosure Income Scheme

VDS: Voluntary Disclosure Scheme

VRS: Voluntary Retirement Scheme

WHO: World Health Organisation

WILL: Wireless in Local Loop

WPI: Wholesale Price Index

WTO: World Trade Organisation

ZBB: Zero-Base Budgeting

Important Financial Institutions

International

1. World Bank

World Bank is not a bank in true sense but a specialised UN agency made of its 186 member countries. Initially, the World Bank was known as International Bank of Reconstruction and Development (IBRD) and International Development Association (IDA). The World Bank group comprises five closely associated institutions: International Bank of Reconstruction and Development (IBRD), International Development Association (IDA), International Finance Corporation (IFC), Multilateral Investment Guarantee Agency (MIGA) and International Centre for Settlement of Investments Disputes (ICSID). The term 'World Bank' refers specifically to two of the five, IBRD and IDA. The World Bank was founded in 1944 and incorporated in the UN system in 1947.

The World Bank functions like a corporate body. The member countries are shareholders of the bank and the number of shares to each country is distributed according to the size of its economy. The United States is the largest single shareholder, with 16.41 percent of votes, followed by Japan (7.87 per cent), Germany (4.49 per cent), the United Kingdom (4.31 per cent), France (4.31 per cent), China (2.55 per cent) and India (2.55 per cent). The rest of the shares are divided among the other member countries. A Board of Governors represents the World

Bank's government shareholders. Generally, these governors are ministers, such as Ministers of Finance or Ministers of Development of the respective countries. The governors are the ultimate policy-makers in the World Bank. They meet once a year at the Bank's Annual Meetings. **The current President of the World Bank Group is David Malpass. The headquarter of the World Bank is based in Washington DC.**

2. International Bank for Reconstruction and Development (IBRD)

It was formulated in 1944 and established in December 1945 on the eve of the end of Second World War at a time when most of the countries, participated directly and indirectly, were passing through economic crisis. IBRD headquarter is in Washington DC. It started functioning in June 1946. The basic objectives of World Bank are: (i) To provide long-term loans to member countries for economic reconstruction and development, (ii) to extend long-run capital investment for balance of payment equilibrium and balanced development of international trade, (iii) to promote capital investment in member countries, (iv) to provide guarantee for loans granted and to ensure the implementation of development projects. Presently, it has membership of 186 countries. As the World Bank and IMF are interrelated any member country get membership to both or to none.

3. International Development Association (IDA)

It was established on September 24, 1960 as a soft loan window of the World Bank. IDA provides interest-free long-term loans to the member countries. The capital resources include net income transferred by IBRD, subscribed capital by member countries, general replenishments by developed countries, etc. IDA helps provide access to better basic services (such as education, healthcare, and clean water and sanitation) and supports reforms and investments aimed at productivity growth and employment creation. Its headquarter is based in Washington DC.

4. International Financial Corporation (IFC)

IFC is a member of World Bank Group. It was established in July 1956. Its main objectives are to provide loans to private sector, coordinate capital and management and induce capitalist countries to invest in developing countries. This institution provides loans to private industries of developing nations without any government guarantee and thus promotes capital investment in order to ensure the financial support to private sector in the developing countries. It also provides advice and technical assistance to promote sustainable development. Presently, it has 181 member countries. The authorised capital of IFC is US $2.45 billion. Its headquarter is in Washington DC.

5. International Monetary Fund (IMF)

International Monetary Fund was established on December 27, 1945, headquartered at Washington DC, USA, on the recommendation of Bretton Woods Conference and also known as one of the Bretton Wood twins, the other being the World Bank (IBRD and its associate financial institutions). It started its operation on March 1, 1947. It was established to promote international monetary cooperation and system of multilateral payments, and to ensure balanced international trade, stable exchange rate, etc., and also to provide economic assistance to the member countries. The value of Special Drawing Right (SDR) is determined by the currencies of five largest exporting member countries (US Dollar, Deutsche Mark, Yen, Franc and Pound Sterling). USA is the largest quota holder with quota of 17.52 percent of the total.

6. United Nations Development Programme (UNDP)

At the United Nations Millennium Summit, world leaders put development at the heart of the global agenda by adopting the Millennium Development Goals (MDGs), which set clear targets for reducing poverty, hunger, disease, illiteracy, environmental degradation and discrimination against women by 2015. On the ground in 166 countries, UNDP uses its global network to help the UN system and its partners to raise awareness and track progress, while it connects countries to the knowledge and resources needed to achieve these goals. UNDP headquarter locations are in New York, Geneva, Copenhagen and Bonn.

UNDP is basically engaged in building democratic governance, poverty reduction, crisis prevention and recovery in case of crisis along with the preparation of world development report. **Achim Steiner is the head of UNDP**.

7. Asian Development Bank (ADB)

It was established in 1966 with an aim to reduce poverty in the Asia-Pacific region. It is a multilateral development financial institution. Its headquarter is in Manila, Philippines. **Presently, it has 67 members. The current**

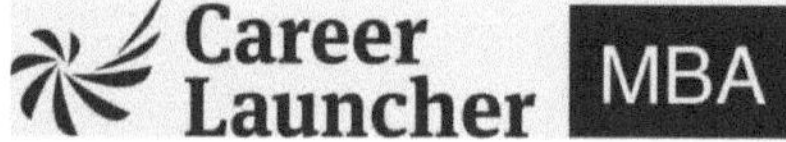

President is Takehiko Nakao, who succeeded Tadao Chino in 2005. The headquarters of the bank is at 6 ADB Avenue, Mandaluyong City, Metro Manila, Philippines. Its basic functions are to extend loans and equity investments to the member developing countries and to provide the necessary technical assistance for the various projects and it also promotes and facilitates investment of public and private capital for development. Asian Development Bank is managed by a Board of Governors, a Board of Directors, a President, three Vice-Presidents and the head of departments and offices. India is a founding member of Asian Development Bank.

National

1. Federation of Indian Chamber of Commerce and Industry (FICCI)

The Federation of Indian Chambers of Commerce and Industry (FICCI) was established in 1927, on the advice of Mahatma Gandhi, to garner support for India's independence and to further the interests of the Indian business community. Starting with 24 members, the number rose to 103 by 1947. Today, with a membership of over 500 Chambers of Commerce, Trade Associations and Industry bodies, it speaks directly and indirectly for over 2,50,000 business units – small, medium and large – employing around 20 million people. FICCI's annual sessions are major economic landmarks where policy issues are spelt out and a two-way communication between the Government and Industry is fostered. This high profile event is addressed by the Prime Minister of India each year. Various sessions take place which analyse the past business trends and offer suggestions for the future. FICCI's 'Think Tank' consists of eminent economists, planners, civil servants and industrialists who meet regularly in structured monthly meetings to discuss important macro level issues confronting the nation. **Presently, Sandeep Somany is the President of FICCI and its headquarter is in New Delhi.**

2. Finance Commission

The First Finance Commission was constituted under Art. 280 by a Presidential Order dated November 22, 1951, under the chairmanship of KC Neogy. The Finance Commission is appointed by the President for a period of five years having five members in all. It shall be the duty of the Commission to make recommendations to the President as to: (a) the distribution between the Union and the States of the net proceeds of taxes which are to be, or may be, divided between them under this Chapter and the allocation between the States of the respective shares of such proceeds; (b) the principles which should govern the grants-in-aid of the revenues of the States out of the Consolidated Fund of India.

15th Finance Commission

Former Planning Commission member N.K. Singh was appointed chairman of the 15th Finance Commission, which, among other things, has been asked to look into the impact of the goods and services tax (GST) on finances of both the centre and states, said a government notification.

The other members of the commission, which is required to submit its report by October 2019, are former economic affairs secretary Shaktikanta Das and former chief economic adviser Ashok Lahiri, Niti Aayog member Ramesh Chand and Georgetown University professor Anoop Singh. The commission will review the current status of the finance, deficit, debt levels, cash balances and fiscal discipline efforts of the union and the states.

It will also recommend a fiscal consolidation road map for sound fiscal management. As per Article 280 of the Constitution, the commission is required to make recommendations on the distribution of the net proceeds of taxes between the centre and the states. The commission also suggests the principles which should govern the grants in aid of the revenues of the states out of the consolidated fund of India.

3. Securities and Exchange Board of India (SEBI)

Securities and Exchange Board of India (SEBI) was established in 1988 to regulate and develop the growth of the capital market. SEBI regulates the working of stock exchanges and intermediaries such as stockbrokers and merchant bankers, accords approval for mutual funds, and registers Foreign Institutional Investors who wish to trade in Indian scrips. Section 11(1) of the SEBI Act propounds that it shall be the duty of the Board to protect the interests of investors in securities and to promote the development of, and to regulate the securities market, by such measures as it thinks fit. **The present Chairman of the SEBI is Ajay Tyagi and SEBI is headquartered in Mumbai.**

4. National Association of Software and Service Companies (NASSCOM)

It represents some 700 Indian companies. In a decade, the non-profit group has become the single voice of India's IT sector, guiding the government, sponsoring seminars and conferences, and churning out rosy forecasts for Indian technologists. **Ms. Debjani Ghosh, former MD, Intel**

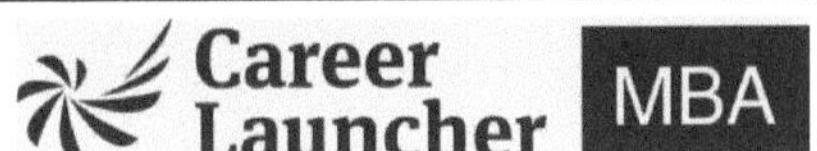

South Asia, is the current and first women President of NASSCOM, succeeding Mr. R Chandrashekhar, President, NASSCOM on completion of his term in March, 2018. The group has offices in Delhi, Mumbai, Bangalore and Hyderabad.

5. National Stock Exchange (NSE)

The National Stock Exchange of India Limited has genesis in the report of the High Powered Study Group on Establishment of New Stock Exchanges, which recommended promotion of a National Stock Exchange by financial institutions (FIs) to provide access to investors from all across the country on an equal footing. Based on the recommendations, NSE was promoted by leading financial institutions at the behest of the Government of India and was incorporated in November 1992 as a tax-paying company unlike other stock exchanges in the country with its headquarter in Mumbai. **Presently, Vikram Limaye is the Managing Director and CEO of NSE.**

On its recognition as a stock exchange under the Securities Contracts (Regulation) Act, 1956, in April 1993, NSE commenced operations in the Wholesale Debt Market (WDM) segment in June 1994. The Capital Market (Equities) segment commenced operations in November 1994 and operations in Derivatives segment commenced in June 2000.

6. Bombay Stock Exchange (BSE)

The Stock Exchange, Mumbai, popularly known as 'BSE' was established in 1875 as 'The Native Share and Stock Brokers Association'. It is the oldest one in Asia, even older than the Tokyo Stock Exchange, which was established in 1878. It is the first Stock Exchange in the Country to have obtained permanent recognition in 1956 from the Government of India under the Securities Contracts (Regulation) Act,1956. BSE is now a corporatised and demutualised entity and is now known as BSE Ltd.

The Exchange, while providing an efficient and transparent market for trading in securities, debt and derivatives upholds the interests of the investors and ensures redressal of their grievances whether against the companies or its own member-brokers. It also strives to educate and enlighten the investors by conducting investor education programmes and making available to them necessary informative inputs. It has more than 4700 companies listed on it thus making its the World's no. 1 stock exchange in terms of numbers of listed companies on the stock exchanges throughout the world. **The Present MD and CEO of BSE Ltd. is Mr. Ashish Chauhan.**

7. National Bank for Agriculture and Rural Development (NABARD)

National Bank for Agriculture and Rural Development Act, 1981, was passed by the Indian Parliament and NABARD was established on July 12, 1982 with an initial capital of Rs. 100 crore. The capital is enhanced to Rs. 2,000 crore subscribed by Government of India and Reserve Bank of India. NABARD is established as a development Bank, in terms of the Preamble of the Act, 'for providing and regulating credit and other facilities for the promotion and development of agriculture, small-scale industries, cottage and village industries, handicrafts and other rural crafts and other allied economic activities in rural areas with a view to promoting integrated rural development and securing prosperity of rural areas and for matters connected therewith or incidental thereto.

NABARD took over the functions of the erstwhile Agricultural Credit Department (ACD) and Rural Planning and Credit Cell (RPCC) of RBI and Agricultural Refinance and Development Corporation (ARDC). Its subscribed and paid-up capital was Rs.100 crore which was enhanced to Rs. 500 crore, contributed by the Government of India (GoI) and RBI in equal proportions. It is now enhanced to Rs. 2,000 crore. **Presently Harsh Kumar Bhanwala is the chairman of NABARD.**

8. Industrial Finance Corporation of India (IFCI)

At the time of independence in 1947, India's capital market was relatively under-developed. Although there was significant demand for new capital, there was a dearth of providers. Merchant bankers and underwriting firms were almost non-existent. And, commercial banks were not equipped to provide long-term industrial finance in any significant manner.

It is against this backdrop that the government established the Industrial Finance Corporation of India (IFCI) on July 1, 1948, as the first development financial institution in the country to cater to the long-term finance needs of the industrial sector. The newly-established DFI was provided access to low-cost funds through the central bank's Statutory Liquidity Ratio or SLR which in turn enabled it to provide loans and advances to corporate borrowers at concessional rates.

This arrangement continued until the early 1990s when it was recognized that there was need for greater flexibility to respond to the changing financial system. It was also felt that IFCI should directly access the capital markets for its funds needs. It is with this objective that the constitution of IFCI was changed in 1993 from a statutory corporation to a company under the Indian Companies Act, 1956. Subsequently, the name of the company was also changed to 'IFCI Limited' with effect from October 1999.

IFCI has fulfilled its original mandate as a DFI by providing long-term financial support to all segments of Indian industry. It has also been chiefly instrumental in translating the government's development priorities into reality. Until the establishment of ICICI in 1956 and IDBI in 1964, IFCI remained solely responsible for implementation of the government's industrial policy initiatives. Its contribution to the modernization of Indian industry, export promotion, import substitution, entrepreneurship development, pollution control, energy conservation and generation of both direct and indirect employment is noteworthy. **Presently Dr. Emandi Sankara Rao is the MD and CEO of IFCI and its headquarter is in Delhi.**

9. Confederation of Indian Industry (CII)
The Confederation of Indian Industry (CII) works to create and sustain an environment conducive to the growth of industry in India, partnering industry and government alike through advisory and consultative processes.

CII is a non-government, not-for-profit, industry-led and industry-managed organisation, playing a proactive role in India's development process. Founded over 107 years ago, it is India's premier business association, with a direct membership of over 4,800 companies from the private as well as public sectors, including SMEs and MNCs and indirect membership of over 50,000 companies from 226 national and regional sectoral associations.

CII helps in changing trends by working closely with government on policy issues, boosting efficiency, competitiveness and expanding business opportunities for industry through a range of specialised services and global linkages. It also provides a platform for sectoral consensus building and networking. Major emphasis is laid on projecting a positive image of business, assisting industry identify and execute corporate citizenship programmes.

With 37 offices in India, 13 overseas in Afghanistan, Australia, Austria, Belgium, China, France, Israel, Italy, Malaysia, Singapore, South Africa, UK, USA and institutional partnerships with 216 counterpart organisations in 94 countries, CII serves as a reference point for Indian Industry and the international business community. **Presently, Ms. Shobana Kamineni is the President of CII. Its headquarter is in Delhi.**

Performance of Indian Economy under various Plans

Planning Commission
The Planning Commission was set up by a Resolution of the Government of India in March 1950 in pursuance of declared objectives of the Government to promote a rapid rise in the standard of living of the people by efficient exploitation of the resources of the country, increasing production and offering opportunities to all for employment in the service of the community. The Planning Commission was charged with the responsibility of making assessment of all resources of the country, augmenting deficient resources, formulating plans for the most effective and balanced utilisation of resources and determining priorities. Jawaharlal Nehru was the first Chairman of the Planning Commission. Planning Commission was replaced by National Institution for Transforming India, also called NITI Aayog on January 1, 2015.

National Institution for Transforming India (NITI Aayog)
The National Institution for Transforming India, also called NITI Aayog, was formed via a resolution of the Union Cabinet on January 1, 2015. NITI Aayog is the premier policy 'Think Tank' of the Government of India, providing both directional and policy inputs. While designing strategic and long term policies and programmes for the Government of India, NITI Aayog also provides relevant technical advice to the Centre and States.

The Government of India, in keeping with its reform agenda, constituted the NITI Aayog to replace the Planning Commission instituted in 1950. This was done in order to better serve the needs and aspirations of the people of India. An important evolutionary change from the past, NITI Aayog acts as the quintessential platform

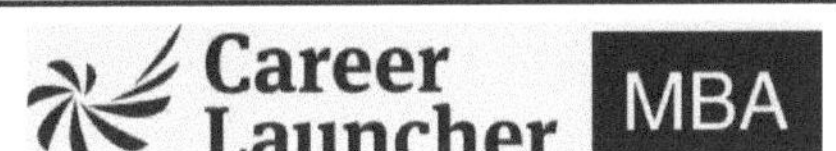

of the Government of India to bring States to act together in national interest, and thereby fosters Cooperative Federalism.

The current Team Members of **NITI Aayog**

Chairperson
Shri Narendra Modi, Hon'ble Prime Minister

Vice Chairperson
Dr. Rajiv Kumar

Full-Time Members
Dr. Bibek Debroy
Shri V.K. Saraswat
Prof. Ramesh Chand

Chief Executive Officer
Shri Amitabh Kant

First five-year plan (1951–56)
During the first five-year plan, India was facing severe food shortage and a climbing inflation rate. Keeping in view these problems, the agriculture sector including irrigation and power projects, was given the higher priority. India also had to bring some sort of equilibrium in the distribution of income. The total outlay allocated was Rs. 2,069 crore (later revised to Rs. 2,378 crore) in which about 45 per cent was to be spent on public sector. Most of the targets were met successfully and the price level lowered. The main aim of rise in the rate of investment also gained moderate success.

Second five-year plan (1956–61)
In the background of the success of first five-year plan, it was felt that Indian economy had reached a stage where more priority should be given to heavy and basic industries of the economy. The main goal was to promote a pattern of development that would result in the establishment of a defined socialistic pattern. The main objectives of this plan were to increase national income by 25 per cent, rapid industrialisation and more even distribution of economic power. Total proposed outlay was Rs. 7,900 crore which was just double of the previous five-year plan with the aim to increase the rate of investment to 11 per cent.

Third five-year plan (1961–66)
This plan was aimed at securing self-sustaining growth as the planners felt that the Indian economy had reached the take-off stage. The main objectives of this plan were to achieve self-sufficiency in the production of food grains, expand basic industries and employment opportunities and reduction in the disparities of income, wealth and economic power. This plan was aimed at the increase in the national income by 30 per cent and per capita income by 17 per cent. Due to the conflict with China in 1962 and with Pakistan in 1965, major shift towards defence expenditure occurred. The proposed outlay for this plan was Rs. 11,600 crore in which the actual public sector outlay was Rs. 8,500 crore.

Annual Plans
Because of conflicts and two successive years of severe drought, the fourth plan was delayed by three years. During the war period, India also faced reduction in foreign aid for consistent economic development. This period also witnessed the devaluation of currency, inflationary recession, general rise in price level and erosion of available resources. So in-between 1966 and 1969, three annual plans were formulated and these were termed as 'plan holiday'.

Fourth five-year plan (1969–74)
This plan was aimed at stable growth and self-reliance with reduction in fluctuation in agricultural production and the dependency on foreign aids. This plan also gave emphasis on improving the condition of less privileged and weaker sections by reduction of concentration of wealth and income. This plan was aimed at the growth of national income by 5,5 per cent and increasing net domestic product from Rs. 29,071 crore to Rs. 38,306 crore. The proposed outlay for this plan was Rs. 24,880 crore.

Fifth five-year plan (1974–79)
This plan was introduced against the backdrop of severe economic crisis because of heavy inflation and hike in oil price in the international market. The plan was aimed at growth with social justice and to bring inflation under control along with stability in the economic status with targeted annual growth rate of 5.5 per cent in the national income. This plan also gave emphasis on the increasing the rate of domestic saving. However, the Janta Party terminated this plan in the fourth year (1978) when it came to power. The proposed outlay for this plan was Rs. 53,410 crore in which the actual public sector outlay was Rs. 39,430 crore.

Sixth five-year plan (1978–83 and 1980–85)

There were two sixth five-year plans because of change of the government at the centre. One was made by the Janta Party government (1978-83) and was terminated by reinstated Congress government which introduced another plan (1980-85). Janta Party's plan stressed at higher production with greater employment opportunities for people living below poverty line. Congress government rejected the Janta Party's plan and brought back the Nehru model of planned growth with an objective of reducing poverty by expanding the economy. 'Garibi Hatao' and strengthening the infrastructure of both the primary and secondary sectors were the main objectives. Extra stress was laid on tackling the interrelated problems through a systematic approach. The sixth five-year plan succeeded in achieving reasonable rate of economic growth. The actual expenditure in the public sector was Rs. 1,09,290 crore (proposed public sector outlay was Rs. 97,500 crore). The total proposed outlay for this plan was Rs. 1,58,710 crore. Average annual growth rate of the plan was 5.2 per cent.

Seventh five-year plan (1985–90)

This plan stressed on such policies and programmes which aimed at rapid growth in food grain production, increased employment opportunities and productivity within the defined parameters of the plan like self-reliance, modernisation, social justice, etc. Due to consistent favourable weather conditions, food grain production growth was 3.23 per cent while GDP grew at an average rate of 5.8 per cent, 0.8 per cent more than the targeted growth rate. The total expenditure of the seventh plan was Rs. 2,18,729.62 crore (21.52 per cent more than the proposed outlay of Rs. 1,80,000 crore) in the public sector. The total proposed outlay was Rs. 3,48,150 crore.

Annual plans (1990-91, 1991-92)

The eighth plan could not be launched as per schedule because of a series of changes in the governments at the Centre. This led to two annual plans based on the same objectives as those of the eighth plan and major thrust was given to employment and social transformation.

Eighth five-year plan (1992-97)

After discussion on a series of approaches, the fourth version of the five-year plan was finally approved as the country was going through severe economic crisis caused by worsening balance of payment situation, heavy external debts, very high budget deficits, growing inflation rate and recession of industries. In order to pursue higher growth rate, several structural adjustment policies were introduced gradually. The government introduced the process of fiscal reforms for the first time with a vision of bringing dynamism to the economy. The main objectives were accelerated economic growth and improvement in the quality of life of the common man. The plan was aimed at an average annual growth rate of 5.6 per cent with average industrial growth rate of 7.5 per cent. The total expenditure during the eighth plan was Rs. 4,95,669 crore (revised) at current prices while the proposed public sector outlay was Rs. 4,34,100 crore. In this plan, the average annual growth rate of 6.8 per cent was achieved against the targeted 5.6 per cent.

Ninth five-year plan (1997-2002)

This plan was aimed at growth with social justice and equality. In this plan, priority was given to accelerating the growth rate of economy with stable price, agricultural and rural development with emphasis on the provision of basic minimum services like drinking water, education, health care, shelter, etc. and control over population growth. The targeted GDP growth rate was envisaged at 7 per cent per annum, then was revised to 6.5 per cent due to change in the national and global economic scenario, but the ninth plan achieved GDP growth rate of 5.35 per cent only because of decline in the growth rate in agriculture and manufacturing sector. The ninth plan also failed to achieve target rate of growth of saving and investment and to check the growth of unemployment. The public sector outlay for the ninth five-year plan was placed at Rs. 8,59,200 crore (33 per cent more than the eighth plan) while the outlay actually realised was Rs. 7,05,818 crore (seen as the failure of both the Centre and the state).

10th five-year plan (2002-2007)

The 10th plan targeted an average annual growth rate of GDP by 8.1 per cent for the plan period to be achieved by a steady acceleration in the course of the plan period from around 6.7 per cent targeted in 2002-2003, to 9.3 per cent in the terminal year 2006-2007. This was expected to lay the basis for a growth rate of above nine per cent during the eleventh plan period.

Sectorally, the 10th plan targeted growth of agricultural GDP at four per cent per year, aiming to reverse the deceleration in the second half of the 1990s – from 3.2 per cent in the period 1980-1996 to 2.6 per cent in the period 1996-2002. GDP growth of around 8 per cent was to require industrial sector growth of over 10 per cent.

India's Vision for the 11th Five Year Plan :
The 11th Plan provides an opportunity to restructure policies to achieve a new vision based on faster, more broad - based and inclusive growth. It is designed to reduce poverty and focus on bridging the various divides that continue to fragment our society. The 11th Plan must aim at putting the economy on a sustainable growth trajectory with a growth rate of approximately 10 per cent by the end of the Plan period. It will create productive employment at a faster pace than before, and target robust agriculture growth at 4% per Year.

It must seek to reduce disparities across regions and communities by ensuring access to basic physical infrastructure as well as health and education services to all. It must recognize gender as a cross - cutting theme across all sectors and commit to respect and promote the rights of the common person. Rapid growth is an essential part of our strategy for two reasons. Firstly, it is only in a rapidly growing economy that we can expect to sufficiently raise the incomes of the mass of our population to bring about a general improvement in living conditions. Secondly, rapid growth is necessary to generate the resources needed to provide basic services to all. Work done within the Planning Commission and elsewhere suggests that the economy can accelerate from 8 per cent per Year to an average of around 9% over the 11th Plan period, provided appropriate policies are put in place.

With population growing at 1.5% per Year, 9% growth in GDP would double the real per capita income in 10 Years. This must be combined with policies that will ensure that this per capita income growth is broad based, benefiting all sections of the population, especially those who have thus far remained deprived. A key element of the strategy for inclusive growth must be an all out effort to provide the mass of our people the access to basic facilities such as health, education, clean drinking water etc. While in the short run these essential public services impact directly on welfare, in the longer run they determine economic opportunities for the future.

The private sector, including farming, micro, small and medium enterprises (MSMEs) and the corporate sector, has a critical role to play in achieving the objective of faster and more inclusive growth. This sector accounts for 76% of the total investment in the economy and an even larger share in employment and output. MSMEs, in particular, have a vital role in expanding production in a regionally balanced manner and generating widely dispersed off - farm employment. Our policies must aim at creating an environment in which entrepreneurship can flourish at all levels, not just at the top.

Twelfth five year plan (2012-2017):
The basic objectives for the Twelfth plan is "faster,more inclusive and sustainable growth".Its aim to renew Indian economy and use the funds from government in improving the facilities of education, sanitation and health. The plan would infuse a huge fund of 47.7 lakh crore rupees that will help to accomplish the economic growth to an average level of 8.2 percent. 12th five-year plan is guided by the policy guidelines and principles to revive the following Indian economy, which registered a growth rate of meager 5.5 percent in the first quarter of the financial year 2012-13. The plan aims towards the betterment of the infrastructural projects of the nation avoiding all types of bottlenecks. The UID (Unique Identification Number) will act as a platform for cash transfer of the subsidies in the plan. The plan aims towards achieving a growth of 4 percent in agriculture and to reduce poverty by 10 percentage points, by 2017.

This plan also proposes a growth target of 8 percent. As far as infrastructure sector is concerned, there is a proposal of increasing the investment in this sector to 9 per cent of the GDP by the end of the Plan period.

Niti Aayog has launched three-year action plan from April 1 after the end of 12th Five Year Plan on March 31. Niti Aayog has also been entrusted the work on the 15-year Vision Document and a seven year strategy, which would guide the government's development works till 2030.

Some other major targets are:
- Increasing green cover by one million hectare every year and adding 30,000 MW of renewable energy generation capacity in the Plan period.
- To reduce emission intensity of the GDP in line with the target of 20-25 reduction by 2020 over 2005 levels.
- Raising agriculture output to 4 per cent for the full Plan.
- manufacturing sector growth to 10 per cent for the full Plan.
- Target of adding over 100,000 MW of power generation capacity in the 12th five year plan.

Stock Exchanges in India

S. No	Name of the Stock Exchange	Addresses
1	OTC Exchange of India	92, Maker Towers F, Cuffe Parade, Mumbai - 400005
2	The Uttar Pradesh Stock Exchange Association Ltd.	Padam Towers, 14/113, Civil Lines, Kanpur - 208001
3	Jaipur Stock Exchange Ltd.	Stock Exchange Building, JLN Marg, Malviya Nagar, Jaipur - 302017
4	Madras Stock Exchange Ltd.	P O Box no 183, New No: 30, (old no:11), Second Line Beach, Chennai - 600001
5	Cochin Stock Exchange Ltd.	MES Dr P K Abdul Gafoor Memorial Cultural Complex, 36/1565, 4th Floor, Judges Avenue, Kaloor, Cochin - 682017
6	Bangalore Stock Exchange Ltd.	Stock Exchange Towers, 51, 1st Cross, J C Road, Bangalore - 560027
7	National Stock Exchange of India Ltd.	Exchange Plaza, Bandra-Kurla Complex, Bandra(E), Mumbai - 400051
8	Gauhati Stock Exchange Ltd.	H/NO, 57 2A, 2nd Floor, Shine Tower, Sati Jaymati Road, Arya Chowk, Rehabari, Guwahati - 781 008.
9	The Ludhiana Stock Exchange Ltd.	Feroze Gandhi Market, Ludhiana - 141001
10	The Calcutta Stock Exchange Association Ltd.	7, Lyons Range, Kolkata - 700001
11	Bhubaneshwar Stock Exchange Ltd.	Stock Exchange Bhavan, P-2, Jayadev Vihar,P.O. – Chandrasekharpur, Bhubaneswar – 751 023"
12	The Delhi Stock Exchange Ltd.	DSE House, 3/1, Asaf Ali Road, New Delhi - 110002
13	Vadodara Stock Exchange Ltd.	Fortune Tower, Sayajigunj, Vadodara - 390005
14	Ahmedabad Stock Exchange Ltd.	Kamdhenu Complex, Opp, Sahajanand College, Panjarapole, Ambawadi, Ahmedabad - 380001
15	Madhya Pradesh Stock Exchange Ltd.	Palika Plaza, Phase II, 201, 2nd Floor, MTH Compound, Indore - 452001
16	Pune Stock Exchange Ltd.	Shivleela Chambers, 752, Sadashiv Peth, RB Kumthekar Marg, Pune - 411030
17	Bombay Stock Exchange Ltd.	Phiroze Jeejeebhoy Towers , Dalal Street, Mumbai - 400023
18	Inter connected Stock Exchange of India Ltd.	International Infotech Park, Tower 7, 5th Floor, Sector 30, Vashi, Navi Mumbai - 400703
19	MCX Stock Exchange Ltd	Exchange Square, 3rd Floor, Suren Road, Chakala, Andheri (East) Mumbai - 400 093.

The last two exchanges formed and their role

National Stock Exchange

In the 1990's when the Indian economy was moving in too many directions the country was facing severe shortage of resources in the form of investment despite a healthy saving rate. India was looking for strong financial infrastructure through widening the investor base within the country for which it had to institute some sort of remedies to reduce the structural weakness and inefficiencies prevailing in the stock market, primary market and other financial sectors like banking and insurance. The newly formed Securities and Exchange Board of India under GV Ramakrishna brought various malpractices prevailed in the existing stock markets like benami possessions, outdated trading, settlement mechanism, lack of transparency in transactions, time gap between actual purchasing and physical delivery, improper disclosure, price manipulation, inside trading, lack of liquidity, etc., into the limelight. Prior to this Narsimhan Committee, formed to recommend the implemental measures to strengthen the financial sector, had been in favour of more powers to SEBI in order to bring about transparency. It was also required for attracting more Non-resident Indians and Foreign Institutional Investors. This led to the formation of Pherwani Committee to explore the various stock exchange reforms. Pherwani Committee suggested the establishment of central depository trust,

scripless trading supplemented by increased use of technology, a national market system, efficient and uniform settlement cycle, etc. This led to the formation of National Stock Exchange.

The existing pioneer Bombay Stock Exchange, which had dominated the market because of its hitherto unassailable position, being an exclusive broker's association, did not support the concept of Stock Exchange regulations. They did not like the regulations coming in their way, which could harm their interest. They also tried to create hurdles through strike and law suits. Eventually, the National Stock Exchange came into existence in 1994, promoted by Industrial Development Bank of India, Industrial Credit and Investment Corporation of India, Industrial Finance Corporation of India, all Insurance Corporations, selected commercial banks and others in response to the Government of India's request to bring more transparency and efficiency in the stock trade. It was because of National Stock Exchange the market saw the elimination of existing traditional fish market style of floor trading. The National Stock Exchange has been instrumental in introducing a nationwide network of computerised trading with more than 280-odd interconnected centres and automated screen-based trading for foreign institutional investors. It also had shortened the settlement period and made it efficient and transparent.

Trading at the National Stock Exchange can be categorized into Wholesale Debt Market and Capital Market. The former mode of trading is similar to money market but here the transactions related to government securities, treasury bills, public sector unit bonds, commercial paper, etc. In National Stock Exchange, both recognised trading members (representing themselves and clients), and participants like banks can trade.

Thus, the National Stock Exchange introduced an integrated and more professional stock market trade into the country, where investors could now trade on an equal footing. Increasing Internet use and dematerialised form of trade now attracted more and more people aware of the stock market practices and attracted by its user-friendliness. Since capital market is a major resource of capital coming through small, institutional and foreign investors, National Stock Exchange has a vital role to play in the growth of Indian economy.

Over The Counter Exchange of India (OTCEI)

The exposed functional inefficiencies and lack of transparency of the traditional trading system created a demand for an organisation, that was capable of providing better and more efficient services. In response to this need, the Over The Counter Exchange of India came into the picture. Incorporated in 1990, under the Securities Contracts Regulation Act, 1956, OTCEI was set-up to help promoters to raise finance for new projects in a cost effective manner while providing transparency in the trading operations. OTCEI introduced many new concepts to the Indian capital markets like screen-based nationwide trading, sponsorship of companies, market making and scripless trading.

Starting its business in 1992, OTCEI was the country's first electronic exchange, was supported by the country's premier financial institutions - Unit Trust of India, Industrial Credit and Investment Corporation of India, Industrial Development Bank of India, SBI Capital Markets, Industrial Finance Corporation of India, General Insurance Corporation and its subsidiaries and CanBank Financial Services, which practically assured its success.

Some of the unique features of OTCEI are: only receipts of actual share certificates are issued (These receipts can be used for other types of transaction) which remain with the custodian; the investor gets the actual rate and amount of trading made by him/her instantly; and faster settlement and transfer process in comparison to other exchanges is the inevitable outcome.

Part – III
General Knowledge
Tests 1 to 5

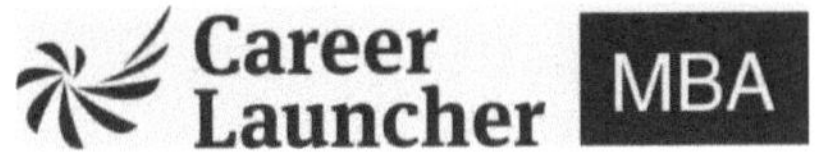

Career Launcher MBA

Test – 1

Number of questions: 40   **Time Allowed: 20 mins.**

1. Who was the person behind the 'Kuka movement'?
   (a) Kunwar Singh   (b) V. B. Phadke
   (c) Guru Ram Singh   (d) Sir Syed Ahmad Khan

2. In the 552 — strong Lok Sabha, how many members are there from the Union Territories?
   (a) 10   (b) 20
   (c) 30   (d) 40

3. Which of the following personalities gave 'The Laws of Heredity'?
   (a) Robert Hook   (b) G. J. Mendel
   (c) Chearles Darwin   (d) William Harvey

4. Name the personality who was also known as Deshbandhu.
   (a) S. Radhakrishanan (b) G. K. Gokhale
   (c) Chittaranjan Das   (d) Madan Mohan Malviya

5. Which of the following is NOT the language enshrined in the eighth schedule of the Indian Constitution, as the language of the state?
   (a) Nepali   (b) Kashmiri
   (c) English   (d) Konkani

6. The capital of Uttarakhand is
   (a) Masoorie   (b) Dehra Dun
   (c) Nainital   (d) None of these

7. *Geet Govind* is a famous creation of
   (a) Banabhatt   (b) Kalidas
   (c) Jayadev   (d) Bharat Muni

8. Which of the following represents the Finance Commissions that have been set-up so far?
   (a) 10   (b) 11
   (c) 12   (d) 15

9. World Trade Organization came into existence in
   (a) 1992   (b) 1993
   (c) 1994   (d) 1995

10. According to the Constitution of India, which of the following is NOT one of the main organs of the Government?
    (a) Legislature   (b) Bureaucracy
    (c) Executive   (d) Judiciary

11. In which year did the Cabinet Mission arrive in India?
    (a) 1942   (b) 1943
    (c) 1945   (d) 1946

12. Panchayati Raj comes under
    (a) Residual list   (b) Concurrent list
    (c) State list   (d) Union list

13. Which of the following constitutional amendments was responsible for deleting the right to property from the list of fundamentals rights?
    (a) 43rd amendment   (b) 44th amendment
    (c) 48th amendment   (d) 52nd amendment

14. *Harshcharita* and *Kadambari* are the works of
    (a) Kalhan   (b) Panini
    (c) Banabhatta   (d) Patanjali

15. When did the war of Americans Independence take place?
    (a) 1770   (b) 1772
    (c) 1774   (d) 1776

16. Which of the following countries is NOT a member of SAARC?
    (a) Maldives   (b) Bhutan
    (c) Malaysia   (d) Nepal

17. Bloemfontein is the judicial capital of
    (a) South Africa   (b) Denmark
    (c) Columbia   (d) The Netherlands

18. Which of the following planets is NOT a terrestrial planet?
    (a) Mercury   (b) Venus
    (c) Earth   (d) Saturn

19. What is the minimum age required to become the President, Vice-President of India or Governor of Indian state?
    (a) 21 years   (b) 25 years
    (c) 30 years   (d) 35 years

20. The Treaty of Versailles was signed in
    (a) 1914   (b) 1916
    (c) 1919   (d) 1923

General Knowledge

21. Which of the following personalities was the first to climb Mount Everest twice?
(a) Tenzing Norway   (b) Tamba Tsheri
(c) Nawang Gombu   (d) Phu Dorjee

22. The controversial Tehri Dam was built over
(a) Ganga   (b) Godavari
(c) Bhagirathi   (d) Narmada

23 Which of the following constitutional amendments was responsible for the inclusion of Konkani, Manipuri and Nepali languages in the eighth schedule of the Constitution?
(a) 68th amendment   (b) 70th amendment
(c) 71st amendment   (d) 76th amendment

24. Vincent van Gogh was a
(a) German poet   (b) Dutch painter
(c) Polish scientist   (d) French musician

25. Who was the first premier of Pakistan?
(a) Liaquat Ali Khan
(b) Mohammad Ali Jinnah
(c) Ali Mohammad Khusro
(d) Mohammed Ayub Khan

26. Telephone was invented by
(a) J. L. Baird
(b) Alexander Graham Bell
(c) K. Macmillan
(d) None of them

27. The famous Chinese traveller Fa-hien came to India during the reign of
(a) Harshvardhan   (b) Chandragupta II
(c) Kanishka   (d) Samudragupta

28. Name the Governor-General and the first Viceroy of India during whose tenure the 1857 revolt took place.
(a) Lord Rippon   (b) Lord Curzon
(c) Lord Canning   (d) Lord Hardinge

29. The absorption of ink by a blotting paper is based on
(a) Newton third law of motion
(b) Bernoulli's theorem
(c) Pascal's law
(d) Capillary action

30. The point in the orbit of any artificial satellite of earth which is at the maximum distance from the earth is known as
(a) Perigee   (b) Aphelion
(c) Antipodes   (d) Apogee

31. Mother Teresa won the Nobel Prize of peace in
(a) 1977   (b) 1979
(c) 1982   (d) 1984

32. Topographical map of India is approved by
(a) Archaeological Survey of India
(b) Geographical Survey of India
(c) Surveyor General of India
(d) None of these

33. This country is known as the 'Sugar Bowl of the World'. Identify it from the given options.
(a) Brazil   (b) Cuba
(c) Mexico   (d) Algeria

34. The North-East Frontier Agency became the Union Territory of Arunachal Pradesh in
(a) 1947   (b) 1950
(c) 1963   (d) 1972

35. Maastricht Treaty is related to
(a) environment pollution
(b) European unification
(c) landmines
(d) biological weapons

36. National Science Day is observed on
(a) January 4   (b) February 28
(c) March 11   (d) August 5

37. Capital of East Timor is
(a) Kiev   (b) Dili
(c) Grozny   (d) Bratislava

38. Can you identify this bowler who is the first in the history of the world cricket to have claimed 500 wickets in the One day Internationals?
(a) Shane Warne   (b) Wasim Akram
(c) Courtney Walsh   (d) Muttiah Muralitharan

39. The first woman Chief Minister of an Indian state is
(a) Sarojini Naidu   (b) Indira Gandhi
(c) Sucheta Kripalani   (d) Rajkumari Amrita Kaur

40. This organelle of the human body is known as the 'powerhouse of the cell'. Name it from the given options.
(a) Golgi bodies   (b) Mitochondria
(c) Lysosomes   (d) Chloroplasm

Test – 2

Number of questions: 40

Time Allowed: 20 mins

1. This disease is caused by the deficiency of protein. Can you identify it from the given options?
   (a) Goitre
   (b) Kwashiorkar
   (c) Hypokalemia
   (d) Dermatosis

2. We all know very well that the Pacific Ocean is the earth's largest ocean. Which of the following represents the percentage area (approximately) of the earth covered by it?
   (a) 25% (b) 35% (c) 40% (d) 45%

3. This place is the wettest place on earth. Can you identify it from the given options?
   (a) Mount Waialeale
   (b) Cherapoonji
   (c) Mawsynram
   (d) None of these

4. The number of non-permanent members of the UN Security Council is
   (a) 5 (b) 10 (c) 15 (d) 20

5. According to the latest population Census, the state with the least population density is
   (a) Sikkim
   (b) Mizoram
   (c) Andaman & Nicobar Islands
   (d) Arunachal Pradesh

6. The number of Union Territories in India is
   (a) 5 (b) 6 (c) 7 (d) 8

7. The maximum duration for which the President's office can remain vacant is
   (a) 1 month
   (b) 2 months
   (c) 3 months
   (d) 6 months

8. Which of the following represents the minimum age required to become the member of the Rajya Sabha?
   (a) 25 years
   (b) 30 years
   (c) 35 years
   (d) There is no age limit as such

9. As per the Constitution of India, the fundamental rights are ________ in number.
   (a) 5 (b) 6 (c) 7 (d) 8

10. Sakyamuni is another name of
    (a) Mahavir
    (b) Buddha
    (c) Lord Shiva
    (d) Lord Vishnu

11. *The Maratha* and *The Kesari* were the two main newspapers started by
    (a) Lala Lajpat Rai
    (b) Gopal Krishna Gokhale
    (c) Bal Gangadhar Tilak
    (d) Madan Mohan Malviya

12. National emergency arising out of war, armed rebellion or external aggression is dealt under
    (a) Article 280
    (b) Article 352
    (c) Article 356
    (d) Article 370

13. Which of the following personalities is considered to be the originator of Sankhya philosophy?
    (a) Bharat Muni
    (b) Kapila Muni
    (c) Adi Shankaracharya
    (d) Agatsya Rishi

14. Which of the following personalities from India is the only winner of Special Oscar in the history of Indian Cinema so far?
    (a) Mrinal Sen
    (b) Shyam Benegal
    (c) Satyajit Ray
    (d) Mira Nair

15. Mahatma Gandhi founded the ___ newspaper in 1903 at South Africa.
    (a) Indian Opinion
    (b) Harijan
    (c) Indian Speaker
    (d) India News

16. Who wrote *Arthashastra*?
    (a) Kalhana
    (b) Vishakhadutta
    (c) Banabhatta
    (d) Chanakya

17. Chauri Chaura incident, which took place in 1922, find prominence in the India's national movement. Can you identify the state in which Chauri Chaura is located?
    (a) Maharashtra
    (b) Uttar Pradesh
    (c) Rajasthan
    (d) Uttar Pradesh

18. H. J. Kania was the first
    (a) Chief Justice of the Supreme Court of India
    (b) Attorney-General of India
    (c) Solicitor-General of India
    (d) None of them

19. Who among the following is known as 'The Saint of Gutters'?
    (a) Baba Amte   (b) Mother Teresa
    (c) Anna Hazare   (d) None of them

20. The capital of Ethiopia is
    (a) Abuja   (b) Dar-es-salaam
    (c) Adis Ababa   (d) Harare

21. World Human Rights Day is celebrated every year on
    (a) December 1   (b) December 3
    (c) December 10   (d) December 22

22. Which of the following represents the year in which NABARD was established?
    (a) 1976   (b) 1982   (c) 1988   (d) 1992

23. Mesopotamia is the former name of
    (a) Tanzania   (b) Iran
    (c) Iraq   (d) Zambia

24. We All know very well that Gujarat has the longest coastline amongst all. Which of the following represents the length of the coastline of Gujarat?
    (a) 1200 km   (b) 1400 km
    (c) 1600 km   (d) 1800 km

25. This personality was also known as 'Blood and Iron Man of Germany'. Can you identify him from the given options?
    (a) Mustafa Kamal Ataturk
    (b) Benito Mussolini
    (c) Bismarck
    (d) Hitler

26. *Gulliver's Travels* is a famous work of
    (a) James Joyce   (b) Jonathan Swift
    (c) James Hilton   (d) Ernest Hemingway

27. Which of the following represents the original number of officially recognized languages enshrined in the Indian Constitution?
    (a) 14   (b) 16   (c) 18   (d) 22

28. The first Battle of Panipat took place in
    (a) 1498   (b) 1516   (c) 1526   (d) 1532

29. Sukumar Sen was
    (a) the first Chief Justice of the Supreme Court of India
    (b) the first Chief Election Commissioner of India
    (c) the first Speaker of the Lok Sabha
    (d) the first Governor of an Indian state

30. Lal Krishna Advani was the ___ Deputy Prime Minister of India.
    (a) fourth   (b) fifth   (c) sixth   (d) seventh

31. Which of the following heads the table of Precedence of the Government of India?
    (a) Vice-President   (b) Prime Minister
    (c) President   (d) Chief Justice of India

32. Which of the following cricketer holds the world record for being the captain of a team for maximum number of times?
    (a) Allan Border   (b) Alec Stewart
    (c) Sunil Gavaskar   (d) Steve Waugh

33. Which among the following is the oldest High Courts in India?
    (a) Bombay   (b) Madras
    (c) Calcutta   (d) Delhi

34. Wightman Cup is associated with
    (a) table tennis   (b) lawn tennis
    (c) badminton   (d) volleyball

35. Netaji Subhash Institute of National Sports is situated at
    (a) Gwalior   (b) Patiala
    (c) New Delhi   (d) Bangalore

36. This personality is the winner of the maximum number of World Billiards Championship titles from India. Can you identify him from the given options?
    (a) Michael Ferrara   (b) Geet Sethi
    (c) Wilson Jones   (d) Manoj Kothari

37. The Sardar Sarovar Project is based on river
    (a) Godavari   (b) Tapti
    (c) Narmada   (d) Krishna

38. Jyotiba Phule was founder of
    (a) Servants of India society
    (b) Satya Sodhak Samaj
    (c) Home rule movement
    (d) Tatva Bodhini Sabha

39. The height of the tallest mountain of the world — Mount Everest is
    (a) 8,834 metres   (b) 8,838 metres
    (c) 8,842 metres   (d) 8,848 metres

40. He is known as the 'Builder of Modern Turkey'. Can you name him from the given options?
    (a) Marshal Tito
    (b) Anwar Sadat
    (c) Mustafa Kamal Ataturk
    (d) Benito Mussolini

Career Launcher MBA   General Knowledge

Number of questions: 40   **Time Allowed: 20 mins**

1. 'AFP', is the news agency of
   (a) UK   (b) USA
   (c) Germany   (d) None of these

2. Which of the following represents the year in which Alexander invaded India?
   (a) 323 BC   (b) 324 BC
   (c) 326 BC   (d) 328 BC

3. Khyber Pass is in
   (a) Pakistan   (b) India
   (c) Myanmar   (d) Afghanistan

4. The first secretary-general of the United Nations was
   (a) U. Thant
   (b) Trygve Lie
   (c) Boutros-Boutros Ghali
   (d) Javier Perez de Cuellar

5. Southern Railway is headquartered at
   (a) Hyderabad   (b) Bangalore
   (c) Secunderabad   (d) Chennai

6. First ministerial meeting of World Trade Organization (WTO) took place at
   (a) Washington   (b) New York
   (c) Geneva   (d) Singapore

7. The highest producer of milk in world is
   (a) USA   (b) China
   (c) India   (d) Germany

8. The first woman chief justice of high court of India was
   (a) Fatima Biwi   (b) Ruma Pal
   (c) Leila Seth   (d) None of these

9. Identify the correct match:

Date		Celebrated as
(a) May 8	-	World Health Day
(b) May 1	-	World Literacy Day
(c) May 17	-	World Telecommunication Day
(d) June 5	-	World Ozone Day

10. The world record for the fastest double century in tests is held by
    (a) Sanath Jaisurya   (b) Nathan Astle
    (c) Adam Gilchrist   (d) Saeed Anwar

11. The first speaker of the Lok Sabha was
    (a) K.M. Munshi   (b) C.D.Deshmukh
    (c) G.V. Mavalankar   (d) H.J.Kania

12. Which of the following represents the number of member nations of the Non-Aligned Movement?
    (a) 54   (b) 75   (c) 93   (d) 118

13. This personality is known as the Father of Economics. Can you identify him from the given options?
    (a) J.M.Keyens   (b) Adam Smith
    (c) Abraham Maslow   (d) J.K. Galbraith

14. Mount Etna is a famous volcano located in
    (a) Argentina   (b) Italy
    (c) Mexico   (d) Phillipines

15. Where is the Tungabhadra sanctuary located?
    (a) Madhya Pradesh   (b) Uttar Pradesh
    (c) Karnataka   (d) West Bengal

16. The agency of United Nations that was set up to strengthen the international cooperation in the field of education and improve the standards of education is
    (a) UNEP   (b) UNCTAD
    (c) UNESCO   (d) UNDP

17. Reserve Bank of India is headquarted at
    (a) Kolkata   (b) New Delhi
    (c) Mumbai   (d) Chennai

18. *Jana Gana Mana*, was accepted as the National Anthem of India by the Constituent Assembly of India in which of the following years?
    (a) 1950   (b) 1949   (c) 1948   (d) 1947

19. The person who has climbed Mount Everest the most — 17 times — is
    (a) Babu Chheri   (b) Appa Sherpa
    (c) Peter Hillary   (d) T. W. Tenzing

20. Which Indian state has its maximum area under the forest cover?
(a) Maharashtra   (b) Madhya Pradesh
(c) Arunachal Pradesh   (d) Kerala

21. This personality is known as *The Father of Geometry*. Identify him from the given option.
(a) Euclid   (b) Pythagoras
(c) Newton   (d) Laplace

22. The biggest producers of oil within the members of Organization of Petroleum Exporting Countries (OPEC) is
(a) Iraq   (b) Iran
(c) Saudi Arabia   (d) Kuwait

23. The first Indian animation film was produced by
(a) H. S. Bhatwadekar   (b) Dada Saheb Phalke
(c) Hiralal Sen   (d) J. F. Madan

24. Who is the founder of the World Economic Forum?
(a) George McDonald   (b) Jack Barry
(c) Robert Allen   (d) Klaus Schwab

25. Who among the following is the author of *Meghdoot*?
(a) Bana Bhatta   (b) Kalhana
(c) Kalidas   (d) Tulsidas

26. Under whose presidentship, the first session of Indian National Congress took place in Bombay?
(a) A. O. Hume   (b) Dadabhai Naoroji
(c) G. K. Gokhale   (d) W. C. Bannerjee

27. How many members are there in the Rajya Sabha?
(a) 238   (b) 242
(c) 246   (d) 250

28. Panama Canal links which of the following water resources?
(a) Pacific Ocean and Atlantic Ocean
(b) Red Sea and Mediterranean Sea
(c) Red Sea and Caspian Sea
(d) Atlantic Ocean and Arctic Ocean

29. Which of the following rays is NOT harmful?
(a) Ultraviolet rays   (b) X-rays
(c) Infrared rays   (d) Short radio waves

30. Who is considered as the *Father of History*?
(a) Aristotle   (b) Herodotus
(c) Socrates   (d) Plato

31. Who among the following Indian President has also been the speaker of the Lok Sabha?
(a) N. Sanjiva Reddy
(b) R. Venkatraman
(c) Dr. Shankar Dayal Sharma
(d) Giani Zail Singh

32. Over which of the following rivers, the Bhakhra Nangal dam is built?
(a) Ravi   (b) Chenab
(c) Sutluj   (d) Beas

33. The Ottawa process negotiations are related to
(a) environmental pollution
(b) ozone layer's depletion
(c) nuclear weapons
(d) banning of landmines

34. What percentage of the world area is occupied by India?
(a) 1.3%   (b) 2.4%
(c) 4.5%   (d) 5.7%

35. In which of the following years, the General Agreement on Tariffs and Trade (GATT) came into existence?
(a) 1947   (b) 1948
(c) 1969   (d) 1984

36. In a normal healthy man, the quantity of blood is about
(a) 3 litres   (b) 4 litres
(c) 5 litres   (d) 6 litres

37. The credit for the classification of the blood groups goes to
(a) William Harvey   (b) K. Landsteiner
(c) Robert Hook   (d) Z. Janssen

38. Which part of the body gets affected in Pleurisy?
(a) Joints   (b) Lungs
(c) Liver   (d) Throat

39. *Unhappy India* is the name of the book written by
(a) Bal Gangadhar Tilak
(b) Lala Lajpat Rai
(c) Gopal Krishna Gokhale
(d) Dr Rajendra Prasad

40. The venue of the first Asian Games that took place in 1951 was
(a) Bangkok   (b) New Delhi
(c) Tokyo   (d) Manila

General Knowledge

Test – 4

Number of questions: 40   **Time Allowed: 20 mins**

1. International Rice Research Institute is based at
   (a) Bangkok   (b) Manila
   (c) Kuala Lumpur   (d) Tokyo

2. What is the effect on the density of a gas if it is heated under constant pressure?
   (a) It will decrease
   (b) It will increase
   (c) Remains constant
   (d) First it will increase and then decrease

3. The Life Insurance Corporation of India (LIC) came into being in which of the following years?
   (a) 1952   (b) 1954
   (c) 1956   (d) 1958

4. This person has written National Anthem for two nations. Who is he?
   (a) Iqbal
   (b) Bankim Chandra Chatterjee
   (c) Rabindra Nath Tagore
   (d) Sharat Chandra Chatterjee

5. Milk is basically a type of
   (a) emulsion   (b) solvent
   (c) suspension   (d) gel

6. Scientific principle of electric motor was discovered by which of the following scientists?
   (a) Michael Faraday   (b) B. Franklin
   (c) T. A. Edison   (d) Enrico Fermi

7. World Consumer Rights Day is observed on which of the following days?
   (a) March 4   (b) March 15
   (c) March 30   (d) April 7

8. The maximum contribution to the tax revenue collection of the government comes through
   (a) income tax   (b) customs duty
   (c) excise duty   (d) service tax

9. The capital of Portugal is
   (a) Algiers   (b) Lisbon
   (c) Brussels   (d) Madrid

10. Where is the headquarters of world's foremost Human Right's Organization, Amnesty International?
    (a) Berlin   (b) New York
    (c) London   (d) Geneva

11. During whose reign did Huen Tsang visited India?
    (a) Kanishka   (b) Chandragupta
    (c) Ashok   (d) Harsha

12. Which of the following is not an official language of the United Nations?
    (a) Chinese   (b) French
    (c) German   (d) Arabic

13. In which of the following years was the name of G-7 changed to G-8?
    (a) 1994   (b) 1996
    (c) 1998   (d) 1999

14. Where are the headquarters of the World Trade Orgnaization (WTO)?
    (a) Brussels   (b) Geneva
    (c) London   (d) Rome

15. 'White Revolution' is related to
    (a) flood control   (b) fish production
    (c) wheat production   (d) milk production

16. Which of the following days is celebrated as the International Labour Day throughout the world?
    (a) April 1   (b) May 1
    (c) June 1   (d) July 1

17. Brass is an alloy which consists of
    (a) Zinc and Sulphur
    (b) Sulphur and Copper
    (c) Copper and Zinc
    (d) Zinc and Magnesium

18. The youngest mountaineer to have scaled Mount Everest is
    (a) Temba Tsheri   (b) Ang Rita
    (c) Nawang Gombu   (d) Fu Dorjee

19. The World Tourism Day is celebrated on
    (a) August 16   (b) September 3
    (c) September 27   (d) October 7

20 India's first steel plant was set-up at
    (a) Rourkela   (b) Bhilai
    (c) Durgapur   (d) Jamshedpur

21. LIBOR stands for
    (a) Long Island Borrowing Offer Rate
    (b) London Inter Bank Offer Rate
    (c) Luxemburg International Banks Organization
        Regime
    (d) None of the above

22. When was the rupee devalued for the first time
    after independence?
    (a) 1948   (b) 1949
    (c) 1952   (d) 1954

23. Central Drug Research Institute (CDRI) is based
    at
    (a) Jabalpur   (b) Pune
    (c) Lucknow   (d) Hyderabad

24. The nature of Indian Economy can best be
    described as
    (a) socialist   (b) mixed
    (c) capitalist   (d) None of these

25. 'Cue' is a term used in which of the following sports
    disciplines?
    (a) Billiards   (b) Football
    (c) Hockey   (d) Chess

26. Word 'secular', was inserted into the Constitution
    of India with the help of which of the following
    constitutional amendments?
    (a) 38th   (b) 36th
    (c) 44th   (d) 42nd

27. The year in which the first train from Thane to
    Mumbai started in India was
    (a) 1843   (b) 1848
    (c) 1851   (d) 1853

28. A person bends forward to
    (a) reduce atmospheric pressure
    (b) decrease friction
    (c) increase stability
    (d) avoid slip-ups

29. 'Tripitakas', are the sacred text of
    (a) Jainism   (b) Buddhism
    (c) Hinduism   (d) Sikhism

30. Sanjukta Panigrahi is a famous dancer of
    (a) Bharat Natyam   (b) Kathak
    (c) Odissi   (d) Mohini Attam

31. Indian Agriculture Research Institute (IARI) is
    headquartered at
    (a) New Delhi   (b) Mumbai
    (c) Lucknow   (d) Bhopal

32. The name of the first cloned horse is
    (a) Ponny   (b) Prometea
    (c) Proteas   (d) Prozac

33. Brahmos is a/an
    (a) Supersonic Cruise Missile
    (b) Tank
    (c) Submarine
    (d) Fighter plane

34. Lucknow is situated on the banks of which of the
    following rivers?
    (a) Gomti   (b) Godavari
    (c) Narmada   (d) Ganga

35. 'Sugar Bowl of India', is
    (a) Madhya Pradesh   (b) Uttar Pradesh
    (c) Kerala   (d) Karnataka

36. Who among the following is credited with the
    invention of polio vaccine?
    (a) Louis Pasteur   (b) Albert Sabin
    (c) Jonas Salk   (d) Alexander Fleming

37. Which of the following countries is also known as
    'Dairy of Northern Europe'?
    (a) Switzerland   (b) Finland
    (c) Denmark   (d) Belgium

38. Currency of Denmark is
    (a) Rand   (b) Krone
    (c) Pound   (d) Peseta

39. Which of the following is a Central Government
    tax?
    (a) Income tax   (b) Corporation tax
    (c) Sales tax   (d) Octroi

40. English education in India was introduced by
    (a) Lord Dalhousie   (b) Lord Curzon
    (c) Lord Macaulay   (d) Lord Rippon

  Career Launcher MBA   General Knowledge

Number of questions: 40 **Time Allowed: 20 mins**

1. Governor is appointed by the
   (a) Prime Minister
   (b) President
   (c) Chief Justice of India
   (d) Chief Justice of the concerned state high court

2. Find the odd one out.
   (a) A. Ramaswamy   (b) Pankaj Advani
   (c) P. Harikrishna   (d) S. S. Ganguly

3. *My Passage from India*, is a book authored by
   (a) E. M. Foster   (b) Ismail Merchant
   (c) Mulk Raj Anand   (d) Nirad C. Choudhary

4. *Coolie*, is a famous work of...
   (a) Khushwant Singh   (b) V. S. Naipaul
   (c) Mulk Raj Anand   (d) R. K. Narayan

5. This personality is credited with the invention of e-mail. Can you identify him from the given options?
   (a) T. Lee Burns   (b) Larry Page
   (c) Ray Tomlinson   (d) None of these

6. When did the Second Round Table conference took place?
   (a) 1915   (b) 1922
   (c) 1928   (d) 1931

7. 'Ansett' is the name of the domestic airline of which of the following countries?
   (a) New Zealand   (b) Germany
   (c) The Netherlands   (d) Australia

8. Metals which chemically behave both as metals and non-metals is called
   (a) alloys   (b) metalloids
   (c) halogens   (d) chalkogens

9. Which of the following articles of the Constitution deals with financial emergency?
   (a) Article 352   (b) Article 356
   (c) Article 360   (d) Article 370

10. The largest river (in terms of volume of water it carries) is
    (a) Nile   (b) Mississippi Missourie
    (c) Amazon   (d) Yangtze

11. The World Environment Day is celebrated thought the world on______ every year.
    (a) May 8   (b) June 5
    (c) July 11   (d) August 27

12. FICCI expands to
    (a) Federation of Indian Companies of Commerce and Instrumentation
    (b) Federation of Indian Chambers of Commerce and Industries
    (c) Federation of International Chambers of Commerce and Industries
    (d) Federation of Indian Conglomerate of Commerce and Industries

13. This place is also known as the 'Manchester of South India'. Identify it from the given options.
    (a) Madurai   (b) Coimbatore
    (c) Bangalore   (d) Thiruvananthapuram

14. Approximately what portion of the world's population reside in India?
    (a) One-third   (b) One-fourth
    (c) One-fifth   (d) One-sixth

15. Decibel is the unit of
    (a) frequency   (b) wavelength
    (c) sound   (d) luminous intensity

16. Which of the following trains is India's first certified ISO-9001 train?
    (a) Mumbai-Delhi Shatabdi Express
    (b) Magadh Express
    (c) Bhopal Express
    (d) AP Express

17. Central Leather Research Institute (CLRI) is based at
    (a) Varanasi   (b) Chennai
    (c) Hyderabad   (d) Kanpur

18. December 1 is celebrated as the ___ throughout the world.
    (a) World Health Day
    (b) World AIDS Day
    (c) World Human Rights Day
    (d) World Habitat Day

19. Who wrote the book *The Algebra of Infinite Justice*?
    (a) Vikram seth   (b) Rohington Mistry
    (c) Anurag Mathur   (d) Arundhati Roy

20. 'Manas Tiger Sanctuary', is in
    (a) Uttar Pradesh   (b) Assam
    (c) West Bengal   (d) Rajasthan

21. Panini was
    (a) a Greek philosopher
    (b) an Indian astronomer and famous
        mathematician
    (c) a sanskrit grammarian of vedic times
    (d) great poet of ancient times

22. *Mein Kempf* is authored by
    (a) Karl Marx   (b) Napoleon Bonaparte
    (c) Adolf Hitler   (d) Benito Mussolini

23. Which of the following is the largest and the
    deepest ocean of the world?
    (a) Arctic   (b) Atlantic
    (c) Pacific   (d) Indian

24. The literacy rate of India is
    (a) 57.86%   (b) 61.34%
    (c) 63.98%   (d) 74.04%

25. Which Indian state has the least literacy rate?
    (a) Bihar   (b) Arunachal Pradesh
    (c) Rajasthan   (d) Orissa

26. SAARC was formed in
    (a) 1982   (b) 1984
    (c) 1985   (d) 1986

27. Which of the following is NOT the member of the
    European Union?
    (a) Greece   (b) Finland
    (c) Norway   (d) United Kingdom

28. ASEAN is headquartered at
    (a) Male   (b) Kathamandu
    (c) Jakarta   (d) Kuala Lumpur

29. This river was also called as the Ganges of the
    South. Name the river from the given options.
    (a) Godavari   (b) Krishna
    (c) Cauvery   (d) None of these

30. Which Indian state is inhabited by 'Jaintiya tribes'?
    (a) Arunachal Pradesh (b) Mizoram
    (c) Manipur   (d) Meghalaya

31. The capital of Greece is
    (a) Warsaw   (b) Athens
    (c) Oslo   (d) Ottawa

32. This country is known as the cockpit of Europe.
    Identify it from the given options.
    (a) Poland   (b) Belgium
    (c) Turkey   (d) Sweden

33. *Natyashastra* is a famous work of
    (a) Banabhatta   (b) Bharatmuni
    (c) Kalhana   (d) Kalidas

34. In which of the following years did United Nations
    (UN) come into existence?
    (a) 1941   (b) 1943
    (c) 1944   (d) 1945

35. Eduskusta is the name of the Parliament of
    (a) Norway   (b) Finland
    (c) Austria   (d) Italy

36. The line that demarcates the boundary between
    India and Pakistan is
    (a) MacMahon Line   (b) Durand Line
    (c) Radcliffe Line   (d) None of these

37. Which of the following represents the number of
    judges in The International Court of Justice?
    (a) 12   (b) 15
    (c) 18   (d) 21

38. Obstetrics is
    (a) a branch of medicine that deals with pregnancy,
        labour and child birth
    (b) a branch of medicine that deals with child
        diseases
    (c) a branch of medicine that deals with eye related
        diseases
    (d) a branch of medicine that deals with kidney
        diseases

39. Which of the following years you would associate
    with the foundation of Indian National Congress
    (INC)?
    (a) 1875   (b) 1881
    (c) 1883   (d) 1885

40. The weight of the man will be ___ on the surface
    of the moon of his actual weight.
    (a) one-third   (b) one-fourth
    (c) one-fifth   (d) one-sixth

Career Launcher MBA   General Knowledge

Answers Keys

Test – 1

1	c	2	b	3	b	4	c	5	c	6	b	7	c	8	d	9	d	10	b
11	d	12	c	13	b	14	c	15	d	16	c	17	a	18	d	19	d	20	c
21	c	22	c	23	c	24	b	25	a	26	b	27	b	28	c	29	d	30	d
31	b	32	c	33	b	34	d	35	b	36	b	37	b	38	b	39	c	40	b

Test – 2

1	b	2	b	3	c	4	b	5	d	6	c	7	d	8	b	9	b	10	b
11	c	12	b	13	b	14	c	15	a	16	d	17	b	18	a	19	b	20	c
21	c	22	b	23	c	24	c	25	c	26	b	27	d	28	c	29	b	30	d
31	c	32	d	33	c	34	b	35	b	36	b	37	c	38	b	39	d	40	c

Test – 3

1	d	2	c	3	d	4	b	5	d	6	d	7	c	8	c	9	c	10	b
11	c	12	d	13	b	14	b	15	c	16	c	17	c	18	a	19	b	20	c
21	a	22	c	23	b	24	d	25	c	26	d	27	d	28	a	29	d	30	b
31	a	32	c	33	d	34	b	35	b	36	c	37	b	38	b	39	b	40	b

Test – 4

1	b	2	a	3	c	4	c	5	c	6	a	7	b	8	c	9	b	10	c
11	d	12	c	13	c	14	b	15	d	16	b	17	c	18	a	19	c	20	d
21	b	22	b	23	c	24	b	25	a	26	d	27	d	28	c	29	b	30	c
31	a	32	b	33	a	34	a	35	b	36	c	37	c	38	b	39	a	40	c

Test – 5

1	b	2	b	3	b	4	c	5	c	6	d	7	d	8	b	9	c	10	c
11	b	12	b	13	b	14	d	15	c	16	c	17	b	18	b	19	d	20	b
21	c	22	c	23	c	24	d	25	a	26	c	27	c	28	c	29	c	30	d
31	b	32	b	33	b	34	d	35	b	36	c	37	b	38	a	39	d	40	d

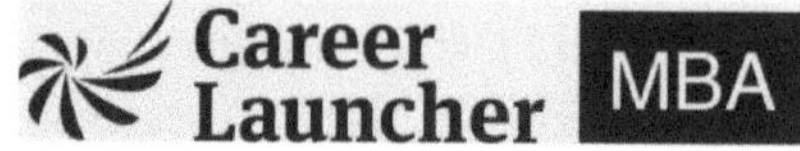

Printed by Libri Plureos GmbH in Hamburg,
Germany